THE
ENCYCLOPEDIA
OF
GHOSTS

OTHER BOOKS BY DANIEL COHEN

FOR YOUNG READERS

THE ENCYCLOPEDIA OF GHOSTS

BY DANIEL COHEN

ILLUSTRATED

DODD, MEAD & COMPANY · NEW YORK

Library of Congress Cataloging in Publication Data

Cohen, Daniel.
   The encyclopedia of ghosts.

   Bibliograhy: p.
   1. Ghosts—Dictionaries.   I. Title.
BF1444.C64   1984   133.1   84-10172
ISBN 0-396-08308-0

PICTURE CREDITS

Illustrations on the following pages are used by permission and through the courtesy of Culver Pictures, Inc., 63; Robert Estall, 101, 236, 239; Bruce Frisch, 98; Harry Price Library, University of London, 72; New York Historical Society, New York City, 5, 6; New York Public Library, 4, 62, 75, 108, 109, 119, 121, 126–29, 165, 175, 189, 225, 271, 274, 275; Photographic Library of Jarrold Colour Publications, 42, 268.

The illustrations on pages 140 and 145 are reprinted, by permission, from Konrad Gesner, *Curious Woodcuts of Fanciful and Real Beasts,* Dover Publications, Inc. (New York, 1971), 11, 34.

Contents

Introduction

People either believe in ghosts or they don't. They are either afraid of them or they are not. But there is a paradox here, for those people who believe most deeply in the possibility of contact between the living and the dead are those who are most likely to regard ghosts as benign and comforting presences, while people who don't really believe in ghosts are most likely to regard them as some sort of horrible visitation and are absolutely terrified of meeting one.

In this book there will be accounts for the believers and the nonbelievers, for those who are seriously interested in the subject of psychical research (or parapsychology, as it is more often called today) and for those who just like to hear a good ghost story. Sometimes the line between these two areas becomes a bit fuzzy or disappears entirely.

The subject of ghosts is an enormous one, for people at all periods in history and in all different cultures have held some beliefs about contacts between the living and the spirits of the dead. Though we don't know what Neanderthal man thought about ghosts, we do know that he buried his dead with awe and reverence. The world of primitive peoples is filled with ghosts and spirits, some helpful, some harmful, but most very powerful beings which must be treated with great respect. The traditional ghost,

ix

he of the moans and clanking chains, goes back at least to the time of the Romans as the account of Athenodorus's Ghost in this volume will show.

It isn't all dragging chains up and down dusty corridors. There are a number of phenomena intimately associated with ghosts, the poltergeist, for example. The word means noisy spirit, and it describes a condition in which objects are moved or thrown about, strange noises are heard, but no ordinary cause for the disturbances can be detected. At one time such phenomena were attributed to witchcraft. Today parapsychologists are most likely to attribute the poltergeist activity to the release of some sort of psychic energy. Skeptics insist that most poltergeist activity is the result of fraud—the "naughty little girl" theory. But in fact many of the most famous and influential ghost stories in history are in reality poltergeist stories.

Or take the "crisis apparition," that is, when the image of someone who has just died, is about to die, or is facing danger or a serious illness suddenly appears to a distant friend or relative. Is such an apparition really a ghost—even if the person is still alive? Technically perhaps not, but anyone who has had such an experience will unhesitatingly affirm that he or she has "seen a ghost."

Some researchers delight in making fine distinctions between such things as apparitions, phantoms, spirits, hauntings, etc. Personally I have found such distinctions generally unnecessary and often confusing—an attempt to come up with a scientifically respectable–sounding classification system that falls flat.

This book is divided into some broad general and, I hope, obvious categories, for the sake of convenience more than anything else. I fully realize that a number of these accounts could appear under different headings. I hope no one wants to quibble about it.

The reality of cases presents a more serious problem. Some of the stories here are legendary or folkloric. Rarely, however, is the origin of the story or legend known as it is in the case of the so-called Angels of Mons. I would certainly regard the tale of the headless specter of Queen Anne Boleyn stalking the corridors of the Tower of London with her head tucked underneath her arm as a legend. Yet there are people who apparently really believe the tale and become offended when they are told it isn't true. A good part of this problem arises because the essence of telling a good ghost story is to tell it with a straight face and with absolute conviction. No campfire ghost story is ever supposed to be less than absolutely true. It isn't essential that the teller actually believe the story. It is essential only that he sounds as if he believes it.

On the other hand, I have often met people who will tell the most incredible stories, sometimes personal experiences with ghosts, that I am convinced they really do believe. I don't necessarily believe what they are saying, nor should anyone else, but they do.

So in general I have tried to refrain from passing judgment on the "truth" of this or that story. Truth—difficult enough to discern in most areas—is virtually impossible to find in the realm of ghosts. Some of the stories seem to me to be so clearly legendary that I have classed them as such. Others are either known or widely suspected to be fakes—these too have been labeled. Though I'm quite sure there are those who will argue that the Amityville Horror really did happen just as it said in the book.

Another serious problem that confronted me in this project was what to include and what to leave out. Obviously no single volume or set of volumes could contain all of the accounts of ghosts and ghostly phenomena throughout history and throughout the world. This book concentrates on accounts from the English-speaking world and on those that have taken place within the last four hundred years or so, though this is certainly not a hard and fast rule. But even within those limitations one could hardly hope to include every ghost story. Not only would the reader (and the writer) be overwhelmed by the sheer mass of material, such an attempt would be terribly repetitious and tedious. One would be in grave danger of being numbed by an endless procession of white and gray ladies, spectral monks and nuns and ghostly knights. Mysterious rappings and footsteps in the corridor at midnight can be boring if repeated often enough. Many popular ghost legends are merely variations on a single popular theme. There are, for example, hundreds of variations of the celebrated tale of the phantom hitchhiker. I have tried to include cases that are famous, significant, representative, or unique. I'm sure some will feel that there are some glaring omissions, but I certainly have tried.

Finally, what is it about ghost stories that is so appealing? Lord Halifax was a celebrated collector of ghostly accounts whose work is cited several times in this book. In the introduction to a published collection, *Lord Halifax's Ghost Book*, his son tried to explain the fascination that such tales held for his father. "They appealed to his natural sense of mystery and romance." But there was more:

"And I cannot doubt that the true secret of the appeal made to his thought by the mysterious or so-called uncanny was the glimpse that such narratives or events might seem to afford of the hidden realities of the unseen world."

That I think sums up the raison d'être of the present volume very neatly—romance, mystery, and the possibility of a peek into the unknown.

1

FAMOUS GHOSTS AND GHOSTS OF THE FAMOUS

AARON BURR AND OTHERS   Aaron Burr was one of the most colorful and controversial characters in American history. His ghost has occasionally been reported in lower Manhattan, where he spent much of his life. Even more celebrated are the ghosts of some of those who were associated with Burr.

Burr was born in New Jersey in 1756, and though descended from a family of famous clergymen, he never showed any interest in religion. Aaron Burr studied law and became involved with that band of American colonists who preached independence from England. During the Revolution he served in Washington's army with great distinction. But even as a soldier he displayed a restless and ambitious nature that made it difficult for him to take orders.

After the Revolution, Burr became a successful lawyer and politician. He was very nearly elected president of the United States, losing in a close vote of the House of Representatives to Thomas Jefferson. Direct election of presidents had not yet become a part of the U.S. political system. Burr was made vice-president, but he always harbored a grudge against Alexander Hamilton, who he thought had cost him the presidency. Hamilton didn't like Jefferson, but he hated and distrusted Burr.

This political quarrel between Hamilton and Burr ultimately ended in a duel on July 11, 1804. Hamilton was fatally wounded and taken back to New York, where he died a few days later. Burr had to flee, for dueling though common was illegal and there were warrants out for his arrest. In addition Hamilton's powerful friends swore to avenge his death.

The Burr-Hamilton duel

After the duel Hamilton was first treated at the house of John Francis, his doctor. The house stood at 27 Jane Street in Greenwich Village. He was then taken to his own house a short distance away, where he died. The Hamilton house is long gone, but the house at 27 Jane Street is said to be troubled by strange sounds and doors that open and close mysteriously.

After many adventures Burr was accused of treason and had to flee the country entirely. The only person in the world he really cared about was his beautiful daughter, Theodosia. She often pleaded with her father to return to America. Finally in 1814 he decided to do so, and Theodosia was to take a ship from the South, where she had lived, to New York, where her father was going to land. The ship that was carrying her never arrived. It was most probably lost in a storm off Cape Hatteras, North Carolina, and the ghost of Theodosia Burr has been reported walking the sands of Hatteras.

Aaron Burr

Theodosia Burr

Eliza Jumel

Aaron Burr lived on and became a successful New York lawyer. In 1833 at the age of seventy-seven he married a wealthy widow, Eliza Jumel, who was about twenty years his junior. She was fairly notorious in her own right. She had been a poverty-stricken beauty who married Stephen Jumel, one of New York's richest men. When he died after an accident, it was rumored that Eliza had really killed him. People have reported the ghost of the "murdered" Jumel haunting the mansion he built for his wife.

Though Eliza Jumel and Aaron Burr had been friends and perhaps more even before Jumel's death and they married shortly after she became a widow, their marriage did not last. Eliza accused Burr of running around with other women. Although he was seventy-eight at the time, the charge may well have been true. A divorce was granted just a few days before Burr died.

Eliza Jumel lived on until 1865. She died in the grand Jumel Mansion at the age of ninety-three. The mansion still stands and is a historic site preserved by the City of New York. Children in the area sometimes say that an old woman comes out on the balcony and chases them away. But since no old woman lives in the mansion anymore, it is assumed that this one is really the ghost of Eliza Jumel.

ABRAHAM LINCOLN   Abraham Lincoln is the most mythic of all American presidents. Because of the highly dramatic nature of his life and death he would inevitably be the subject of ghostly legends. But Lincoln seems to have had some genuine interest in ghosts and spirits while he was still alive.

During Lincoln's day spiritualism was extremely popular in America, and it attracted followers from all walks of life. Lincoln's wife, Mary Todd, appears to have been one of the many who was drawn to spiritualist beliefs. Her interest in the possibility of life after death grew after the death of her young son, William, who died while the Lincolns were living in the White House. Naturally there are stories that the boy's ghost has been seen in the White House, but there is no really strong tradition.

There are also stories that Mary Todd Lincoln actually arranged for séances to be held in the White House and that the President himself attended some of them. If he did (and there is no firm evidence on this point), he may have attended only to please his wife, not because he had any belief in spiritualism himself. According to a widely repeated story, at one séance a large piano was levitated when the medium placed her hand upon it. During the darkest days of the Civil War, another medium was supposed to have come to the White House with advice on how to conduct the war that she had been given by great leaders of the past. What this advice was and how it was received by the President is unknown.

Abraham Lincoln himself was a brooding, often melancholy man, particularly during his later years. He might sit silently for hours in what some have said was a mood of deep depression but others have attributed to a state of mystic reverie.

A great deal of attention has been focused on Lincoln's alleged prophetic dreams, particularly a series of dreams in which he was supposed to have foreseen his own death by assassination.

About ten days before he was killed, he reported a dream in which he saw himself in a coffin, and when he asked what had happened, he was told that the President had been killed by an assassin. On the very morning of his assassination, he told friends that he had a dream about being on a ship bound for some unknown place.

W. H. Crook, one of President Lincoln's bodyguards, said that Lincoln was convinced he would be killed because he had a dream warning him of the assassination three days before it happened. The bodyguard said that he had begged Lincoln not to go to the theater on the evening of April 14 but the President was fatalistic and went anyway. That, of course, was the evening on which he was shot by John Wilkes Booth.

There isn't necessarily anything unusual about these reports. Since the stories of Lincoln's dreams are all second- or thirdhand, we do not really know how accurate they are or how much they were colored or inspired by the assassination itself. People often make prophetic dreams or other instances of alleged prophecy fit events that already have occurred. Conscious faking or altering of the "prophecy" is not really necessary; selective memory comes into play, and the mind naturally selects only those details that

Abraham Lincoln

conform to what has happened; the mind also tends to fill in details to make the story fit more closely to the event.

In addition, Lincoln was undoubtedly a moody man who was
often deeply depressed. It should come as no surprise that he
dreamed of assassination, for his life had been threatened many

times. He was not unconcerned about his own safety, but he was genuinely fatalistic about the possibility of being killed.

The stories of séances and prophetic dreams plus the fact that Abraham Lincoln was the first American president to be assassinated have contributed to a supernatural atmosphere that has clung to the Lincoln legend.

After Lincoln's death the ghost stories began. For years people reported hearing ghostly footsteps, presumably those of the murdered President, around the White House. The first person who reported actually seeing the ghost was Grace Coolidge, wife of Calvin Coolidge, thirtieth president. Mrs. Coolidge said that she saw the figure of Lincoln staring out of a window of the Oval Office.

There were a lot of reports of Lincoln's ghost during the terms of President Franklin D. Roosevelt. When Queen Wilhelmina of the Netherlands was staying at the White House, she said that she heard a knock at the door and when she opened it, she found the tall top-hatted figure of Lincoln standing in the hall. It should be recalled that the Queen had a previous interest in spiritualism.

When she reported the strange incident to President Roosevelt the next morning, he didn't seem surprised. He said that the bedroom that the Queen was staying in was also known as the Lincoln Room and that many others had reported seeing the ghost in or near the room.

One of FDR's secretaries said that she saw Lincoln in a more informal pose. He was sitting on the bed in the Lincoln Room pulling on his boots. The sight scared her badly. There is another tale that Lincoln's ghost once tried to set fire to the bed in the Lincoln Room and that the woman who was staying there left immediately.

While relatively few people have actually reported seeing the ghost of Lincoln in the White House, many have reported that they somehow felt a ghostly presence. When FDR's little Scottish terrier, Falla, would begin barking for no particular reason, some would say that the dog could see the ghost but no one else could.

President Harry Truman was once asked about a mysterious knock he heard on his bedroom door in the White House. "Yes, I heard the knock and answered it about three in the morning. There wasn't anybody there. I think it must have been Lincoln's ghost walking the hall." Later Truman admitted that he was joking about the ghost but that he had heard the knock.

After Lincoln's death there were a large number of mediums who claimed that they were in contact with his spirit. Lincoln was a popular subject in spirit photography. His ghostly form was often seen hovering in the background of such photographs. These photographs, however, were invariably fakes and usually crude fakes.

At Lincoln's grave in Springfield, Illinois, his ghost has often been reported. But there are other rumors that Lincoln's body is not really buried in the grave.

There are also a large number of ghostly legends attached to Lincoln's funeral train. After Lincoln died, his body was taken back to Illinois for burial. It was carried on a special funeral train, and all along the route people lined up to see the train pass. The passage of the train received an extraordinary amount of publicity, and it became sort of a national funeral procession.

Ever since then, according to legend, a ghostly train takes the same route every year. The train is covered with black, and the engine manned by skeletons.

The *Albany Times* printed this description of the legendary train:

"It passes noiselessly. If it is moonlight, clouds cover over the moon as the phantom train goes by. After the pilot engine passes, the funeral train itself with flags and streamers rushes past. The track seems covered with black carpet and the coffin is seen in the center of the car, while all about it in the air and on the train behind are vast numbers of blue coated men, some with coffins on their backs, others leaning upon them."

Lincoln's funeral train is the American equivalent of the phantom armies of Europe.

ADMIRAL TYRONE   On June 22, 1893, Lady Tyrone, the wife of Admiral Sir George Tyrone, was giving one of her popular at home parties in her house in London's exclusive Eaton Place. The room was filled with the cream of Edwardian society. Everyone was chattering away, apparently having a good time, when suddenly a hush fell over the room as a figure in full naval uniform walked in without being announced, strode across the floor as the guests fell back to make way for him, and abruptly vanished.

The figure was recognized as that of Admiral Sir George Tyrone by everyone present. And everyone also knew that Sir George was far away with the Mediterranean Fleet. What the guests did not know and could not know was that the admiral was dead, having just drowned in the wreck of the HMS *Victoria*. The reason for the wreck is one of the great naval mysteries of all time.

Admiral Tyrone had been leading one column of the fleet; Admiral Markham in the *Camperdown*, the other. For no reason that has ever been discovered, Admiral Tyrone suddenly signaled the two columns of battleships to turn inward toward one another at a given point. A collision between the *Victoria* and the *Camperdown* was inevitable unless the orders were reversed, but Admiral Tyrone remained adamant and the ships headed directly toward one another. At virtually the last moment the admiral either realized his error or changed his mind, for he ordered "full steam astern." But it was too late, and the *Camperdown* sheared into the *Victoria*, which sank quickly. Survivors of the disaster said that they heard Admiral Tyrone crying out that it was all his fault. But in the best naval tradition, he went down with his ship—and in the best ghostly tradition, he appeared in his wife's drawing room at exactly the same moment.

Bishop PIKE'S SÉANCE   On September 17, 1967, the
Right Reverend James A. Pike, former Episcopal bishop of California, sat in a television studio in Toronto, Canada, with Arthur
Ford, a minister of the Disciples of Christ Church and one of
America's best-known spirit mediums. They were to hold a televised séance that had been arranged by Allen Spraggett, religion
editor of the *Toronto Star* and a frequent writer on psychic sub-
jects.

Ford put on a blindfold—to protect his eyes from the strong TV
lights, he said—and he went into a trance. During the trance
Ford's spirit guide "Fletcher" delivered messages allegedly from
the spirit of Bishop Pike's son, Jim Jr., who had shot and killed
himself in New York about a year earlier.

According to Ford, Fletcher was the spirit of a long-dead
French Canadian who regularly transmitted messages from the
spirit world.

Aside from the setting the séance was a traditional one and the
"messages" from the "spirit" of James Pike, Jr., were the same sort
of consoling, morally uplifting, and rather vague communication
that mediums had been delivering for over a century.

During the séance the spirits of young Pike and others who had
messages for Bishop Pike were supposed to have produced evidence of their genuineness—that is, they were supposed to have
revealed evidence about their earthly lives that could not have
been otherwise known to the medium. Bishop Pike was impressed,
though he acknowledged that much of the information might have
come by normal means, that is, Ford might have learned it from
mutual friends or newspaper reports, but Pike did not think Ford
had done so. He was convinced that during the séance Ford had
indeed been in contact with the spirit of his dead son.

Prior to the séance, Bishop Pike himself had been no hardened
skeptic on psychic matters. Though a clergyman, he had suffered

many of the religious doubts that had tormented the founders of psychical research during the nineteenth century. He was searching for scientific proof of life after death. His interest in psychical research went back several years, and he had already written on the subject.

But it was not an academic or philosophical interest that drew him to Arthur Ford. The suicide of his son was a crushing personal loss. He was in London when he heard of the suicide, and a short time later he attended séances held by the British medium Ena Twigg, who had allegedly been in contact with his son. Before his suicide, Jim Jr. had also shown some interest in spiritualism.

Bishop Pike did not rush to a séance immediately upon learning of his son's death. He was first subjected to what he believed to be poltergeist activity and other strange manifestations which led him to the conclusion that someone was trying to communicate with him from "the other side." The Bishop decided that he had to go to either a medium or a psychiatrist.

Objects, including photographs of Bishop Pike and his son, seemed to disappear mysteriously and then reappear again in unfamiliar places. Strangest of all was the apparent recurrence of the 140 degree angle. Bishop Pike found an alarm clock that had belonged to his son stopped at 8:19. This he believed to be the time of the boy's death by London time. (The New York coroner had estimated the time of his death to be about 3:00 A.M. local time.) The hands of the clock set to 8:19 form a 140 degree angle. Quite suddenly it seemed as if the 140 degree angle appeared everywhere. A batch of opened safety pins found mysteriously on the bishop's bed seemed to form the fatal angle. Books or cards fell on the floor in such a way as to create a 140 degree angle. After delivering a speech one evening, the bishop suddenly "had a great awareness that the hour was important, and almost without thinking, I turned and looked up at the large clock, eight-nineteen! The configuration of the hands hit me with almost physical impact."

It was these experiences that sent Bishop Pike first to Mrs. Twigg and ultimately to the TV studio séance with Arthur Ford.

The reaction to the Ford-Pike séance was sensational. The tape was first shown on Canadian television and then widely shown in America. A story of the séance and the events that led up to it appeared on the front page of *The New York Times*, one of the few times in the long history of that influential newspaper that it has given front-page coverage to a psychic event. Naturally other newspapers and magazines throughout the country picked it up.

There were plenty of scoffers as well, but there is no doubt that this highly publicized séance gave spiritualism its biggest lift in many years. And then the case of Bishop Pike took a final grim and bizarre turn.

In the fall of 1979 Bishop Pike and his wife went to Israel to do research for a book he was planning on the origins of Christianity. On September 1 they left Jerusalem in their rented car, driving in the direction of Bethlehem. It should have been a brief drive, but the road led through some of the most inhospitable desert areas in the world. The bishop took a wrong turn and got lost, and then the car got stuck. Bishop Pike and his wife were stranded without supplies in the middle of the desert. Diane Pike, who was considerably younger and in much better health than her fifty-six-year-old husband, felt that she had the strength to push on in what she was sure was the direction of the Dead Sea, but the Bishop declared that he could go no further. He said that she should try to get help and come back for him. Ten hours after they had become lost, Diane Pike stumbled into an Israeli construction camp and the search for Bishop Pike began.

The news of his disappearance was on the front page of newspapers all over the world. The thought of the colorful and controversial clergyman lost in the very region where tradition says Jesus prayed, fasted, and was tempted held an irresistible fascination. Israeli authorities searched for him with helicopters and mediums tried to locate him with more arcane methods.

Arthur Ford said that he had psychically "seen" Pike alive in a desert cave. Mrs. Twiggs insisted the missing man was "on the border trying to make the transition."

Seven days after the breakdown, Israeli searchers found the body of Bishop James A. Pike. It was on a ledge, not in a cave as Ford predicted or in the spot pinpointed by any other medium. The bishop had apparently died only a short time after his wife left.

Not long after Bishop Pike's death, Arthur Ford also died. While doing research for a biography on Ford, Allen Spraggett and the Reverend William V. Raucher turned up evidence that cast a cloud over the original televised séance. In Ford's files they found old newspaper clippings that contained some of the information that had supposedly been revealed by the spirits during the séance.

Spraggett also quoted a former secretary of the medium who said that Ford often had extensive notes about prospective sitters at his séances because nobody could "perform one hundred percent of the time."

Spraggett acknowledged that the discovery was a "traumatic moment," but according to a March 11, 1973, *New York Times* story, he asserted that Ford was a "gifted psychic who for various reasons, scrutable and inscrutable, fell back on trickery when he felt he had to."

See also: HARRY HOUDINI

FLIGHT 401   On the night of Friday, December 29, 1972, Eastern Airlines Flight 401 from New York to Miami crashed in the Florida Everglades while approaching the Miami airport. There were some seventy survivors of the tragedy, but the majority of the passengers and crew, 101 in all, were killed. The cause of the crash appears to have been a combination of pilot error and equipment failure.

Shortly after the crash, rumors began to spread among airline employees that apparitions of Captain Bob Loft and flight engineer Don Repo, both of whom had been killed in the crash of

Flight 401, were being seen on other Eastern flights. The reports
came primarily from plane #318, a plane similar to the one that
had crashed in the Everglades. Most of those who saw the apparitions knew the dead men before the crash. Here is the record of
two of these sightings taken from a popular book on the subject:

"L-101—location not specified . . . flight engineer came to flight
deck before doing 'walk around' preflight inspection and engi-
neering panel check . . . saw man in Eastern Second Officer's uniform sitting at his seat at the panel. . . . The engineer quickly
recognized him as Don Repo. . . . The apparition of Repo said
something like: 'You don't need to worry about the preflight. I've
already done it.' . . . Almost immediately the three dimensional
image of Repo disappeared, vanished. . . .

"Capt. Loft . . . seen again in first-class section in New York
(JFK) by flight captain and two flight attendants. . . . They talked
to him and he disappeared. . . . Flight was canceled . . . told me by
captain involved . . . asked me to keep his name confidential."

These rumors reached the ears of writer John G. Fuller, who
had already made a reputation researching and writing on fringe
topics such as UFOs. Fuller began his own investigation, talking to
as many witnesses to the apparitions as possible and trying to follow through the theory that the reason that plane #318 had such
a large number of sightings was that salvaged parts from the
crashed plane had been used in it. Fuller said that he ultimately
was able to get in touch with the spirit of Don Repo through the
use of a Ouija board.

The result of his investigations was the popular book *The Ghost
of Flight 401* published in 1976. The book makes an interesting
"ghost story," but as evidence for the existence of ghosts it has little weight. The bulk of the evidence is anecdotal and often anony-
mous, so it has been impossible for other researchers to check the
accuracy of the reports. The book was made into a TV movie.

See also: THE AMITYVILLE HORROR, THE EXORCIST

HARRY HOUDINI   The great magician Harry Houdini was the most ferocious, tenacious, and successful enemy of fraudulent spirit mediums. Yet he appears to have seriously entertained the possibility of communication with the dead, and since his death communications with his spirit have been reported frequently.

Houdini was a complex and in many ways strange man whose devotion to his mother was legendary. After her death he apparently earnestly sought some reassurance of her spirit's survival and some means of communicating with his dead mother. One of Houdini's friends was Sir Arthur Conan Doyle, creator of Sherlock Holmes and a convinced spiritualist. Doyle's wife was also an amateur medium, and Houdini apparently attended some séances in the Doyle home. During one of these séances Houdini was given a message supposedly from his dead mother. However, the message was written in English; Houdini's mother had been born in Europe and never learned to write English. Doyle stated blandly that Houdini's mother must have learned to write English in the spirit world. This enraged the magician, who considered the statement an insult to the memory of his mother and he never spoke to Doyle again.

Houdini was disgusted by the activities he saw in other spiritualist séances, and this turned him into the crusader who went on the road to expose the fakery of mediums. Doyle, by the way, never believed that Houdini could reproduce mediumistic feats by trickery. He clung to the opinion that Houdini himself was a medium but for some perverse reason chose to deny that fact and slander other mediums.

Whatever Houdini's original motivation, he did turn his antispiritualist activities to personal gain. Where he had once appeared onstage to perform tricks and escapes, he now appeared to deliver antispiritualist lectures and demonstrations. He also wrote books and articles on the subject. Antispiritualism became part of his act. Naturally he quickly became viewed as the prime enemy of spiritualism. The spirit controls of many mediums predicted his imminent destruction and death.

In fact, Houdini did die quite unexpectedly on Halloween 1926. His antispiritualist activities plus the fact that he died on the traditional festival of the dead have led to an extraordinary number of rumors concerning his death.

One rumor was that Houdini had prepared a message that he would communicate from beyond the grave if that were possible. The message was supposed to be in a code that the magician and his wife, Beatrice, had once used during a stage mentalist act and was known only to them.

A lot of mediums claimed that they had received Houdini's message, but Beatrice Houdini would not endorse any of them until two years after Houdini's death when she got a letter from an American medium named Arthur Ford. What followed was an extremely confusing series of events—and just exactly what happened and why is not clear even to this day. Beatrice Houdini apparently endorsed Ford's claim and held a number of séances with him. But a newspaper reporter then said he overheard Ford and Beatrice conspiring together to make up the story so that they could make money on a lecture and show tour. Many of Houdini's magician friends claimed that there never was a message and that the celebrated Houdini "code" was a simple one that was well known both in and outside the magical profession. Beatrice Houdini herself was distraught and ill, and when she recovered somewhat she claimed that some of the things that she had said earlier had not been accurate but that it was her illness and delicate emotional state that had caused her to become confused and make mistakes. She denied ever conspiring with Ford but said that there never had been a Houdini message either. She did, however, continue to hold séances on Halloween for several years but finally declared that if Houdini had survived death he was not coming back.

However, to this day mediums throughout the world hold Halloween séances, and hardly a year passes without some medium somewhere declaring that he or she has contacted the spirit of the great magician.

It is a curious fate for the man who was known as the most ferocious foe of spiritualism to have become a Halloween stock figure for spiritualist mediums.

See also: WALTER

ℍARRY PRICE   Harry Price was probably the best known "ghost hunter" of modern times. He was prominent in the field of psychical research in Britain for some forty years. He founded the National Laboratory of Psychical Research, now part of the University of London, and wrote extensively on his investigations, though considerable doubt has been raised about his methods and even his honesty during some of his most celebrated investigations.

Shortly after Price's death in March 1948 there was a story that the ghost hunter had himself returned as a ghost. Such accounts are not uncommon about recently dead psychical researchers. After the death of the primary founders of psychical research, mediums all over the world reported that they were in contact with the founder's spirits. Price's appearance, however, was somewhat more dramatic.

Early in the spring of 1948, a young Swedish man known under the pseudonym Erson awoke to find an elderly, slightly balding man standing by his bedside. This figure began to speak in a language that Erson could not understand but that he took to be English. Despite the language barrier the figure was able to get across to Erson the information that his name was Price.

The figure that called itself Price began appearing to Erson fairly regularly and was seen by the man's wife and daughter as well. The figure did not seem at all misty and "ghostlike" but rather quite solid, so Erson tried to photograph it. The photos showed nothing, and Price laughed at the attempts.

Since he was confronted by an English-speaking apparition, the Swede tried to learn a little English and was able to hold at least rudimentary conversations with his ghostly visitor. Price told Erson that he had been involved in the investigation of ghosts. He also urged Erson to go to a particular hospital for treatment of a difficult health problem. At the hospital Erson discussed not only his health but his ghost with one of the doctors. The doctor happened to be interested in psychical research, which Erson was not, and he was able to identify the ghostly figure as Harry Price. The doctor checked further and found that Price had died at about the time the figure first appeared to Erson. Why the spirit of the ghost hunter should appear to a man in another country who did not know him, had no interest in his work, and did not even speak his language was something no one could fathom.

See also: BORLEY RECTORY, CROSS CORRESPONDENCES, ROSALIE

JEREMY BENTHAM   The influential, if eccentric philosopher Jeremy Bentham was the founder of the philosophy of Utilitarianism, which was extremely popular in the early nineteenth century. It was Bentham who coined the phrase "the greatest good for the greatest number."

As the name of his philosophy implies, Bentham was very keen on things being practical and useful, and that included the bodies of the dead. He thought that it was very wasteful to have corpses simply stuck away in the ground when they could be preserved and put on display for the inspiration of future generations. This was particularly true for admirable figures such as himself. Accordingly, when he died in 1832, he ordered his friends to have his corpse embalmed, stuffed, and set up in a glass case at the entrance of the University College of the University of London, where it was to serve as an inspiration to generations of his followers. Unfortunately the head was not particularly well preserved and has been replaced by a wax image.

Things didn't work out quite the way Bentham expected. Rather than being an object of honor his mummified remains are regarded as a macabre curiosity. And the devoutly materialistic Bentham would doubtless be distressed to hear that his ghost is said to haunt the halls of the college.

K ATIE KING   Katie King is the ghost of a person who may have never existed. She comes from a large family of ghosts which may be equally imaginary. The King family of ghosts are the products of spiritualism. They first made their appearance in 1852 in a log cabin in Athens County, Ohio. The cabin was owned by one Jonathan Koons, who claimed to be a medium, and it was the scene of many lively séances. One who attended Koons's séances described a full-scale spirit concert: ". . . the fiddle, drums, guitar, banjo, accordian, French harp, tea bell, triangle, etc., played their parts."

These activities attracted a great deal of local attention, and Koons charged admission to view and hear the proceedings. In the early and very unsophisticated days of spiritualism there were a number of establishments similar to Koons's cabin. Though a full record of the activities of Jonathan Koons is lacking, it is not unfair to assume that he was more of a conjurer and performer than he was medium. In short he was almost certainly a fake and not a very clever one at that, for he soon faded from the history of spiritualism—but he left behind a legacy—the King family.

The King family made their first known appearance at Koons's séances. John King, the patriarch of the clan, was supposed to have been a pirate in life, and his language at séances was often rough and colorful. In addition to the old pirate, there were some fifty-six other Kings who showed up at Koons's séances. Most of the other Kings had little or no personality and have returned to the world from which they are supposed to have come without leaving

John King

a trace. However, John's ghostly daughter, Katie, has attained a genuine immortality as one of the great ghosts or spirits of history.

John King, and particularly Katie began to appear at the séances of other mediums. This was not unusual in spiritualist séances of the time. Celebrated spirit guides, be they the spirits of famous people or of individuals like John and Katie King, who may or may not have existed, were often used by several different mediums, just as today the same celebrities make the rounds of many different talk shows.

Katie King became a regular guest at the séances of the flamboyant Italian medium Eusapia Palladino. Katie was not an important part of the Palladino séances, for she was primarily a physical medium who specialized in producing ghostly sounds and moving objects about the darkened séance room. Palladino was found by investigators to be using fraud on several occasions, but even today she has her defenders, who say that while she did indeed use trickery some of the time, at other times she produced genuinely paranormal phenomena.

Katie King was to become a true ghostly star through her association with the young English medium Florence Cook. Florence Cook was the first or one of the first mediums to produce material-

Florence Cook   *The "spirit" of Katie King*

izations of the entire human body in the light—or at least the
half-light of a gaslit séance room. Florence would sit in a dark
curtained recess of the room—usually called the cabinet—allegedly to protect her from the light while she was in a trance state.
After a while a white garbed form calling herself Katie King
emerged from the cabinet.

During the tests the medium was sometimes tied to her chair,
and there were other elementary controls. But skeptics insisted
that the "spirit" of Katie King was really Florence Cook in a sheet.
Indeed photographs of the medium and the spirit show that they
looked exactly alike. While Florence had her circle of believers
there were many more who scoffed at her séances as examples of
crude and obvious trickery that would appeal to only the most
gullible and stupid.

The saga of Florence and Katie would probably be nothing
more than an obscure footnote to spiritualist history if the genuineness of the ghostly phenomena had not been investigated and

confirmed by Sir William Crookes—one of the most respected scientists in the world.

Crookes was a physicist, developer of a tube that made possible the development of the X-ray. He was also elected president of the Royal Society, the most eminent scientific society in the world at that time.

Crookes became involved in spiritualism in the late 1860s and participated in investigations of a number of spirit mediums. Though he was clearly a believer in spiritualist phenomena, his initial investigations appear to have been fairly careful. He was certainly no addle-headed fool, and even after his involvement with spiritualism, he continued to make significant contributions to physics.

In 1874 Florence Cook's materializations of Katie King were being widely attacked as fraudulent, even by many spiritualists. Florence said that she would submit to an investigation by competent authorities, and she chose as the investigator Sir William

Imaginative drawing of Katie King at a séance

Crookes, a man whose reputation appeared to be above reproach. Crookes agreed to conduct the tests. At first he admitted to some difficulties in trying to get Florence to agree to any sort of reasonable controls. But as the tests went on, she became more agreeable, and many of the later séances were held in Crookes's own home under conditions which he controlled completely.

The major charge that was always brought against Florence Cook was that, like Clark Kent and Superman, Florence and Katie were never seen together. Crookes was well aware of the charge. He described this scene at a séance held March 12, 1874, in his home.

"Katie had been walking amongst us and talking for some time; she retreated behind the curtain which separated my laboratory, where the company was sitting, from my library, which did temporary duty as a cabinet. In a minute she came to the curtain and called me to her saying, 'Come into the room and lift my medium's head up, she has slipped down.' Kate was then standing before me clothed in her usual white robes and turban headdress. I immediately walked into the library up to Miss Cook, Katie stepping aside to allow me to pass. I found Miss Cook had slipped partially off the sofa, and her head was hanging in a very awkward position. I lifted her onto the sofa and in so doing had satisfactory evidence in spite of the darkness that Miss Cook was not attired in the 'Katie' costume but had on her ordinary black velvet dress and was in deep trance."

Crookes insisted that it was only three seconds between the time he saw the white-robed Katie and the time he picked up the medium; there was not enough time to change from one costume to the other. Still it wasn't quite seeing them together. But even that was to come.

In a séance on March 29, Katie invited the scientist into the darkened "cabinet." He carried a small phosphorus lamp, and by its dim light he saw Florence Cook, clad in black velvet, crouching on the floor "to all appearances perfectly senseless." Standing behind her garbed in the usual spirit white was Katie King. "I passed

Professor Crookes tests the medium and the spirit

the lamp up and down so as to illuminate Katie's whole figure and satisfy myself thoroughly that I was really looking at the veritable Katie ... and not the phantom of a disordered brain." After a while Florence Cook began to move. Katie motioned for Crookes to go to another part of the cabinet; after that he "ceased to see Katie but did not leave the room till Miss Cook woke up."

And that was not the end of the wonders. Crookes took a series of photos of Katie, including one of himself walking arm in arm with the spirit. He wrote, "It was a common thing [during the photographic sessions] for the seven or eight of us in the laboratory to see Miss Cook and Katie at the same time under the full blaze of electric light." There is even supposed to be one photo of Katie and Florence Cook together, but this does not appear to have survived.

Crookes also reported witnessing a tearful farewell scene between the spirit and the medium, with Katie telling "Florrie" she must leave now because "my work is done."

Crookes's tests of Florence and Katie lasted some three years. At the end he insisted, "I say, to assume the Katie King of the last three years to be the result of imposture does more violence to one's reason and common sense than to believe her to be what she herself affirms."

The case of the ghost and the scientist is one of the strangest in the entire history of psychical research. It is so bizarre that today most psychical researchers who believe in the existence of spirits still hesitate to mention the investigation as proof of the existence of spirits and ghosts.

There seem to be only three possible explanations for the extraordinary series of events. First that Katie really was a ghost. Yet the evidence that Crookes collected is so singular, so much more elaborate than that collected in any other ghost investigation that even the convinced are cautious.

A second possibility is that Florence Cook was a fraud and Crookes a deluded fool. Harry Houdini said of Crookes, "There is not the slightest doubt in my mind that this brainy man was hoodwinked." But to be deluded under the circumstances he describes and over so long a period, Crookes would have to have been no ordinary fool—he would have had to border on the idiotic. Given the high quality scientific work Crookes did during the period with Florence Cook and long afterward, this seems rather clearly not to be the case.

Which leads to a third possibility. This world famous scientist

was not a dupe but an active participant in one of the most fla-
grant hoaxes in history. But why? He seems to have nothing to gain
from such a fraud. He suffered a good deal of scorn at the hands of
his scientific colleagues. Would his devotion to the spiritualist
cause make him take part in such fakery? Or might there have
been another, more personal reason? In 1962 psychical researcher
Trevor Hall went over all the evidence he could find and came to
the conclusion that the scientist and the attractive young medium
were lovers and the séances were simply excuses for their trysts.
There is certainly an air of suppressed sensuality in Crookes's descriptions of Florence in his séance reports. Hall also dug up an
account written by a friend of Florence Cook's who said that she
confessed the whole thing before she died.

But maybe Sir William Crookes had the last word on this subject. Shortly after Hall's book on the Cook-Crookes affair was
published, a London medium named Grace Rosher said that she
was contacted by the spirit of the long-dead Crookes, who denied
the whole thing. "I cannot imagine how such an absurd suggestion
could be made," said the spirit.

LADY HOWARD   There are certain notorious figures in history around whom ghostly legends tend to cluster. Such a figure is
Lady Francis Howard, a celebrated beauty at the court of James I.
Lady Howard had four husbands and was reputed to have poisoned two of them. Along with one of her husbands, she was sent
to the Tower for the poisoning of Sir Thomas Overbury, one of the
most sensational murder cases of the time, but she was later released.

According to Dartmoor folklorist Ruth E. St. Leger-Gordon,
"For all these crimes Lady Howard now pays a penalty after
death. Every night, according to one version of the tale, she assumes the shape of a large black dog, in which guise she runs beside a coach of bones driven by a headless coachman. The goal of

the expedition is Okehampton Castle. . . . Upon arrival she, still in dog-guise, plucks one blade of grass which she carries in her mouth back to her old home site at Tavistock. When every blade of grass in the Castle grounds is removed in this way at a rate of one per night, the penance will be completed and the poor lady will be able to rest in peace. Judging by the amount of mowing still necessary around the ruins . . . she has many more nocturnal journeys before her."

St. Leger-Gordon also points out that Lady Francis Howard had no connection with Okehampton Castle. Okehampton once belonged to the family of Lady *Mary* Howard, a contemporary of, but no relation to, the notorious Lady Francis. The confusion of names and the unquenchable desire to spin a good tale has consigned the perfectly innocent Lady Mary to a horrible and apparently eternal fate, at least in folklore.

MARIE LAVEAU   Marie Laveau was known as the voodoo queen of New Orleans. She was, quite literally, a legend in her own time. No one knows who she really was, where she came from, or how old she was when she died. There are some stories that hold she never really died, while others say that there were several women who took the name Marie Laveau and the stories connected to them have become confused.

The earliest report of Marie Laveau comes from the 1830s, when she was said to be leading voodoo dances in the spot in New Orleans known as Congo Square. She quickly developed a reputation as a seller of powerful magic charms and potions. Many people both black and white visited her little house on Saint Ann Street with requests for magical aid. Marie sold cures for disease, love potions to attract people, and poisons to get rid of them. That was all common enough in New Orleans when belief in voodoo was still strong. But Marie was reputed to have greater-than-average powers for a voodoo priestess.

One story tells of two Frenchmen who were sentenced to be hanged. Their friends came to Marie for help, and she vowed to them that the men would not be hanged as scheduled. On execution day the two men were brought to the gallows in the public square. Up to that point the day had been bright and sunny, but as the nooses were slipped around the necks of the condemned men, a violent thunderstorm broke. The crowd that had gathered to watch the execution fled. The executioner managed to get the trapdoor open, but the wet ropes slipped off the Frenchmen's necks and they landed unhurt on the ground.

As in so many of these tales, fate could be delayed but not denied, and the men were successfully executed at a later date. But Marie had kept her word—the men were not hanged as scheduled.

Fifty years after she was first supposed to have appeared in Congo Square, Marie was still there holding ceremonies, and according to witnesses she didn't look a day older. After that she disappeared, killed in a hurricane in the 1890s, say some stories. Others say that she survived the hurricane and was seen floating down the river on a log singing voodoo songs.

There is no doubt that there really was a Marie Laveau—probably two of them. The first original Marie died around 1881, and her death was reported in the newspapers of the time. Her place was then taken by another woman, perhaps her daughter, who continued to practice voodoo magic for another ten years or so until she died or gave up voodoo and disappeared.

That is what the historians say. Legend views the story differently. According to legend Marie Laveau changed herself into a big black crow that can still sometimes be seen flapping around the old St. Louis cemetery. Other stories hold that her spirit has been changed into a large dog or a snake.

At the St. Louis cemetery there are two unmarked tombs, and people think that Marie Laveau is buried in one of them, but no one is sure which. Even today people sometimes leave voodoo offerings on these tombs.

Marie's ghost has been said to appear frequently in the vicinity of the cemetery. One person said that the ghost hit him across the face when he failed to recognize her.

The site of Marie's old house at 1020 St. Ann Street is also rumored to be haunted by the ghosts of Marie and her followers, who are still performing their voodoo rituals from the spirit world.

MARTIN LUTHER

ARTIN LUTHER   What may or may not have been the spirit of an angry Martin Luther appeared to an Englishman in the early seventeenth century. The story that lay behind the appearance began in Germany. Luther's discourses were under a papal ban, and during the religious wars an ardent Lutheran named Casper von Sparr found a copy of the discourses. Fearing that they might be destroyed, he decided that a good way to insure their survival would be to have the copy smuggled to England and then translated into English. The task was given to an English diplomat named Captain Bell, who took the book with him to London.

Bell was a busy man and a somewhat careless one. Months went by as the manuscript lay unopened and gathering dust in his library. Then one night Bell awoke to see an awful figure standing by his bed. It had a long beard that reached to its waist, and he could see its bones through transparent flesh. No insubstantial phantom this, it shot out a hand and grabbed Bell by the ear.

"Sirrah!" it roared, "will you not take time to translate that book which is sent you out of Germany? I will provide you with both a place and a time to do it!" The spirit then vanished, but Bell was a badly shaken man. However, the ghost was as good as its word, though in a most unpleasant way. Within a few days Bell incurred the displeasure of the Lord Chancellor and as a result was thrown into prison without trial for ten years. During that time he had little else to do except translate Luther's discourses.

Though the spirit that appeared to Captain Bell is often thought to be that of Martin Luther, it did not look like Luther, nor did it speak in German as Luther would have. It may have been a projection of Bell's own troubled conscience.

PATIENCE WORTH   One of the most prolific "writing spirits" of all times was a girl who reportedly died in the seventeenth century but reappeared as a spirit control in the early years of the twentieth century. This spirit called herself Patience Worth.

Patience operated through the agency of Mrs. Pearl Curren, a St. Louis housewife who was much attracted to spiritualism. On July 8, 1913, while Mrs. Curren was using a Ouija board this message came through:

"Many months ago I lived; Again I come—Patience Worth my name." Later Patience provided details of her life. She was born in England in the seventeenth century, migrated to America, and was killed by Indians. But she failed to provide the sort of information that could be checked historically. In other respects, however, Patience was extremely chatty.

She progressed from the Ouija board to speaking directly through Mrs. Curren while Mr. Curren took down the dictation. She even learned to operate a typewriter using Mrs. Curren's fingers.

Patience turned out an incredible stream of stories, poems, sermons, and aphorisms which some people thought had literary merit.

A St. Louis newspaper man named Caspar W. Yost wrote articles and finally a best-selling book on the subject. "Patience's" own writings also became extremely popular. There were Patience Worth clubs and even a magazine was devoted to her.

However, interest in Patience soon faded, and skeptics pointed out that there was a great deal in Mrs. Curren's own background that could have accounted for her knowledge (limited though it was) of Patience's life.

See also: MUSIC FROM THE DEAD

THE SPIRIT OF SAMUEL   The Bible has little to say on the subject of ghosts. The attitude of the ancient Hebrews toward ghosts seems to have been more suspicious than skeptical. Anyone who had dealings with ghosts or spirits of any sort was somehow performing an unnatural and ungodly act, for which he was likely to suffer.

The most celebrated "ghost story" in the Bible recounts just such a case and reveals a great deal about the ancient Hebrew attitude toward ghosts and people who had any traffic with them.

Facing a military crisis, King Saul felt that God had turned away from him and denied him access to prophecy. "And when Saul enquired of the Lord, the Lord answered him not, neither by dreams . . . nor by prophets." So Saul decided to try and obtain his prophecy by other means, by resorting to necromancy, questioning the dead about the future. Traditionally the dead were supposed to be able to foresee coming events, but to the Hebrews necromancy was an accursed practice.

Still it seems as if Saul had no trouble finding someone who was skilled in the practice. She was an old woman from Endor, a phrase often translated as Witch of Endor. The King wanted the old woman to summon up the spirit of the prophet Samuel. The woman was very wary because King Saul himself had previously banned all attempts at conversing with the dead and other acts of necromancy on pain of death. But times had changed, and Saul was desperate. He assured the woman that she would not be punished. So she conjured up the spirit of Samuel, "An old man . . . covered with a mantle."

The pious old prophet was not at all pleased at having been summoned up in so impious a manner. "Why hast thou disquieted me, to bring me up?" he demanded. King Saul explained that the Lord would no longer answer his questions, but he thought that Samuel might. That made Samuel even angrier: "Wherefore then dost thou ask of me, seeing the Lord is departed from thee, and is become thine enemy?"

Samuel did issue a prophecy, but it was a grim and terrible one. Not only would the Israelites lose to the Philistines, but Saul and his sons would die as a result of the battle. The next day a thoroughly demoralized King Saul led his army to defeat. His sons were killed in the battle, and in despair Saul killed himself with his own sword.

See also: PROPHETIC CORPSES

WALTER   During the early years of the twentieth century, American spiritualism was dominated by the medium Mina Crandon, known in spiritualist circles as Margery. Margery was the wife of a respectable and prominent professor of surgery at Harvard Medical School. Margery's spirit control was her dead brother Walter, who had been killed in a train accident in 1911.

Margery became well-known outside of spiritualist circles in 1922 when she tried to claim a prize offered by the magazine *Scientific American* to anyone who could show genuine mediumship. One of the members of the *Scientific American* committee that was to judge the genuineness of the phenomena produced by the medium was the magician Harry Houdini, already known as a fierce opponent of mediums and spiritualism.

Margery, with Walter's aid, had apparently produced some astonishing effects in several séances where the magician was not present, and by 1924 it seemed as though the prize was to be awarded to her. But Houdini objected, and more séances were arranged in which the magician imposed strict controls. He designed a cabinet in which the medium could be enclosed with only her head and hands visible.

During one of the séances a folding ruler was found in the cabinet. Houdini accused Margery of smuggling the ruler into the cabinet so that she could manipulate a small box containing a bell that was supposedly rung by spirit hands. Walter, on the other hand, accused Houdini of planting incriminating evidence, and

Houdini (right) *tests Margery*

during the séance he became very abusive and threatening. In the end the committee voted against awarding Margery the prize. However, after Houdini's death in 1926 one of his assistants said that he had placed the ruler in the cabinet on Houdini's instructions. Naturally spiritualists jumped on this confession. But surprisingly some magicians also think that Houdini may have framed the medium, because he hated her and knew she was a fraud but had been unable to prove it. That debate will never be settled.

But there was other, less ambiguous evidence of Margery's trickery. One of the proofs that Walter was supposed to give of his existence was that during a séance he would impress his thumbprint in dental wax. However an investigator found that Walter's thumbprint was identical to that of Margery's dentist, who had helped her to develop the method of taking prints. The dentist apparently had nothing to do with the fraud, and of course Margery never admitted or explained anything. Despite the fingerprint fiasco and other exposures, Margery remained prominent not only in spiritualist circles but also in psychical research. It is an era in psychical research that modern parapsychologists look back upon with some embarrassment.

See also: HARRY HOUDINI

2

CLASSIC

CASES

ATHENODORUS'S GHOST   One of the oldest "true" ghost stories on record comes from the pen of Pliny the Younger, who lived in Rome in the first century A.D. Like his more famous uncle, Pliny the Elder, the younger was a careful and accurate recorder of what he had seen and heard. Through his letters historians have been able to learn a great deal about life in Rome at the height of the empire.

There is nothing in his writings to indicate that Pliny was a particularly credulous or superstitious man. Yet he was much impressed by a ghost story that he had heard, and he was prepared to vouch for the truth of it. He told the story in a letter to his patron, Lucias Sura.

"There was formerly at Athens a large and handsome house which none the less had acquired a reputation of being badly haunted. The folk told how at the dead of night horrid noises were heard: The clanking of chains which grew louder and louder until there suddenly appeared the hideous phantom of an old man who seemed the very picture of abject filth and misery. His beard was long and matted, his white hair disheveled and unkempt. His thin legs were loaded with a weight of galling fetters that he dragged wearily along with a painful moaning; his wrists were shackled by long cruel links, while ever and anon he raised his arms and shook his shackles in a kind of impotent fury. Some few mocking skeptics who were once bold enough to watch all night in the house had been well-nigh scared from their senses at the sight of the apparition; and what was worse, disease and even death itself proved the fate of those who after dusk had ventured within those accursed walls. The place was shunned. A placard 'To Let' was posted but year succeeded year and the house fell almost to ruin and decay."

Then, continued Pliny, the philosopher Athenodorus reached the city, looking for a home to rent. Like most philosophers he was short of cash, and so he needed a house that could be rented cheaply. He spied the dilapidated old house with the 'To Let' sign and inquired how much the rent would be. "Being not a little surprised at the low figure, he put some more questions, and then there came out the whole story." The philosopher decided to take the house anyway.

It was the philosopher's custom to sit up late at night writing in his study, and on his first night in the haunted house, he refused to change his routine. In fact, he decided to work on a particularly difficult problem so that his mind would be fully absorbed and would not play tricks on him and cause him to see things that were not there.

"He was soon absorbed in philosophical calculations, but presently the noise of a rattling chain, at first distant and then growing nearer, broke on his ear. However, Athenodorus being particularly occupied with his notes, was too intent to interrupt his writing until, as the clanking became more and more continuous, he looked up and before him stood the phantom exactly as it had been described.

"The ghastly figure seemed to beckon with its finger, but the philosopher signed with his hand that he was busy and again went to his writing. The chains were shaken angrily and with persistence upon which Athenodorus quietly arose from his seat and taking the lamp, motioned the spectre to lead before."

The ghost led the philosopher through the house and into a garden. At a spot in the garden shrubbery, the ghost signed and disappeared. Athenodorus marked the spot and then went back into the house and retired for the night. He slept soundly. The next morning he went to the local magistrates and told them what he had seen. He suggested that the spot at which the ghost had disappeared be investigated. This was done, and when the investigators started digging, they unearthed a human skeleton just a few feet below the surface. Ancient and rusted chains still clung to the bones. The remains were carefully collected and properly buried. The house was then cleansed by various rituals and after that was never again troubled by ghosts or bad luck.

This story may be the origin of the popular idea of ghosts who drag clanking chains. It is interesting to compare the description of the ghost in this account with Charles Dickens's description of Marley's Ghost in *A Christmas Carol.*

THE CHELTENHAM HAUNTING   While there are literally hundreds of reputedly haunted houses in England, this case is one of the most famous and certainly one of the most closely investigated. It has been called "the most famous case of haunting since the Society of Psychical Research was formed"—high praise indeed.

For many years the location of the haunted house and the names of the individuals involved were deliberately kept secret. The haunting took place in a large Victorian house at Cheltenham in the county of Gloucestershire. The house was called Garden Reach.

The house was built in the 1860s and first purchased by a man named Henry Swinhoe. He lived there for some years with his wife, to whom he was devoted. After her death, however, he went to pieces and began drinking heavily. He had been a widower for some two years when he married a woman named Imogen, who thought that she could reform him, but she failed and quickly became a heavy drinker herself.

There is some dispute about the character of these two individuals. Henry Swinhoe's descendants claim that he was not a heavy drinker before he married Imogen and that she had driven him to drink.

Garden Reach

There is no dispute, however, about the fact that both of the Swinhoes had become violent alcoholics and quarreled constantly. Many of the quarrels centered around the first Mrs. Swinhoe's jewelry, which Henry had hidden somewhere in the house. It was later learned that he had hidden the jewels under the floorboards in a front room and that they were to serve as a nestegg for the children of his first marriage. Imogen thought she should have them. Imogen left her husband before his death, in July 1876, and never returned to Cheltenham. She died a few years later but unaccountably left instructions that she was to be buried at Cheltenham in a churchyard not a quarter of a mile from the house in which she had lived so unhappily. She had died, according to a medical report of the time, as a result of excessive drinking.

After Swinhoe's death the house was bought by an elderly gentleman who survived there only six months. His widow moved out, and the house remained empty for five years.

In April 1882 the house was rented by a Captain F. W. Despard, but the haunting itself did not begin until June of that year. The principal witness in this case was the family's eldest daughter, Rosina, who kept a detailed record of the appearance of the ghost. Rosina Despard, a young woman in her twenties when the haunting began, was a high-quality witness. She was a strong-willed, extremely intelligent individual who later went on to become a doctor—very unusual for a woman in Victorian times—and held several important medical posts. Her descriptions of encounters with the ghost are remarkably detailed. Equally remarkable is Miss Despard's coolness in the face of her ghostly encounters.

She first saw the ghost one evening after she had gone up to her room. There was a noise of someone passing the door, and when she opened the door, she saw "the figure of a tall lady, dressed in black, standing at the head of the stairs. After a few minutes she descended the stairs and I followed for a short distance, feeling curious what it could be. I had only a small piece of candle and it suddenly burnt itself out, and being unable to see more, I went back to my room."

Her description of the figure was very clear.

". . . a tall lady dressed in black of a soft woolen material, judging from the slight sound in moving. The face was hidden by a handkerchief held in the right hand. This was all I noticed then: but on further occasions when I was able to observe her more closely, I saw the upper part of the left side of her forehead, and a little of the hair above. Her left hand was nearly hidden by her sleeve and a fold of her dress. As she held it down, a portion of the widow's cuff was visible on both wrists, so that the whole impression was that of a lady in widow's weeds. There was no cap on the head, but the general effect of blackness suggests a bonnet, with long veil, or a hood."

The ghost was quite solid and not at all "ghostlike" in appearance. It was also remarkable for its habit of appearing at practically any time of the day or night, usually for short periods, though Rosina once observed it for half an hour. Rosina was not the only witness; at least five others in the house testified to seeing the ghost, and there were reports of another half-dozen witnesses though they were never interviewed by investigators.

Not everybody in the house saw the ghost, however. Captain Despard and his wife never saw it. On several occasions Miss Despard saw the ghost enter the room where her father or other members of her family were sitting. She would point the ghost out to them, for she could see it quite clearly, but was astonished to discover that others saw nothing.

Some investigators have proposed that the strange lady in black was no ghost at all but Captain Despard's mistress, whose existence he simply refused to acknowledge. Victorian morality drove people to elaborate stratagems of denial, but since the appearance of the woman in black continued for several years, the mistress theory seems rather farfetched.

Miss Despard tried to photograph the ghost several times, but it never appeared in good light while she had a camera. On two occasions she tied threads across the stairs, but the ghost seemed to glide right through them.

"I also attempted to touch her but she always eluded me. It was not that there was nothing to touch but that she always seemed to be beyond me, and if followed into a corner, simply disappeared."

Once a group of children made a ring around the ghost, but it just walked out between two people and vanished. Dogs were sensitive to its presence; cats failed to react at all.

Miss Despard tried to speak to it, but it seemed incapable of speech. Once when addressed directly, the ghost seemed to sort of gasp, though no sound was heard. While it could not vocalize, its very distinct footsteps could be heard regularly even by people who did not see the ghost.

When the haunting began, the ghost had a very substantial shape, but as time went on, it became less distinct. After 1886 it had assumed a very ghostly appearance indeed. It seemed to disappear entirely after 1889 though soft footsteps were reported until 1892.

Rosina Despard's journal of the haunting was sent to the Society for Psychical Research, and Frederick Myers, one of the founders of the SPR and later its honorary secretary, investigated the case. He did not see the ghost himself, but he did interview many of those who had, and he was very impressed by the quality of the witnesses and the evidence that they gave. He called the case "one of the most remarkable and best authenticated on record."

Miss Despard also investigated the history of the house, and it was she who came to the conclusion that the figure must be that of Imogen Swinhoe, perhaps returned from the grave and still searching for the hidden jewels.

The Despards moved out of Garden Reach after about ten years, and by that time the ghost had faded. The house was sold to a church group that renamed it St. Anne's and turned it into a girls' school. Accounts differ as to whether the ghost caused any trouble at the school. One account says that the ghost was never seen, while another insists that the proprietors had to abandon the school because of "constant trouble from the ghost."

In the 1970s a writer named Andrew MacKenzie said that he had uncovered evidence of even later appearances by the Cheltenham ghost. He reported the case of a man named John Thorne, who lived near the old haunted house. In October 1958 Thorne said he woke up one night to find a strange woman in his bedroom. It was very dark, and he could not see her very well, but he got the impression that she was wearing the clothes of the past century. He woke his wife and turned the lights on, but the figure disappeared and his wife told him he was dreaming. Three years later Thorne's brother, William, and teenage son, who were staying at the house, had a similar experience. William thought he heard footsteps in the hall, and when he looked out of the open door, he saw a woman in a long black dress who was holding a handkerchief up to her face. He remembered that the room suddenly became very cold.

The next morning when William told his brother what had happened, John Thorne replied, "Thank goodness. I thought I had been dreaming." He then recounted the story of the woman he had seen three years earlier.

It was several years later that William Thorne ran across a magazine article about the original "Cheltenham haunting" and realized that the figure he had seen looked almost exactly like the one described by Rosina Despard.

The original house has now been subdivided into flats, and no unusual happenings have been reported there since 1962.

THE CROSS CORRESPONDENCES   Organized psychical research began in the year 1881 with the founding of the British Society for Psychical Research. The founders were a distinguished group of scholars, led by philosopher Henry Sidgwick, who believed that there was more to the universe than materialistic science was revealing. Much of early psychical research was involved with an investigation of the claims of spiritualist mediums.

As the founders of psychical research began to die off, they often returned as spirit controls for mediums throughout the world. During the early years of the twentieth century, it seemed as if the departed founders were engaged in a vast, worldwide word game. The result was that extraordinary series of messages that came to be known as "the cross correspondences." A few weeks after the death of Frederick Myers, one of the founders of the SPR, a medium who had worked regularly with the group began getting messages from Myers's spirit. Soon other mediums who had worked with the SPR also reported messages from Myers.

Most of these messages were recorded by automatic writing, and the communications continued off and on for some thirty years. To many psychical researchers, it seemed as if Myers and the others were frantically attempting to establish their survival by sending complex messages from beyond the grave.

The special feature of this communication was that there were many references to the same topic, or "cross correspondences," in

Henry Sidgwick

the messages received by different mediums. Since the mediums lived in different parts of the world, there seemed little chance of collusion with one another to construct these complicated interlocking messages. If such messages could not be attributed to fraud or coincidence, then they would have to be regarded as proof that the mediums were controlled by spirits "from the other side," by the spirits of the dead psychical researchers.

Myers and his friends had been literary scholars, and the topic chosen for a cross correspondence was usually a literary one. Here, according to D. J. West, a member of the Society for Psychical Research is "an extremely simple example of a cross correspondence." It is called the Laurel Wreath case.

"One day Mrs. Piper [a well-known medium] when in a trance repeated the word 'laurel' several times. Next day when supposedly controlled by the spirit of F. W. H. Myers, she said, "I gave Mrs. Verrell [another medium] laurel wreath.' . . . An examination of her [Mrs. Verrell's] script showed that on an occasion three weeks before she had written 'Apollo's laurel bough,' 'Lauretaus,' 'A laurel wreath,' 'coronea laureta,' and various other references to laurel and laurel wreath." Again three weeks after Mrs. Piper's reference to laurel, Mrs. Verrell's script contained "Laurel leaves are an emblem. Laurel for the victor's brow."

It must be repeated that this is an extremely simple example. More typically the correspondences involved dozens of references, allusions to obscure phrases, and so forth. West comments that it "all looked like deliberate attempts to set the investigators a puzzle." Over the thirty years that the cross correspondences were being produced, the mediums turned out hundreds of thousands of pages of automatic writing. At least one man, J. G. Piddington, spent most of his life studying them and trying to make some order out of this overwhelming mass of material.

Some serious psychical researchers regard the cross correspondences as the best evidence for communication from beyond the grave. Others are not nearly as enthusiastic. They think that the thousands upon thousands of pages that make up the cross correspondences are just too complicated, too open to differing interpretations, to be conclusive. The skeptics believe that some researchers have seen "significant" messages that simply weren't there. In such a huge mass of material, they contend that there would be many perfectly ordinary conventional linkages of words as in the Laurel Wreath case. Besides, some wonder, if communication were possible, why would the founders of psychical research choose to communicate in so complex and obscure a manner?

See also: G. P., HARRY PRICE

THE DRUMMER OF TEDWORTH   The first ghost story that was ever investigated was the case that came to be known as The Drummer of Tedworth. It should properly be called a poltergeist case.

The events took place in the town of Tedworth, England, in March 1662. A traveling showman named William Drury was arrested for using counterfeit documents. The local magistrate, John Mompesson, set Drury free but confiscated his drum. Drury had once been a drummer in the army, and he considered the drum an important part of his act. He was very attached to it and quite upset when it was taken away from him. Within a few days all manner of strange things began happening to the Mompesson home.

The house was assailed by a loud drumming sound which grew worse after Drury's confiscated drum was destroyed. The Mompesson children were lifted out of bed by an unseen hand. At night the covers were torn off Mr. Mompesson's bed and his shoes were thrown at him. Other objects in the house were thrown around. Books were hidden, chamber pots were emptied onto beds, and in general life in the Mompesson house became difficult, uncomfortable, and very noisy.

All of this is typical poltergeist activity, but there was more. One servant was terrified by the vision of "a Great Body with two red and glaring eyes." Such apparitions are not typical in poltergeist cases.

The people of the time attributed such phenomena to witchcraft, and the case attracted the attention of Joseph Glanvill, the chaplain to King Charles II. Glanvill was an intelligent and educated man and an important one. He believed in the reality of witchcraft and had been an active witchcraft investigator, but unlike many other witch hunters he was neither a credulous fool nor a monster. He really tried to establish the facts of a case rather than being simply swept along by superstition and hysteria. Joseph Glanvill might be classed almost as the father of modern psychical research and the case of The Drummer of Tedworth was the first attempt at a serious investigation of such phenomena.

Glanvill traveled to Tedworth to question the witnesses firsthand. He witnessed some of the strange events himself. While he was at the Mompesson house, one of the maids said "it was come."

Joseph Glanvill

Glanvill hurried up to one of the bedrooms. "There were two little modest Girls in the Bed, between seven and eleven Years old as I guessed." Glanvill heard a scratching in the bed, "as loud as one with Long nails could make upon a Bolster." This went on for about half an hour and was followed by a noise which sounded like a dog panting. There was also some movement in the bedding. He published his evidence and conclusions in a book and provided us with our first complete account of the investigations of a poltergeist. Here is an excerpt:

"Upon the fifth of November 1662 it [the drummer] kept a mighty noise and a servant observing two boards in the children's room seeming to move, he bid it give him one of them. Upon which the board came (nothing moving it that he saw) within a yard of him. The man added, 'Nay, let me have it in my hand.' Upon which it was shoved quite home to him. He thrust it back and it was driven to him again, and so up and down, to and fro, at least twenty times together, till Mr. Mompesson forbade his servant such familiarities. This was in the daytime and seen by a whole room full of people."

Glanvill reported many similar marvelous events at the Mompesson home. The obvious explanation in the seventeenth century was witchcraft; the angry drummer had somehow bewitched the magistrate's house. Early in 1663 Drury was again arrested in a nearby town; the charge was not witchcraft but pig stealing. He was found guilty and sentenced to be transported to the American colonies, but Drury escaped from the convict ship and made his way to a town just a few miles from Tedworth. He bought another

Page from Glanvill's book. The "drummer" is shown in the upper left-hand corner.

drum and began beating it in the town square. Within twenty-four hours Magistrate Mompesson had him arrested on the charge of witchcraft.

Drury apparently confessed or, more accurately, boasted of causing the disturbances in the Mompesson home, though he did not say how. Still, he was acquitted on the charge of witchcraft, but on the original charge of pig stealing he was again condemned to transportation to the colonies, and this time he did not escape.

When Glanvill wrote up the case, he considered two possible explanations, witchcraft and trickery. Someone told him that the disturbances had been caused by "two young women in the house with a design to scare thence Mr. Mompesson's mother." But Glanvill rejected the idea of trickery for he did not see how any human being or group of human beings could possibly have been responsible for all the strange happenings. He could also discover no possible motive for the trickery. "And what interest could any of his [Mompesson's] family have had (if it had been possible to have managed it without discovery) to continue so long and so troublesome and so injurious an imposture."

But one can find in Glanvill's report some evidence of a human agency behind the disturbances. Every once in a while a member of the household would become so enraged at "the drummer" that he would pick up a weapon and charge at the source of the disturbance. This show of force would always make the disturbance stop.

Once Mompesson himself saw some wood move in a chimney room and grabbed a pistol and fired at the moving wood. Later blood was found nearby and on the stairs and in several other places in the house.

But as far as we know, no one ever confessed to faking the phenomena. If trickery was involved in the drummer case, many of the events could not possibly have taken place as reported. But since the descriptions of the most spectacular events are all secondhand and often taken months after the event, we cannot be sure of the accuracy of the descriptions.

THE GREEN GHOST OF VAUVERT   In the mid–thirteenth century the very pious King Louis IX of France gave a house near Paris to six monks from the Order of St. Bruno. However, from the window of their new house, the monks could see a much finer residence nearby. It was the palace of Vauvert. The palace had been built as a royal residence by King Robert but had been unused for many years.

Vauvert, though deserted, never had the reputation of being haunted until the monks of St. Bruno became its neighbors. From then on, frightful shrieks and howlings were heard from the palace every night. People reported seeing strange lights in the window of the deserted palace. Finally a huge green specter with a long white beard was seen regularly at an upstairs window howling and shrieking at passersby.

The stories of these ghostly goings-on at Vauvert soon reached the ears of the King himself, who was shocked and set a royal commission to investigate. The monks of St. Bruno also professed to be shocked, but they hinted to the commission that if they were allowed to inhabit the palace, they would soon expel the ghost.

The King was relieved and delighted to hear that the holy monks offered to undertake the dangerous task of getting rid of the ghost. A deed was drawn up making the palace of Vauvert the property of the monks of St. Bruno, and once they moved in, the disturbances ended forever.

Though solid information on this case is scanty, there seems good reason to believe that this is one of the oldest and most successful ghostly frauds on record.

THE GHOST AND THE JUDGE   One of the great problems in investigating ghost reports is that human memory is extremely fallible. Stories of even the most credible and honest witnesses cannot be trusted, not because the witness has necessarily told a lie, but because human memory is almost unbelievably unreliable. One expert on memory has called what we remember of our past an "imaginative reconstruction." This is particularly true when we try to recount extraordinary events that happened a long time ago. Nowhere in the annals of psychical research is this unfortunate fact illustrated more clearly than in the case of Sir Edmund Hornby.

In 1875 Sir Edmund Hornby was a jurist in charge of British interests in the Orient. His official title was chief judge of the Supreme Consular Court of China and Japan. The court was located in Shanghai, where the judge lived. He was an important and highly respected individual, certainly not the sort of man who could easily be accused of seeing things or making up ghost stories. So when Sir Edmund told people of the remarkable meeting that he had on the night of January 19, 1875, they tended to believe him.

The judge had heard cases during the day, and as was his custom, he wrote out his decisions after dinner, put them in an envelope, and gave them to his butler. His butler was then instructed to give the envelope to the newspaper reporter when he arrived for a summary of the judgments was to appear in the next day's paper. The judge then went to bed.

He was awakened from a sound sleep by a loud knocking at his bedroom door. The judge shouted, "Come in," and a figure that he recognized as the reporter entered the room. The judge resented the intrusion and angrily told the reporter that his butler had all the information the reporter needed. But the reporter made no apologies and gave no sign of leaving. He said only that he regretted having to wake the judge up, but that he had looked for the judge in his study first and, not finding him there, tried the bedroom.

Sir Edmund was now furious at the man's insolence. He was ready to jump out of bed and throw the man out of the room, yet there was something strange about the reporter's appearance that

A British judge

made him hesitate. The reporter looked very pale; perhaps he was ill, so the judge simply asked him politely to leave.

Instead of leaving, the reporter advanced into the room and sat down at the foot of the judge's bed. He moved slowly and stiffly as if he were in pain. Sir Edmund looked at the clock; it was twenty past one in the morning. The reporter also looked over at the clock. "Time presses," he said. Then he asked the judge for a summary of his decision and took out a small notebook in which to write down what he was told.

"I will give you nothing of the kind," thundered the judge. "Go downstairs and find the butler and don't disturb me. You will wake my wife. Otherwise I shall have to put you out. . . . Who let you in anyway?"

"No one."

"Confound it, what the devil do you mean? Are you drunk?"

"No, and never shall be again," the reporter replied. Then he repeated his request for the judge's decision. "Time is short."

"You don't seem to care about my time," growled the judge. "This is the last time I will ever allow a reporter to enter my house."

The reporter's reply stopped him short. "This is the last time I shall ever see you anywhere."

Sir Edmund was worried now, for the reporter was acting so strangely that there was no telling what the man might do. He also didn't want to awaken his wife, who was asleep in the next room. So he gave the reporter the summary that he had requested. As the judge talked, the reporter scribbled quickly in his notebook, apparently taking down the judge's words in shorthand. When the summary was finished, the reporter thanked the judge and left. The clock was striking half past one; the whole incident had taken about ten minutes.

The next morning Judge Hornby received a shock when he was told that the reporter who had disturbed him had died that very night. But what was truly shocking about the story was the time which the reporter had died. He had gone to work in his room that evening. At about midnight his wife came down to ask when he was coming to bed. He said that he had only the judge's decision to get ready; then he would be finished.

At about one-thirty, when he had still not come to bed, the reporter's wife became worried, and when she went down to look in on him, she found him dead on the floor. At his side lay his notebook, and written in the notebook were these words: "In the Supreme Court before the Chief Judge: The Chief Judge gave judgment this morning in the case to the following effect. . . ." The remainder trailed off into an illegible scrawl.

At an inquest it was determined that the reporter had died at approximately one o'clock, of a heart attack.

The judge was quite naturally extremely curious about what had happened and tried to find out as much as he could about the circumstances surrounding this extraordinary occurrence. The reporter's wife and servants insisted that he had never left the house the night of his death. The judge's own servants assured him that no one could have come into his house since all of the doors and windows had been locked. His wife, who had been sleeping in another room, thought she recalled hearing voices during the night, but she did not know to whom the judge had been speaking or what had been being said.

Now this strange occurrence put Judge Hornby in a dilemma, for he did not want to let a lot of people know about it, fearing (probably correctly) that they wouldn't believe him and that this would damage his reputation. But he couldn't keep completely quiet about it either. So he repeated the tale to only a few close friends, whom he swore to silence.

No secret can be kept forever, but this story made the rounds very slowly, and it wasn't until nine years after the event that two British psychical researchers, Edmund Gurney and Frederic Myers heard of it. They checked with Judge Hornby, and he dictated the story as it was told here and gave Gurney and Myers permission to use it in one of their books.

Gurney and Myers were experienced psychical researchers who had spent years collecting accounts of ghostly appearances. They thought that this was one of the very best they had ever heard, primarily because of the character of the witness, Sir Edmund Hornby. The judge swore that the account he had given them was absolutely correct. "As I said then, so I say now—I was not asleep, but wide awake. After a lapse of nine years my memory is quite clear on the subject. I have not the least doubt I saw the man—I have not the least doubt that the conversation took place between us." The judge had no possible reason for lying and had the reputation of a sane and sound witness. It was the perfect ghost story, and so it seemed for several months after Gurney and Myers published their account. Then the psychical researchers received a letter from Mr. Frederick H. Balfour, member of a prominent British family and a relative of the president of the Society of Psychical Research itself, another totally trustworthy witness. Balfour knew a lot about the events in Shanghai in January 1875.

The name of the reporter was not mentioned in the original account, but Balfour knew it was the Reverend Hugh Lang Nivens, editor of the *Shanghai Courier*. Rev. Nivens, he said, had not died at night but between eight and nine in the morning after having had a good night's rest.

In the judge's account he described how his wife was asleep in the next room, but Balfour said that at the time of the alleged meeting with the apparition, the judge was not married. His first wife had died some two years earlier, and while the judge did remarry, it was not until March 1875, three months after Nivens died. The judge said that he "remembered" details from the inquest into the Reverend Nivens's death, but since the death had been from natural causes, no inquest was ever held.

The "ghost" wanted to get a particular decision that was to be announced on January 20, and the judge gave it to him. The last words in Nivens's reporter's notebook were supposed to concern that decision. Yet there was no record that any such decision had been delivered on January 20.

There were not a few minor contradictions between Balfour's account and the recollections of Judge Hornby; they were in conflict on practically every major detail of the event. When Judge Hornby saw the Balfour letter, he was astonished.

In thinking the matter over, he agreed that his "vision" of the dead reporter must have come some three months after the death, not on the same night. But he insisted that he had not fabricated the story but told it exactly as he remembered it. "If I had not believed, as I still believe, every word of it [the story] was accurate and that my memory was to be relied on, I should not ever have told it as a personal experience."

G. P. Probably the most extraordinary series of mediumistic séances in the history of psychical research is what has been called the G. P. series. These séances are extraordinary because of the individuals involved. Leonora Piper, the celebrated American medium, and Richard Hodgson, an Englishman who had been an investigator for the Society for Psychical Research in Britain and who came to America to head the American Society of Psychical Research, were the principal participants.

Hodgson was no gullible fool. He was a keen and skeptical in-

Mrs. Piper

Richard Hodgson

vestigator who had exposed so many mediumistic frauds that some of those in the field accused him of running the Society *against* Psychical Research. Many mediums who had met him would cheerfully have wrung his neck.

G. P. was supposed to be the spirit of George Pellew, a young English friend of Hodgson's who died suddenly in February of 1892. Sometime before his death Pellew had attended a séance with Mrs. Piper (under a false name) but apparently had not been very much impressed by the medium.

A few weeks after Pellew's death, a spirit calling himself G. P. introduced himself at one of the Piper séances. Another friend of Pellew's who was in attendance recognized some of the information about Pellew that the spirit revealed.

Other friends of the dead Pellew were brought to séances. They were not only struck by how much G. P. seemed to know about Pellew, but how much the spirit's voice, coming from Mrs. Piper, seemed to resemble that of the dead man. Hodgson attended these séances regularly.

During most of the séances, however, G. P. communicated by means of automatic writing, while the medium's regular spirit guide, named Dr. Phinuit, did most of the talking. Mrs. Piper would be slumped over in a deep trance. She would speak in the voice of Dr. Phinuit while her hand rapidly wrote messages from G. P. The total effect was extremely eerie.

The strange proceedings continued night after night for months. One of the most significant incidents in the series took place during the winter of 1892. Attending the séance was James Howard, who had been a close friend of Pellew's. Hodgson was recording the events. Mrs. Piper was in a deep trance, her body completely limp and—to all outward appearances—lifeless.

Howard had already been at several séances, but he was not convinced that he was in contact with the spirit of his dead friend. "Tell me," he demanded, "something known only to G. P. and myself."

The medium's hand began to twitch. She grabbed a pencil and

started writing with great speed. Hodgson picked up the sheets and read them aloud as she finished. Howard agreed that the information was generally correct. Then the medium wrote the word "Private" and pushed Hodgson away.

He wrote, "I retired to the other side of the room, and Mr. Howard took my place close to the hand where he could read the writing. He did not, of course, read it aloud and it was too private for my perusal. The hand reached the end of each sheet, tore it off from the block book, and thrust it wildly at Mr. Howard, and then continued writing. The circumstances narrated, Mr. Howard informed me, contained precisely the kind of test for which he had asked and he said that he was 'perfectly satisified, perfectly.' "

Hodgson was not yet perfectly satisfied. He gathered thirty more of Pellew's friends, none of whom personally knew the medium. He also brought in 120 other people. He wanted to see if the spirit of G. P. could identify Pellew's friends from a group of total strangers. G. P. picked out every one of the thirty without a single mistake. G. P. was also said to have given information on the location of a tin box of Pellew's private papers which was supposedly lost after his death.

Ultimately the skeptical Hodgson was converted to belief in Mrs. Piper. "I cannot profess to have any doubt but that they [the dead] . . . have survived the change that we call death, and they have direct communication with us whom we call living, through Mrs. Piper's entranced organism."

Despite his "conversion" Hodgson continued to expose mediums that he thought to be fraudulent.

Hodgson suddenly and unexpectedly dropped dead in January 1906, and shortly after his death his "spirit" began to pop up at séances including the séances of Mrs. Piper herself.

Hodgson may have been a brilliant researcher, but as a spirit he was a flop. Many of George Pellew's friends were impressed that when G. P. was speaking through Mrs. Piper, they were really in contact with the spirit of their dead friend. Hodgson's friends did not feel the same way at all. The psychologist and psychical researcher William James attended some of the séances and said that they revealed nothing that Mrs. Piper might not have learned in perfectly ordinary ways during her long association with Hodgson.

See also: THE CROSS CORRESPONDENCES

Tнε HYDESVILLE HAUNTING   The ghostly phenomena that afflicted a house in the little hamlet of Hydesville in upstate New York turned out to have enormous significance. Yet the beginnings of the Hydesville haunting were simple and quite familiar.

The strange happenings began in March of 1848 in the humble cabin of John D. Fox, unsuccessful farmer and part-time blacksmith. The Fox family had lived in the Hydesville house for only a few months. Before they moved in, the house had been occupied by a long succession of tenants. Primarily it had been used as a temporary dwelling by families looking for larger and more suitable quarters in the vicinity. The house had a reputation for being shabby and uncomfortable but not for being haunted.

The house at Hydesville

Fox sisters

Four members of the Fox family lived in the little house. Mr. Fox was a morose and silent man and a staunch Methodist. People said that before he had turned to religion, he had been a drunkard for many years. Religion, however, had not improved his disposition. Mrs. Fox had the reputation of being a good though not terribly bright woman who had suffered much during the years when her husband drank.

With the couple lived two daughters, Margaretta, sometimes called Margaret or Maggie, who was fifteen years old, and Kate (also called Katie, Cathie, or Catherine), who was not quite twelve. There were two other Fox children older than Maggie and Kate who no longer lived with their parents. A son, David, lived a few miles from Hydesville. A married daughter, thirty-four-year-

old Leah Fish, lived in the nearby city of Rochester. Leah was separated from her husband at that time and ultimately was married
several times.

During the last week of March 1848, the Fox household was
shaken by a series of strange noises for which no cause could be
found. Most of the noises came from the room in which Maggie
and Katie slept. The family was at first disturbed and then frightened. But after a while they decided that whatever it was that was
making the noises meant no harm and they became curious. But
there seemed no rational explanation to account for the noises. So
far a fairly conventional poltergeist case, right down to the teen or
preteen girls around whom the phenomena centered.

The next step was to attempt to communicate with whatever it
was that was making the noises. One night, when the girls were in
a rather playful mood, they began asking the unknown noisemaker
some questions. To everyone's surprise they began getting answers
to the questions. When they asked the age of one of the girls, the
correct number of knocks was given. This so astonished Mr. and
Mrs. Fox that they called some of the neighbors in to see, or rather
to hear, what was going on.

One of the neighbors, William Duesler, wrote the following account of what he witnessed:

"Mrs. Fox then asked if it would answer my questions if I asked
any, and if so, rap. It then rapped three times. [This was the signal
for yes.] I then asked if it was an injured spirit, and it rapped. I
asked if it had come to hurt anyone who was present, and it did
not rap. I then reversed the question, and it rapped. I asked if I or
my father had injured it (as we had formerly lived in the house),
and there was no noise. Upon asking the negative of these questions the rapping was heard. I then asked if Mr.——— [John C.
Bell] (naming a person who had formerly lived in the house) had
injured it, and if so, manifest it by rapping, and it made three
knocks louder than common, and at the same time the bedstead
jarred more than it had done before. I inquired if it was murdered
for money, and the knocking was heard. I then requested it to rap

The first of the spirit rappings

when I mentioned the sum of money for which it was murdered. I then asked if it was one hundred, two, three or four, and when I came to five hundred the rapping was heard. All in the room said they heard it distinctly."

Such "rapping poltergeists" had been heard in the past, but not in Hydesville or the vicinity. As word of the spirit rappings spread, hundreds flocked to the Fox house to witness the marvel. They came on horseback, by wagon and coach. The little town had never seen such excitement before.

The rapping spirit indicated that its body had been buried in the cellar of the house. The Foxes dug up the cellar, and according to one account they found some human teeth and bones and parts of a broken bowl. But this story, like so much about the Hydesville rappings, has been disputed.

Now it happened that John C. Bell, the ghost's accused murderer, was living in a town not a dozen miles from Hydesville. He rushed back to confront his accuser face-to-face (or face to what-ever). But he was unable to question the spirit directly. Instead Bell went to his friends and former neighbors and asked them all to sign statements testifying to his innocence and to his good character and reputation. Some forty-four persons signed such a statement, and Bell had it printed up and distributed in pamphlet form.

However, there was at least one person in Hydesville who did not care for John C. Bell at all. She was Lucretia Pulver, who had worked as a maid in the Bell family when they lived in Hydesville in 1844. Lucretia had been fourteen years old at the time. She said that she remembered seeing a peddler who had come to the house during the summer of 1844 and had promised to return. But the peddler was never seen again. According to Lucretia, one day after the peddler's disappearance, she had been sent away from the house. She claimed that a few days later she saw Mrs. Bell mending two old overcoats, which she believed might have belonged to the peddler. She also mentioned seeing some loose earth in the cellar. The murdered peddler's grave perhaps? A couple of other people including Lucretia's mother also attested to their belief that something unusual, and possibly sinister, had happened in the Bell house during the summer of 1844.

The rapping spirit who was so garrulous about so many things turned surprisingly tactiturn when it was asked to give information about itself. The Fox sisters, for no good reason that anyone can recall, named the spirit Mr. Splitfoot. The spirit indicated that his (it was assumed to be a man) initials were C. R. and that he had once lived in Orleans County, New York, and that he had five children. Attempts to confirm these meager leads came to nothing. Clearly, John C. Bell could not be charged with murder on the basis of such flimsy evidence. The authorities dismissed the whole affair as the creation of a couple of mischievous girls.

On the basis of the past history of such events, one would expect the Hydesville rappings to have been a ninety-day wonder. Remembered, if at all, as only an unimportant footnote in the record of these phenomena. But they became much more than that; they became the spark that ignited the movement that was known as spiritualism. During the next half-century spiritualism was to become an important movement that would sweep the world. While spiritualism is no longer the movement it was back in the nineteenth century, spiritualist meetings are still held in many communities in the United States and Europe and the influence of spiritualism is felt in some of the popular religious cults of South America.

Spiritualism also inspired the beginnings of psychical research, that branch of investigation that is now more popularly known as parapsychology.

How could this happen? How could such a simple and really unspectacular event create such a reaction? Of course, no one can say with complete certainty, but the time and the place were clearly factors. The world was ready for spiritualism. In the years just prior to the Hydesville events, there had been a great deal of speculation in the United States and elsewhere about the possibilities of communicating with the dead. Hydesville itself is located in a part of New York State that is known as the Burnt Over District—Burnt Over because it has been consumed by so many religious enthusiasms. For example, the Mormon Church started in the very same region. Then there was the personality of the Fox girls. Often individuals who have reported poltergeist experiences when they are young will either deny them or simply no longer discuss them once they get a bit older. The Fox sisters made a career of spiritualism. And there is always a large element of luck.

During the height of interest in the rappings themselves, the crowds around the Fox house grew so large and boisterous that the family decided in the interest of peace and quiet that the girls should be sent away for a while. First Maggie and Kate were sent to the home of their brother, David, but the rappings followed them, as did the horde of curiosity seekers. The girls were then split up; Kate remained at her brother's house, while Maggie was sent to Rochester to stay with her sister Leah.

In Rochester the rappings grew, if possible, even more pronounced. They were accompanied by a host of other activities typical of a poltergeist. Objects were thrown about, beds were shaken, and tables and chairs moved mysteriously around the room. Along with the raps there came mysterious groans, grunts, and a sound that Leah described as "the gurgle of coagulated blood being emptied from a bucket."

But rather than being mindless and destructive, as the traditional poltergeist, this one remained generally cheerful and became remarkably cooperative. It even helped friends of the Foxes work out a rapping code that could be used to send messages more complex than yes or no. The first message delivered in this code was, "We are all your dear friends and relatives."

Thus the significance of the rappings had expanded dramatically. No longer was the source of the noises simply the spirit of a murdered peddler intent on bringing his murderer to justice. The rappings now opened up a channel of communication to the world of the dead. It was the "spiritual telegraph," as its supporters called it. The word telegraph was popular at this time because four years earlier Samuel Morse had made his first successful experiments with the telegraph, and the world was still astounded by the apparent miracle of sending coded messages over a wire. The rappings of the spirits and the tappings of the telegraph machine sounded very much alike. To many the spiritual telegraph was no more incomprehensible and miraculous than Samuel Morse's telegraph, though considerably more wonderful and more important.

The gift of stimulating messages from the spirit world proved to be contagious. Soon the rappings began to follow Leah as well as her younger sisters. When one of the Fox girls stayed in a boardinghouse, other girls in the house quite suddenly developed the ability to produce rappings.

The Fox sisters may have been shy about their "gift" at first, but they soon lost all traces of shyness. From private performances, or sittings, as they came to be called, the Fox sisters moved onto the

public stage. In conjunction with a local hypnotist, Dr. George
Capron, Leah and Maggie participated in a series of lectures and
demonstrations in Rochester. Hundreds attended the initial dem-
onstration, and though there was some hostility from the audience,
the series was accounted a great success and the group went on the
road, attracting large crowds wherever they appeared. By 1850
they felt secure enough to take their demonstrations to New York
City, where they were extremely popular.

There were skeptics, loads of them, but the Fox sisters also won
some influential converts to their cause. The most influential was
Horace Greeley, the editor of the *New York Tribune* and one of
the most important figures in the history of American journalism.

Investigations into the Fox sisters' abilities began. In 1851 a
group of Buffalo, New York, doctors observed Leah during a performance and declared that the noises were produced when she
snapped her knee joints. Leah hotly denied the charge.

There were more tests, usually unsuccessful ones, and there
were confessions by relatives and former asssociates of the Fox sisters that the whole thing was a fake. The Foxes continued to deny
all, and they remained popular for years though their careers in
spiritualism were overshadowed by more flamboyant mediums.

In 1888 the world of spiritualism was rocked when Maggie and
Catherine Fox made public statements that they had faked the
Hydesville rappings from the beginning and that spiritualism itself
was a fraud.

According to the sisters, the rappings had begun as sort of a
childish joke to frighten their mother, but when Leah became involved, she saw a way of capitalizing on the excitement and making money.

The sisters, despite their former fame, had become paupers and
alcoholics by the time they made their confession. Convinced
spiritualists simply refused to believe them, saying that they had
become turncoats for money. Ultimately Margaret recanted her
confession and was welcomed back into the spiritualist fold.

See also: THE COCK LANE GHOST

ROSALIE   The extraordinary story of the little-girl ghost called Rosalie began on December 8, 1937. Harry Price, who was one of Britain's most highly publicized psychical researchers and a man who was known under the title the Ghost Hunter, was contacted by a lady he knew. She told Price that she wanted him to attend a private séance at which the spirit of a little girl named Rosalie invariably materialized. She made Price swear that he would never identify any of those who attended the séance or the place at which it was held. The family, she said, wanted absolutely no publicity because they were afraid that the spirit might be frightened away. People who attend séances are often sensitive about publicity, so these conditions did not strike Price as being at all unusual. And thus began one of the more intriguing mysteries in the history of psychical research.

On Wednesday, December 15, 1937, Price went to what he called "one of the better-class London suburbs." He was admitted to a large mid-Victorian house by a parlormaid shortly after 7 P.M. Inside he met Mr. and Mrs. X, as Price called them, and their daughter, aged about seventeen. Over supper he was told the story of Rosalie.

A friend of Mrs. X, a Frenchwoman Price called Mme Z, had married an English officer at the beginning of World War I. The officer was killed in 1916 leaving his wife with an infant daughter, Rosalie. The tragedy for Mme Z was compounded in 1921 when Rosalie died of diphtheria.

Some five years after her daughter's death, Mme Z began to sense the presence of the girl's spirit. The feeling grew stronger, and soon Mme Z not only began to hear her daughter's voice and see her form but was actually able to grasp her hand. Mme Z discussed these events with Mr. and Mrs. X, who were already involved with psychic phenomena. They suggested that regular séances be held at their house in order to summon the spirit of Rosalie. These séances began in the spring of 1929 and continued more or less regularly on Wednesday evenings up until the time that Price was called in. Usually those attending the séance were only Mr. and Mrs. X, their daughter, and Mme Z, though an occasional outsider like Price was admitted. Rosalie appeared at almost every séance.

After dinner Price was introduced to Mme Z and to a young man Price called Jim, who was also to attend the séance.

Harry Price was an experienced psychical researcher and well aware of the fact that many séances were faked. He had exposed some of these fakes himself. He examined the house, with particular attention to the séance room. He interviewed all of the servants. When it was time to begin the séance, he locked the door and put the key in his pocket. He then sealed the door and all the windows with tape and initialed the tape. He spread powder in front of the fireplace in order to detect footprints of anyone coming or going that way. These were all precautions to prevent anyone from slipping into the room once the lights were turned out.

When the room was sealed, Price minutely examined couches, drawers, rugs, and every other item in the room. He found nothing in the least suspicious. He examined the clothing of Jim and Mr. X, but at this time Victorian morality still applied and Price admitted that he "could not very well search the three ladies." Still, he was convinced that they were concealing nothing on their persons.

The séance began at about 9 P.M. The six participants sat in a circle of chairs in the center of the room. Mr. X switched off the light, and the group chatted quietly in total darkness for about twenty minutes. Then Mr. X turned on the radio to provide some music. The illuminated panel of the radio cast a dim light in the room. A short time later Mr. X switched off the radio and told the sitters to be absolutely still. Mme Z began to call "Rosalie" and she sobbed softly.

Mrs. X whispered to Price that Rosalie was in the room. The investigator could hear the shuffling of feet, and he felt something warm touch his hand, but since the room was pitch-dark he could

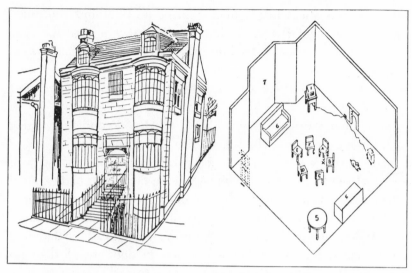

Sketch of the house in which the séance was said to have been held

see nothing. Price then asked if he could touch the spirit, and he was given permission to do so. He stretched out his hand and touched what he took to be the nude figure of a little girl of about six years of age. Her long hair fell to her shoulders. He took her right hand and felt her pulse; it was about ninety beats a minute. He put his ear to her chest and heard her heart beat.

Price had some plaques covered with a substance that glowed in the dark and cast a dim greenish light. He asked permission to uncover the plaques and was told that he could. In the faint greenish light Price saw what he described as "a beautiful child who would have graced any nursery in the land."

Price asked the little girl some questions but did not receive any significant answers. Shortly the whole scene became very emotional with Mrs. X and Mme Z sobbing loudly. The luminous plaques were covered, and the séance ended around eleven o'clock.

When the lights were turned back on, Price examined all of the seals and the powder. They were exactly as he had left them. He took a quick tour of the house but found nothing unusual. He was convinced that the séance could not have been faked, and he rushed to his club to write his report.

But the report did not appear in print until 1939, nearly two years after the event. Naturally it created a sensation and was widely quoted or republished.

In his report Price concluded that if the séance had been faked, it would have required an incredibly elaborate deception involving trapdoors, a revolving wall, or some such stage device in order to sneak a living child into the room. He asserted that none of those who had participated in the séance was making any money out of it and they didn't want any publicity, indeed, that they had gone to great lengths to avoid it.

Even critics of psychical research agreed that fraud under such circumstances would have been extremely unlikely. But they raised an even more fundamental question—had the séance taken place at all? Curiously, in the many months between the time of the supposed séance and the publication of Price's report, he mentioned the case to only one other individual and he swore her to silence.

As the clamor for more information grew, Price insisted that he would have to respect the privacy of those who had been involved. Later he said that at the end of August 1939 the X family and Mme Z went on a motoring tour of France but the war broke out and they were separated. Mme Z was never heard from again, and presumably the spirit of Rosalie disappeared with her.

The critics were far from satisfied. Why, they asked, would anyone with a grain of sense go driving around France in August 1939 when the outbreak of war seemed inevitable? Why didn't "Jim," who had attended the Price séance, or someone who had attended one of the many earlier séances in which Rosalie presumably appeared step forward? How about the servants or some friend of the family who could at least confirm that the séances had taken place making a statement? There was complete silence. The only person who could or would confirm the existence of the spirit child Rosalie or indeed of the X family and Mme Z was Harry Price. The whole thing depended on his word and his word alone.

How reliable was Harry Price? Opinions differ. He had been one of England's most prominent psychical researchers, but he had often been criticized by colleagues for his flamboyant and publicity-seeking style. By 1937 his career was in trouble, and the National Laboratory of Psychical Research, which he had established, collapsed from lack of financial support.

At about the time the Rosalie case was published, Price was becoming involved with an even more sensational case—the haunting of Borley Rectory, which was to make him more famous than ever. By 1941 he seemed to regret that he had ever said anything about Rosalie in the first place; at least he stopped talking about the little-girl ghost, though he never admitted that the incident had not taken place.

In the mid-1950s some psychical researchers tried to check out the only solid bit of information Price had left (Price himself died in 1948), his description of the house in which the séance had been held. After painstaking research they concluded that even the house was fictitious.

See also: BORLEY RECTORY, HARRY PRICE

THE VERSAILLES ADVENTURE   The feeling or belief that one has seen a figure from the past is, as this volume shows, an extremely common one. The belief that one has actually stepped into the past and is able to view not only the forms of those long dead but the scenery as well is less common, but it does form the basis for one of the most singular and fascinating episodes in the history of psychical research.

The story began on the afternoon of August 10, 1901. Two Englishwomen, Ann Moberly and Eleanor Jourdain, who were touring France, visited the great palace of Versailles outside of Paris. (Later, when they wrote up their experiences of that day, they

The Petit Trianon

used the pseudonyms Elizabeth Morrison and Francis Lamont.) Both women were teachers, intelligent and well educated, but neither of them had any particular interest in French history in general or Versailles in particular. Nor had they any previous interest in or knowledge of psychical research or ghosts. They were in all respects quite ordinary tourists.

The pair was strolling toward the Petit Trianon, a smaller palace on the grounds of the main palace. The Petit Trianon had been a favorite spot of the unfortunate Queen Marie Antoinette. The two women saw a small gate, went through it, and their adventure began.

"To our right we saw some farm buildings looking empty and deserted; implements were lying about; we looked in, but saw no one. The impression was saddening; but it was not until we reached the crest of the rising ground where there was a garden that we began to feel as if we had lost our way, and as if something were wrong."

The two women found the atmosphere increasingly oppressive. The buildings and gardens around them looked somehow unreal, as if they were part of a stage set. They met two men who were wearing long greenish coats that looked like official uniforms of some sort. The men told them to go straight on. The feeling that something was very wrong became more and more acute. They passed a small building which they called a kiosk. Beyond it they saw a dark pockmarked man wearing a wide-brimmed hat and a heavy cloak. The expression on the man's face was "very evil," and they were almost afraid to walk past him.

They saw "a young girl standing in a doorway, who wore a white kerchief dress to her ankles"; there was a lady sketching, and finally when they came to a country house, a young man offered to show them around to the front of the house. When they arrived there, they felt that they had returned to the twentieth century.

Oddly enough the two women did not talk about the incident for a full week. Wrote one, "nor did I think about it until I began writing a descriptive letter of our expeditions of the week before. As the scenes came back one by one, the same sensations of dreamy unnatural oppression came over me so strongly that I stopped writing and said to Miss Lamont 'Do you think the Petit Trianon is haunted?' Her answer was prompt. 'Yes I do!' "

The women agreed not to talk further about the incident until they had written out separate accounts of what they had experienced and compared them. The written accounts were similar enough to make the women believe that they had jointly experienced something very strange. They decided to do further research on Versailles.

Over the next two years the women spent hours searching books and memoirs concerning the French palace. They came to the conclusion that they had stepped back into the past at a period shortly before the French Revolution overwhelmed King Louis XVI and Queen Marie Antoinette. From old maps and descriptions they believed that they could reconstruct exactly where they had walked that day. They thought they could identify one of the individuals they had seen. The dark-skinned, pockmarked man must have been the Queen's Creole friend the Comte de Vau-

Marie Antoinette

dreuil, who was often at the palace. They believed that they were even able to fix the date upon which they had entered the past as August 5, 1789.

Three years after their first adventure, on July 4, 1904, the two women again visited Versailles. Nothing was the same. "The kiosk was gone. Instead of a shaded meadow continuing up to the wall of the terrace, there is now a broad gravel sweep beneath it . . . Exactly where the lady was sitting we found a large spreading bush of apparently many years' growth." The crowds in the modernized Trianon gardens in no way resembled the quaintly garbed individuals they had seen on their first visit. "The commonplace, unhistorical atmosphere was totally inconsistent with the air of silent mystery by which we had been so much oppressed. People went wherever they liked, and no one would think of interfering to show the way."

The two women finally wrote up their Versailles experience in a book called *An Adventure.* The case became and remains one of the most interesting and puzzling in the history of psychical research. It was the basis for an excellent British television dramatization which was also shown widely in the United States in 1983 and 1984.

The major reason that this case has been taken so seriously is the very high caliber of the witnesses. There is, after all, no confirming evidence that Miss Moberly and Miss Jourdain saw what they said they saw. We just have to take their word for it. But everyone who has studied the case has assumed that their word was good. They were two highly respected and respectable individuals who never sought money or fame from their experience. There has never been a hint that either woman was a habitual liar or in any way mentally unbalanced. The witnesses seemed just as puzzled about what they had experienced as everyone else.

Despite this the case rests on an extremely shaky foundation for it relies entirely on the memory of the two witnesses, and as both psychology and psychical research have demonstrated, the human memory is highly unreliable in such matters.

In the 1930s an English psychical researcher named R. J. Sturge-Whiting went over the whole case. By a careful search he located all of the places the women had described in their account and concluded that all were at Versailles in 1901 when the two women made their visit. The people they had seen were gardeners, amateur artists, and ordinary tourists, the sort that visited the palace regularly. What about their identification of the Comte de Vaudreuil? The description was very general. Surely there must have been more than one dark pockmarked man in history. It is not stretching coincidence too far to imagine that such an individual may also have been one of the tourists at Versailles on August 10, 1901.

Most psychical researchers today would probably put the entire wonderful Versailles adventure down to a combination of mistaken identity, overactive imagination, and selective memory.

3

HAUNTINGS

THE BLOODY GHOST   St. James's Palace in London was
built by Henry VIII for his queen Anne Boleyn on the site of a former leper hospital. But it is not the ghost of the King or his most
tragic Queen or of the poor and despised lepers that haunt the site.

The most prominent and ghastly ghost of Saint James Palace is
the specter of a small man with his throat cut and his mouth hanging open. He sits propped up in a bed against a wall in the
"haunted room," and the entire scene is drenched in blood.

This specter has its origins in a sensational incident that took
place on May 31, 1810. The duke of Cumberland, George III's
dreadful and debauched son, had returned to St. James late one
evening. The servants heard the sounds of a fight coming from the
duke's bedroom, but such noises were not uncommon and they
were ignored.

The duke had two valets, Yew and Sallis. When the noise had
quieted down, the duke called for Yew, who found his master covered with blood but otherwise quite cool and composed. The
duke's bloodstained sword lay on the floor. He said that he had
been attacked but had managed to fight the attackers off and had
been wounded in the process. The physician was sent for but
found the duke had been only slightly wounded on his sword hand.

The duke then called Yew and asked him to find Sallis. Sallis was
in his own room sitting up perfectly straight in bed. There was a
deep gash in his throat, so deep that his head had nearly been
severed, and a blood-covered razor was found across the room.

At an inquest the duke insisted that Sallis had tried to murder him and then had committed suicide. The truth appears to have been that the duke had an affair with Sallis's daughter, who then committed suicide. In order to silence Sallis, the duke cut the man's throat with his own sword, then arranged things to look like suicide. The duke was never punished or even brought to trial, but as news of what happened spread, the duke, who had never been popular, was openly booed in the streets and was unable to show his face in London.

See also: THE TOWER OF LONDON

BORLEY RECTORY   Borley Rectory has been called "the most haunted house in England." In a land in which ghosts seem to abound, that is quite a title. Yet Borley has most certainly earned it, or at least so it seemed. For a haunted house Borley had everything from a ghostly nun to a poltergeist, a famous ghost hunter, and a whopping controversy.

Borley was a spectacularly ugly red brick structure built in 1863 by Rev. H. D. E. Bull. According to local legend, there was a ghostly nun who walked the grounds. A path in the garden was even known as the Nun's Walk. There was also a spectral coach complete with fire-breathing horses and a coachman. According to one version of the story, the nun came from a convent that stood nearby, and she tried to elope with a coachman, but she was caught and walled up alive in the convent. There is, however, no concrete historical documentation to back up this grisly but familiar tale. In another version of the legend, the nun tried to elope with a monk, but the couple was caught, the nun was walled up, and the monk was hanged.

The Reverend Bull and members of his family reported seeing the nun on several occasions, but the specter did not seem to frighten them unduly.

Rev. Bull died in 1892 in the Blue Room of the rectory. He was succeeded by his son the Reverend Harry Bull. The second Reverend Bull and his family also reported seeing the various local ghosts from time to time. However, this Rev. Bull was a man with a considerable sense of humor, so one was not always sure when he was joking. At one point he warned that if he was dissatisfied with his successor, he might try to make his dissatisfaction known from beyond the grave in some unmistakable way—"such as throwing moth-balls about, that's it, moth-balls, then you'll know it's me." Rev. Harry Bull died in 1927, also in the Blue Room, which by now was known as the "haunted room" in the rectory. After his death there were reports that mothballs had been seen flying around the deserted rectory. But Rev. Bull made his presence known in an even more unmistakable fashion; his ghost, dressed in the old gray jacket in which he died, was also reported in the rectory from time to time.

The third set of tenants of Borley were the Reverend and Mrs. Eric Smith, and they did not seem to possess the Bull family's easy tolerance for the unearthly. It wasn't the apparitions that bothered them so much as what seemed to be poltergeist activity: doorbells that rang mysteriously, pebbles that were thrown at windows, phantom footsteps in the hall that broke the still of the night. The Smiths reported the phenomena to a local newspaper, and the newspaper contacted England's premier ghost hunter, Harry Price.

Price came down to the rectory for a three-day stay in 1929 and apparently witnessed some of the phenomena himself. He saw the nun in the garden and held a séance in which he said that he contacted the spirit of Rev. Harry Bull. However, Price did not manage to rid Borley of the disturbances, and within a few months the Smiths moved out. Lack of "amenities" was their stated reason.

In October 1930 the Reverend L. A. Foyster (a relative of the Bulls) and his wife, Marianne, moved into the rectory, and they stayed for five years, during which the unusual happenings reached their peak. Much of the activity centered around Marianne Foyster, who was a troubled woman much younger than her husband. She was occasionally struck by an invisible hand or thrown out of bed in the middle of the night, and once she claimed that she had nearly been smothered by her own mattress. There were also mysterious, almost illegible messages that were found scrawled on the walls and on odd pieces of paper appealing for "Light," "Mass," and "Prayers." Rev. Foyster kept a diary of all the events he witnessed at Borley, and he also invited down a number of psychical researchers including Harry Price. Many of the researchers were impressed by what they either saw or heard. Borley Rectory was getting quite a reputation.

Price seemed to suspect that the cause of many of the disturbances was Marianne Foyster herself. He noted that most of the phenomena occurred when she was out of sight or happened to her when she was alone. Whether she caused them unconsciously or by trickery is unknown.

After a couple of years the more spectacular poltergeist activity died down, and the Foysters spent three relatively quiet years at Borley. The couple left the rectory in 1935. Foyster died some ten years later, and Marianne, who according to ghost expert Peter Underwood led "a strange and unhappy life, now resides in Canada where, under pressure, she has told conflicting stories of her life at Borley Rectory, the people she met there and her subsequent life."

After the departure of the Foysters, the rectory was empty, for the new clergyman opted to live elsewhere. Harry Price then had a chance that he had sought for years, to live and work in a real haunted house. He leased the property for a year and brought down a whole team of volunteer investigators to help him with his project.

Borley was subjected to the most intensive investigation of any haunted house in history. The results were published in Price's book *The Most Haunted House in England,* which created a sensation and was at first hailed as a milestone in psychical research.

One of those who read Price's book was Rev. Canon W. J. Phythian-Adams, Canon of Carlisle. He proposed the theory that the ghostly nun was not an English nun, as everyone had assumed, but a French nun named Marie Larrie, who had eloped with her lover to England in the eighteenth century. There she had been betrayed and murdered by her lover and buried in the cellar of one of the houses that stood on the site before Borley was built. The Canon suggested digging, and Price dug in the cellars and found human remains, which some medical experts believed to be those of a young woman.

The bone that attracted most attention was a jawbone which showed evidence of a deep abscess which must have been extremely painful. Many of those who have reported seeing the nun said that she looked "miserable" or "pale and drawn." Was it possible that the poor lady's misery was due to a toothache? The remains were ultimately buried in a London churchyard, but any connection of these remains to the ghostly nun remains purely conjectural.

However, the last word on Borley had not been written. For years Harry Price had his detractors, even within psychical research, and they soon began to chip away at his most famous case.

Price died in 1948, and shortly after his death, a *Daily Mail* reporter described how he had caught Price in the act of manufacturing phenomena at Borley during his original 1929 investigations. This prompted Mrs. Smith, wife of the former rector, to write to the paper and say that they had never believed that the rectory was haunted by anything worse than rats in the first place.

All this could be set down to hearsay and skeptical grumbling. A truly damaging blow to the reputation of Harry Price and the Borley haunting was delivered by three of Price's psychical research colleagues, E. J. Dingwall, K. M. Goldney, and Trevor Hall. In their 1955 book, *Haunting of Borley Rectory*, they described how they reexamined all of Price's original notes and compared them with the final account that he published in his book. In fact very little out of the ordinary happened while Price and his associates were at Borley. Even these modest effects, strange noises and the like, could easily be attributed to entirely natural causes. Price

The remains of Borley Rectory after the fire

had simply exaggerated certain facts and played down or entirely omitted others in order to make his story sound more sensational.

Going back farther in history, the three authors said that practically all of the major poltergeist activity could be attributed to Marianne Foyster, who hated Borley and wanted to move. The nun and the other apparitions were folklore and hearsay, they concluded.

Price had his defenders, and there were others who said an attack on him was unfair because he was no longer around to defend himself. But the evidence presented by Dingwall, Goldney, and Hall was so solid that their reexamination of the case left Price's reputation as a ghost hunter in shreds and severely tarnished the reputation of Borley rectory as "the most haunted house in England." By that time Borley wasn't around to defend itself either. The ugly old rectory burned to the ground in 1939, taking its secrets, if it ever had any, with it.

Even a dead haunted house is not always allowed to rest in peace. Shortly after Borley burned down, Dr. A. J. B. Robertson organized a group which continued to conduct experiments and investigations at the Borley site for several more years. Their report records unusual temperature variations, unexplained noises, strange smells, and lights of unknown origin. Nothing sensational but enough to keep interest in Borley simmering.

Even today, though Borley no longer exists, visitors interested in ghosts come to the area hoping to catch a glimpse of the spectral nun or otherwise get in touch with the supernatural.

See also: HARRY PRICE, ROSALIE

THE BROWN LADY OF RAYNHAM HALL   The ghost that is reported to walk the halls of stately Raynham Hall in Norfolk, England, is in many respects similar to the hordes of gray and white ladies that are supposed to walk the halls of so many other stately English homes. This one wears a brown dress and is therefore known as the Brown Lady, but the great difference is that this particular ghost is supposed to have been photographed. There is also a portrait of the ghost that hangs in the house, but no one seems to know the subject of the picture. There are no particular deaths or other events that are connected with the appearance of this ghost.

Raynham Hall is owned by the Townsand family. The ghostly figure was first reported during the Christmas season 1835. One of the guests who had come down to stay for Christmas was a Colonel Loftus. He was going up to his room one evening when he saw a strangely dressed woman in the hall. He adjusted his glasses to try to get a better look at her, but as he did, she disappeared.

A week later Colonel Loftus got a better look at the figure. In fact, he nearly ran into her in the hall. He described her as being a noble-looking lady wearing a brown satin dress. Her face was bathed in an unearthly light, but what was strange and ghastly about her was that she had no eyes—there were only empty sockets where the eyes should have been. Up close the Brown Lady was not a pleasant sight.

When Colonel Loftus told his story, some of the people staying at the house laughed, but others reported that they too had seen the strange figure, but were afraid to mention it for fear of being laughed at. Colonel Loftus made a sketch of the woman he had seen, and an artist made a painting from the sketch. The painting called *The Brown Lady*, was hung in a room where the figure has frequently been reported.

Some years later the novelist Captain Frederick Marryat was staying at Raynham Hall. He had naturally heard stories of the ghost and asked if he could sleep in "the haunted room," the one in which the portrait of the Brown Lady was hung. He spent some time examining the evil-looking figure in the portrait.

Later that evening Marryat and two companions were walking along an upstairs corridor when they saw the figure of a woman carrying a lamp coming toward them. They hid behind a door as the figure approached soundlessly. Light from the lamp reflected off her brown dress, and as she passed the door, she turned her eyeless face toward them and grinned in a "diabolical manner."

Captain Marryat happened to be carrying a pistol at the time, and he jumped from behind the door and fired point-blank at the frightening figure. If someone had been trying to play a joke on him, the person would have been shot dead. But the bullet passed right through the figure, which promptly disappeared.

The Brown Lady was not reported again until 1926, when it was seen by two boys. But what sets the Brown Lady apart from so many similar specters is what happened on September 19, 1936. Two photographers from the magazine *Country Life* arrived at Raynham Hall to photograph the inside of the house.

One of the photographers, Captain Provand, had just taken a picture of the main staircase of the house and was getting ready to take another. While Captain Provand was leaning over his camera putting in a new plate, the other photographer, Mr. Indre Shira,

Photograph of the Brown Lady

stood holding the flash-gun. Suddenly he shouted that he could see a shadowy figure that looked like the figure of a woman in a veil coming down the stairs. As the figure glided toward the photographers, Shira told Provand to take another shot immediately. Provand, who was still leaning over the camera and did not see the figure, took the picture. When he looked up, the figure was gone. However, when the photograph was developed, it showed a dim and ghostly-looking figure on the stairs. You cannot make out any features or anything other than a general sort of shape. Several photography experts who went to the offices of *Country Life* to examine the original photograph said that it did not look as if it had been faked. But faking a photograph of this type is far from impossible or even difficult for professional photographers. The figure itself is so shadowy that it may also have been the product of some flaw in either the camera or the film. Despite this it is still considered one of the best and most puzzling of the ghost photographs.

The Brown Lady has not been reported since 1936.

See also: SPIRIT PHOTOGRAPHY

THE CALVADOS HAUNTING   Traditional ghost and poltergeist stories come most often from the English-speaking world. Stories of this nature seem relatively rare on the European continent. Yet one of the best of the traditional ghost/poltergeist stories comes from France. The events took place in the latter part of the nineteenth century at a place called Calvados Castle, though château would be a more accurate description.

The château was built in 1835 on the ruins of an older structure, and almost from the start it acquired a reputation for being "haunted" though the nature of the early haunting is unknown.

In 1865 Calvados was inherited by a man whose identity has been shielded under the title Monsieur de X. He lived there with his wife and son, the son's tutor, Abbé Y, and servants, Emile, Auguste, Amelina, and Celina.

As soon as they moved in, they began hearing unexplained noises, but it wasn't until 1875 that the phenomena had become persistent and bothersome enough for M. de X to begin making a record of what happened. He also made an attempt to determine what the cause of the phenomena might be. He began his journal:

"This is October 1875. I propose to note down and record every day what happened during the night before. I must point out that the noises occurred while the ground was covered with snow, there was no trace of footsteps around the château. I drew threads across all the openings, secretly. They were never broken."

The abbé's room seemed to be particularly afflicted. There were loud bangings on the wall. A heavy candlestick moved across the mantelpiece by itself. An armchair that had been securely fastened to the floor began to inch its way toward the fireplace.

For the next several days the house was assailed by a variety of noises. Then, unaccountably, the noises ceased but only for a short time. On October 31 they began again.

"A very disturbed night," wrote M. de X in his journal. "It sounded as if someone went up the stairs with superhuman speed from the ground floor, stamping his feet. Arriving on the landing he gave five heavy blows, so strong that the objects suspended on the wall rattled in their places. Then it seemed as if a heavy anvil or a big log had been thrown on the wall, so as to shake the house. Nobody could say whence came these blows. Everybody got up and assembled in the passage on the first floor. We made a minute inspection but found nothing. We went to bed, but more noises obliged us to get up again. We could only go to rest at about three o'clock."

On the nights that followed, there were more loud noises of unknown origin. One of the noises sounded to the harassed family like a body rolling down the stairs. M. de X had a striking description of another of the sounds that was heard. ". . . some being rushed at top speed up the stairs from the entrance hall to the first floor . . . with a loud noise of tread which had nothing human about it. Everybody heard it. It was like two legs deprived of their feet and walking on their stumps."

In the next phase, which began in about mid-November, a new type of noise was added. ". . . everybody heard a long shriek, and then another, as if of a woman outside calling for help. At 1:40 [A.M.] we suddenly heard three or four cries in the hall, and then on the staircase."

In the days to come the shrieks became worse. "It is no longer the cry of a weeping woman, but shrill, furious despairing cries, the cries of demons or the damned."

Windows and doors opened and closed by themselves. Furniture was thrown about. Significantly, in M. de X's view, Bibles in the house were desecrated. The invisible thing, whatever it was, then began to attack people. Mme de X was struck in the hand with such force that the mark was visible for days.

By January the entire family was virtually beside itself when the house "was shaken twenty times." Finally a priest was called in who performed the rites of exorcism and placed religious medals throughout the house.

Here M. de X's account ends, and it was assumed that the exorcism brought a halt to the manifestations. However, there is also a later account written by the abbé long after he left Calvados and had become a priest. He indicated that the day after the exorcism all of the religious medals disappeared mysteriously and a few days later suddenly materialized out of thin air over M. de X's desk. The noises then began anew. It apparently took a second exorcism to finally end the manifestations.

Clearly M. de X believed his house was subject to some sort of demonic influence. The less religiously inclined would say that the house was haunted. Psychical researchers would probably prefer the more neutral term poltergeist—one of the most violent and persistent on record.

THE COCK LANE GHOST   The modern era of ghost hunting can be said to have begun in the mid–eighteenth century with the strange happenings in a house on a little London street called Cock Lane.

The supposedly haunted house was owned by a man named Parsons. The ghost was that of a Miss Fanny, a distant relative of a stockbroker named Kent who rented the Cock Lane property from Parsons. Miss Fanny had come to serve as Kent's housekeeper (some said mistress) after his wife died.

Kent and Parsons quarreled about money. Kent moved out and sued his former landlord. At about this time Miss Fanny died. The

Cock Lane

official verdict was that she had died of smallpox, but Parsons
hinted darkly that Miss Fanny had been poisoned by his enemy
Kent.

There matters rested for approximately two years. Then at the
beginning of 1762 the area around Cock Lane was alive with the
news that the Parsons house was being haunted by the ghost of
poor dead Fanny. Elizabeth Parsons, daughter of the owner of the
house, a girl of about twelve, said that she had seen the ghost and
the ghost had said that her death was the result of poison. No one

else reported actually seeing the ghost, but many persons heard loud and mysterious knockings and scratchings. The ghost was tagged with the nickname "Scratching Fanny." In many ways the events at Cock Lane resemble those of a typical poltergeist case.

According to Elizabeth, the ghost would not render herself visible to anyone else, but she would answer questions by using a simple knocking code, one knock for yes, two for no. Scratching indicated extreme displeasure.

The possibility of a ghost answering messages in code was taken quite seriously by many. A committee headed by several clergymen decided to sit up all night at the Parsons house in order to investigate the ghost. Here are some of the questions they asked. The answers were delivered by a knock or knocks.

"Do you make this disturbance on account of the ill-usage you received from Mr. Kent?"—"Yes."

"Were you brought to an untimely end by poison?"—"Yes."

A former servant of Fanny nicknamed "Carrots" was present at the interrogation. The ghost was asked, "Can your former servant, Carrots, give information about the poison?"—"Yes."

"How long before your death did you tell your servant Carrots that you were poisoned? An hour?"—"Yes."

Carrots was appealed to, but she said she knew nothing of poison and that Fanny had been quite unable to speak an hour before her death. That shook the faith of some of the interrogators, but the questioning continued.

"If Mr. Kent is arrested for this murder, will he confess?"—"Yes."

"Would your soul be at rest if he were hanged for it?"—"Yes."

"Will he be hanged for it?"—"Yes."

When word of this conversation with the dead got around, little Cock Lane was overflowing with curiosity seekers. Parsons began charging admission to get in to see his haunted house. Everyone in London, even the great Dr. Samuel Johnson, discussed the case of the Cock Lane ghost with great interest and seriousness.

One of the investigators, the Reverend Aldrich of Clerkenwell,

The haunted house in Cock Lane

was pastor of Saint John's Church, where the body of the dead woman was deposited in a vault. The ghost promised Mr. Aldrich that she would follow Elizabeth Parsons to the church vault and give notice of her presence by a distinct knock on her coffin lid.

A large party of ladies and gentlemen gathered at Mr. Aldrich's house near the church. The girl was brought to the house and at about 10 P.M. put to bed. The men were getting ready to go down to the vault when a great commotion erupted in the girl's room. The girl said that the ghost had arrived, and the ladies who were with her in the room affirmed that they heard the familiar scratchings.

But Mr. Aldrich was a hard and suspicious man. He ordered the girl to take her hands from under the covers and held them firmly while he questioned the ghost. There were no answers. Finally he asked the ghost to make its presence known by any sign—touching the cheek or hand of someone in the room, rustling the curtain, any sign at all. Nothing happened.

Still he decided to go through with the second part of the experiment. At about midnight a group went down to the vault and took up positions alongside Fanny's coffin. Here is how one chronicle describes the scene:

"The ghost was then summoned to appear; but it appeared not; it was summoned to knock; but it knocked not; it was summoned to scratch; but it scratched not." Many of those who left the vault were convinced that they had been hoaxed by Parsons and his daughter.

Others did not wish to be hasty and arranged an even more conclusive test. They decided that if the ghost of Fanny was to answer anyone, she would surely answer Kent, her accused murderer. It was in order to see Kent hanged that the ghost had presumably become restless in the first place. So Kent was brought to the vault and loudly asked the dead Fanny if he had indeed murdered her. Again nothing happened.

Still there were those who refused to be convinced, and the rumor spread that Fanny's body had been removed from the coffin before the test so that she would be unable to transmit any messages. So Kent had the coffin opened in front of a group of witnesses, and the body was indeed still there.

Now it was the harassed Kent who took the offensive. He brought suit against Parsons, his wife, a servant in the house, and a printer whom they had hired to publish an account of the haunting. The trial was held on July 10, 1762, and the judge, Lord Chief Justice Mansfield, not only found all the defendants guilty and meted out stiff sentences, he also reprimanded the minister who carried out the first investigations of Scratching Fanny.

Parsons and his associates maintained their innocence throughout the trial. The prosecution was never able to explain how the entire deception had been accomplished. In one instance Elizabeth Parsons was found to have concealed a block of wood under her dress and knocked on it. But this did not explain all of the noises and other phenomena that had been observed. So a few still clung to a belief in the reality of Scratching Fanny.

There is a curious and eerie footnote to the stories. Some years after the Cock Lane excitement died down, a man named J. W. Archer visited the crypt of Saint John's Church at Clerkenwell where the body of Scratching Fanny was entombed. At the time the interior of the vault was in great confusion. He sat down upon a coffin which the sexton's boy, who was holding the lantern for him, said belonged to Scratching Fanny. This made Archer curious so he pried the lid off the coffin, "and saw the face of a handsome woman, with an aquiline nose; the feature remaining perfect, an uncommon case, for the cartilage normally gives way." He reported that the rest of the body was also "perfectly preserved."

Archer saw no trace of the smallpox which was supposed to have killed Fanny, and he recalled that some mineral poisons help to preserve bodies.

"I made particular inquiries at the time of Mr. Bird, churchwarden, a respectable and judicious man; and he gave me good assurance that the coffin had always been looked upon as the one containing the Cock Lane woman."

THE GHOSTLY MONKS OF GLASTONBURY   There is perhaps no more mysterious legend-enshrouded place in England or indeed the entire world than Glastonbury Abbey. Glastonbury Abbey is the site of one of the oldest, if not the oldest, Christian church in the British Isles. Long before it was a Christian church, Glastonbury was a pagan place of worship.

Legend has it that Christianity was first brought to Glastonbury by Saint Joseph of Arimathea, the wealthy Jew who was supposed to have taken Jesus' body and placed it in the tomb he had prepared for himself.

The tower at Glastonbury

King Arthur is said to have been carried off to Glastonbury—it is one of the many places reputed to be the Isle of Avalon where the king "sleeps." And in fact the historical King Arthur may have been buried at Glastonbury. Many legends hold that the Holy Grail was taken to Glastonbury—a most historic and romantic place.

Naturally there are plenty of ghost stories attached to Glastonbury Abbey, including one which asserts that the ghost of King Arthur rides into the courtyard of the abbey every Christmas Eve. This is, of course, a legend, but there is a set of ghosts or spirits at Glastonbury that deserves special attention.

Early in this century an antiquary and archaeologist named Frederick Bligh Bond and his colleague J. Allan Bartlett were appointed to take charge of excavations at Glastonbury Abbey. Since the abbey is very ancient, there is always some sort of archaeological excavation going on in it or nearby, even today.

Bond and Bartlett, however, were no ordinary archaeologists interested only in what they could see and measure. Both believed firmly in ghosts or spirits or something very like them. While at Glastonbury they decided to experiment with automatic writing. One of the men held a pencil in his hand, and the pair talked casually of indifferent matters. Then sometimes the man holding the pencil would find his hand beginning to write. He was not supposed to guide the pencil himself. His hand was believed to be under the control of some sort of outside intelligence.

The first message came through on the night of November 7, 1907. It contained a drawing of a floor plan of Glastonbury, and it was signed Gulielmus Monachus, William the Monk. Messages from other monks, all of whom indicated that they had lived at Glastonbury in about the thirteenth century, followed. The first messages were written in medieval Latin, the language of the monks. But they soon switched to English, though it was a very archaic and strange kind of English. Often the messages were incomprehensible.

The ghostly monks of Glastonbury began sending messages about the original construction of the abbey. They told the archaeologists what they would find and where to dig. That was something that no mortal man could know.

"When you dig excavate the pillars of the crypt six feet below the grass . . . they will give you a clue. The direction of the walls eastward . . . was an angle . . . courtyards twenty-seven long, nineteen wide. Wait and the course will open in the spring. You will learn as you proceed. . . . We have much to do this spring."

One of the automatic drawings made at the abbey.
Notice the signature of the monk in the center.

On the basis of such messages, the two archaeologists claimed to have unearthed a chapel, the existence of which was unknown to any living person and not in any historical records.

Critics, however, complained that the information produced by the automatic writing contained much that was wrong and nothing that could not be gathered by examining existing historical records or from careful observation and deduction.

If the individuals who produced the automatic writing had been ordinary laymen, then we might have to look at the case differently. Even if the messages were vague and occasionally wrong, they were written in medieval Latin and archaic English and they indicated an intimate knowledge of Glastonbury. However, since Bond and his associate were trained archaeologists and scholars, they had all of the knowledge necessary to produce the messages without any help from the spirits. The two men, however, always denied charges of fraud, but skeptics contend that in cases such as this deliberate and conscious fraud is not necessary.

See also: THE SLEEPING KNIGHTS

GLAMIS CASTLE   The huge, gloomy, and imposing structure of Glamis Castle in Scotland may have as many ghostly and terrible tales attached to it as any single structure on earth. The sinister reputation goes back a long way. The castle is mentioned in Shakespeare's *Macbeth*, and some people claim that Macbeth's murder of King Duncan actually took place within Glamis. Visitors are sometimes shown "the room" where the murder took place, and many have reported a "sinister atmosphere." However, Glamis does not seem to have been the site of that particular murder, though plenty of others have taken place within its thick stone walls. Another King of Scotland, Malcolm II, who reigned during the eleventh century, was said to have been murdered in Glamis and since no amount of scrubbing could remove the bloodstains from the stones, the room was walled up.

Glamis Castle

How an eleventh-century murder could have taken place in a castle that was not built until the fourteenth century is impossible to say, but the legend persists anyway. Indeed it is tales of "secret" walled rooms that are most persistent at Glamis.

It is said that at one time towels were hung out of the window of every room in the castle, but there was one room (or in some versions an entire tower) from which no towels could be seen, yet all attempts to locate this hidden room or tower were unavailing.

Legend offers numerous answers to the question of what this secret room contains. One persistent and colorful legend holds that the secret room tale began with the second lord of Glamis in the fifteenth century. He was a magnificently bearded fellow, known primarily for his addictions to drinking, wenching, and gambling, and he was nicknamed "the Wicked Lord" or "Earl Beardie." One version of the legend holds that Earl Beardie was not the lord himself but a drinking companion.

Among the many tales that the more pious spread about him was that he persistently ignored the Sabbath and on one particular Sunday when he was extremely drunk, he roamed up and down the halls of his castle looking for someone who would play cards with him. But no one would risk playing cards on the Sabbath.

Finally Earl Beardie became so enraged that he shouted he would play cards "with the Devil himself." Naturally there was a knock at the castle door, and standing outside was a tall dark man wearing a black cloak and black hat. He inquired of Earl Beardie if he still wished to have a gambling partner. "Yes," roared the earl, "whoever you are."

The Wicked Lord and his sinister-looking visitor went into a small room and slammed the door. From behind the door their voices could be heard shouting and swearing by the frightened servants who crept as close as they dared. They could hear the Lord of Glamis say that he had lost so much that he had nothing left to gamble with. The stranger made a suggestion, but the servants were unable to hear it clearly. Whatever it was, the Wicked Lord agreed.

One of the servants became so curious that he crept right up to the door and put his eye to the keyhole but was nearly blinded by a flash of light. The Lord of Glamis burst out of the room screaming at his servants for spying on him. When he turned to go back into the room, the stranger had gone and had taken his soul with him.

Earl Beardie died about five years later, and it is said that his ghost still drunkenly roams the halls of Glamis castle looking for someone to play cards with. But the secret room is also supposed to contain the ghost of Earl Beardie and the form of the stranger playing cards till Judgment Day.

Another version of the legend holds that the secret room contains the remains (and ghosts) of several ancient enemies of the lords of Glamis who were walled up there and allowed to starve to death.

But the most widely repeated version of the secret room legend is somewhat more recent in origin. The early lords of Glamis were much like Earl Beardie, they drank and gambled away what fortune they possessed, and by the mid–seventeenth century they had nothing left and their castle had fallen into ruins. The estate was then inherited by a different sort of man, Patrick Lyons, who by hard work and thrift rebuilt not only the family fortune but the castle itself. The king made him the earl of Strathmore, but after the first earl's death the old family addiction to wild and expensive living reasserted itself.

It was during the eighteenth century that the secret room legend really appears to have gotten started. It was said that the hidden locked room contained a hideous secret known only to the earl of Strathmore himself, his heir, and the steward of the castle. The secret was to be revealed to the heir on his twenty-first birthday.

Usually heirs to the earldom made light of the idea of a secret until they turned twenty-one and then they changed. Of one it was written, "It is unquestionable that for many years after the revelation of the secret, Claude [Lord Strathmore] was quite a changed man, silent and moody, with an anxious scared look on his face. So evident was the effect on him that his son, when he came of age in 1876, absolutely refused to be enlightened."

His wife, however, was extremely curious about the mystery, and she once asked the steward what the secret was. The steward gravely assured her, "If your ladyship did know, you would not be a happy woman."

In 1880 a Scottish newspaper carried a story about a workman at the castle who had accidentally knocked a hole in the wall. Behind the wall he found a secret passage, and at the end of the passage there was a locked door. At that point the workman became badly frightened and told the steward what he had seen. A short time later this workman disappeared, and it was said that he had been given a large sum of money and told to emigrate to Australia and never to tell anyone what he had found.

The most popular theory today is that the room contains or contained one of the heirs to the estate. This theory runs that in 1821 the first son of the eleventh earl of Strathmore was born horribly deformed and was not expected to live. The family put out the information that the baby had died shortly after birth, but in fact it was placed in the secret room, where it was expected to expire shortly. However, contrary to medical predictions the deformed infant survived.

In time a second son was born and became heir to the estate, but the deformed eldest brother and the true heir was still alive in the secret room. This secret had to be imparted to all who wrongfully inherited the earldom. In fact, the deformed brother outlived four earls of Strathmore, and each had to be told of the hidden chamber and what was in it.

It was said that the earls of Strathmore actually encouraged rumors of ghosts in the secret chamber in order to draw attention away from the real secret.

A somewhat more exotic variation of this story holds that the deformed child grew into a "monster" of great size and enormous strength. Peter Underwood in *Gazetteer of Scottish & Irish Ghosts* says, "The creature is said to have lived to an incredible age, one person who should know maintains that he died in 1941. . . . The last Lord Strathmore felt sure that a corpse or coffin was buried somewhere in the walls and a walk high up on the roof is still known as the Mad Earl's Walk, perpetuating the legend and dating perhaps from an escape attempt or the place where the poor monster was exercised."

There is also a gray or white lady who wanders the halls of the castle. She may be the ghost of Janet Douglas, wife of James, the sixth lord of Glamis. James died suddenly one morning after eating breakfast. His wife was suspected of poisoning him, but no evidence could be found and the case was dropped.

Six years later Janet Douglas found herself in much more serious trouble. She was accused of plotting to poison the King of Scotland and of practicing witchcraft. Knowledge of poisons was just thought to be a branch of witchcraft. Evidence was not needed in a witchcraft case, and Janet Douglas was tried, condemned, and executed at Castle Hill in Edinburgh, Scotland, in 1537.

Another tradition, however, holds that she was actually condemned to be walled up alive in a room in the castle and it is her spirit that haunts the hidden room, or by her powers of witchcraft she is still alive inside that sealed room after more than four hundred years.

This list hardly exhausts the supernatural or semisupernatural creatures that are connected by legend with Glamis castle. Says Underwood, "There is the Queen Mother's bedroom where no one could sleep soundly when it was a bedroom; the tongueless woman who looks out of a barred window, or runs across the park pointing to her bleeding mouth; and the ghostly little Black boy, who sits on a stone seat by the door into the Queen Mother's sitting room and is supposed to be a Negro servant who was unkindly treated over two hundred years ago."

And Underwood adds, "There is even a vampire legend at Glamis." This is the tale of a woman servant at the castle who was caught in the act of sucking the blood of one of her victims. She was said to be walled up alive (or at least undead) in the secret room, or a secret room. However, since that is not the proper way to get rid of a vampire, the danger that someday the wall may be broken down and the evil creature released still exists at the castle.

IGNATIUS THE BELL RINGER   The ghostly or spectral monk is one of the most common figures in all British ghostlore. Typical of such ghosts is the one that haunts the Elm Vicarage near Wisbech. It is supposed to be the ghost of a monk named Ignatius who died nearly eight hundred years ago.

At that time a monastery stood on the site now occupied by the vicarage. The area was often threatened by floods, and it was one of Ignatius's responsibilities to watch the rising floodwaters and warn his brothers if there was any danger. One night while on watch Ignatius fell asleep and thus failed to ring the warning bell when the floodwaters rose. As a result water rushed into the monastery, several monks were drowned, and Ignatius was in disgrace. For his carelessness he appears to have been doomed to haunt the site ever since. The bell that he failed to ring has also taken on a spectral form, and it can be heard ringing the night before any member of the parish is to die.

Despite this rather ominous history Ignatius appears to be a benign, even helpful spirit. Those who have lived at the vicarage usually first become aware of his presence by hearing unexplained footsteps at night. After that goes on a while, Ignatius himself makes an appearance. According to the wife of Rev. A. R. Bradshaw, who saw the ghostly monk many times, the ghost would appear first as a fine outline, and then the outline would gradually be filled in with the figure of a man in his mid-thirties "with dark curly hair and thin ascetic features." He was always dressed in a rather shabby brown monk's habit and sandals.

Ignatius would appear, usually at dusk, in various parts of the house. Once Mrs. Bradshaw actually brushed against him while he was passing down an upstairs corridor. The monk turned to her and said, "Do be careful." Since the ghost spoke first, Mrs. Bradshaw thought that this was an excellent opportunity to ask him who he was. The response was, "Ignatius the bell ringer."

One night Mrs. Bradshaw was sleeping in a bedroom that was usually reserved for guests. She was awakened in the middle of the night by a feeling of pressure on her throat. She saw a vague black shape bending over her and what appeared to be a pair of gnarled hands clutching at her throat. She was unable to move. The dog that usually slept at the foot of her bed was growling and snapping at the thing, but to no effect. Suddenly she saw Ignatius; he reached for the hands clutching at her throat and pulled them away. Mrs. Bradshaw rushed into the room in which her husband was sleeping and told him of the experience. At first he thought that she had simply had a horrible nightmare, but when he looked at her throat he found that it was bruised and red. The marks persisted for several weeks.

Later, when Mrs. Bradshaw saw Ignatius again, she asked him who had attacked her and was told that it was the ghost of a man who had been murdered in that room. Later he told her that she would not be seeing him as often in the future for having saved her life had helped to complete his long penance for his past sin, and he was hopeful that complete forgiveness and eternal rest would soon be his.

HAMPTON COURT Cardinal Wolsey, principal advisor to King Henry VIII, had a magnificent residence built for himself up the Thames from London. The palace was called Hampton Court. The palace was so magnificent that it is said Henry envied the cardinal; he was also suspicious of the cardinal's great power. Arousing envy and suspicion in a monarch as autocratic and potentially violent as Henry VIII was a dangerous business, and Wolsey was driven from office and soon died. Had his health been better, the King would probably have had him executed. Henry

Henry VIII

took over Hampton Court, and it became one of his favorite residences. Today Hampton Court, magnificently restored and only a short boat ride from the center of London, is one of England's most celebrated tourist attractions.

As might be imagined, many ghosts are said to haunt the stately halls of the Tudor palace. Oddly Henry VIII's is not one of them, and Cardinal Wolsey has been spotted only once or twice. Some of Henry's six wives are more in evidence. Henry's third wife, Jane Seymour, bore him a son at Hampton Court and died a week later. Her ghost is said to be seen gliding along the area known as the Clock Court carrying a lighted candle.

The most famous and tragic of the many Hampton Court ghosts is that of Lady Catherine Howard, another of Henry's wives. She was eighteen when she married the fat, ill, and aging monarch. Within a few months of the marriage, there were rumors about her behavior; they were probably true, and in any case Henry believed them, and that was all that mattered. He had her arrested, and she well knew that her most probable end would be the chopping block at the Tower. On the night of her arrest at Hampton

Court, Lady Catherine broke free from her captors and raced along the gallery in an attempt to see her husband and plead for her life. Henry, who was in the chapel, ignored her pleas, and she was dragged away shrieking and sobbing.

On the anniversary of her arrest, her ghost is said to come shrieking down what has come to be known as the Haunted Gallery. Her screams are also reportedly heard in the little room from which she escaped and to which she was dragged back.

An artist sketching in the Haunted Gallery saw a hand with a large and very unusual ring on it emerge from behind a tapestry. Though the hand did not remain in sight for long, he managed to sketch it. The ring on the hand was later identified as one belonging to Catherine Howard.

The ghost of another of the wives Henry had executed, Anne Boleyn, has occasionally been reported at Hampton Court. Visitors say that they recognize her from a portrait that hangs in the palace. But she is more frequently associated with the Tower of London.

Archbishop Laud, one of Henry's other victims, is sometimes

Catherine Howard

seen at Hampton Court, but he makes a much more spectacular appearance in the library at St. John's College, Oxford, where he can be seen rolling his head across the floor.

Hampton Court has its own White Lady, a ghostly form in a flowing white gown that is seen most often at the dock near the river.

Hampton Court also has a Gray Lady, a tall gaunt woman in a long gray robe, but the identity of this specter has been established as Mrs. Sybil Penn, nurse for Henry's children, Edward VI, Mary Tudor, and Elizabeth. Mrs. Penn was much loved by those she had cared for. She had been given a pension and an apartment in Hampton Court. When she died on November 6, 1586, she was buried at nearby St. Mary's Church, Hampton. All was quiet for a couple of centuries, and then the church was struck by lightning, and Mrs. Penn's grave and monument were moved, but in the process her remains were scattered. A short time later a family named Ponsoby, who occupied the apartment at Hampton Court that had once belonged to Mrs. Penn, began complaining of strange noises. The most persistent noises were those of a woman's voice and a spinning wheel.

In an attempt to discover the source of the noises, a wall was broken through, and inside was found a sealed chamber that contained, among other things, a very old spinning wheel. Though no one could say for sure, it is very possible that this was the spinning wheel once used by Mrs. Penn.

It was about that time that the gray-robed figure began to be seen in the halls around the apartment. There is a statue of Mrs. Penn at Hampton Court, and the ghostly figure is supposed to resemble the figure in the statue.

There is also a child ghost dressed in the fashion of a page boy from the time of Charles II. And a whole group of gorgeously attired ghosts were once spotted by a police constable in the garden.

See also: THE TOWER OF LONDON

*T*HE HAUNTED AIRFIELD   The airfield at Montrose in Scotland has two ghosts, one of an unnamed biplane pilot who was killed in a crash in 1913, the other of an officer of the RAF during World War II who was also killed in a crash at the field.

The old biplane pilot made his most dramatic appearance in the autumn of 1916. He had already been seen by several of the pilots and by the commanding officer of the base. Then one night there was an alarm that a marauding German plane had been spotted somewhere in the vicinity. A Hurricane taxied out in an attempt to intercept the invader. A half hour of searching was fruitless, and the plane was ordered to return to base. However, on the chance that an enemy plane might actually be in the vicinity, the commander decided against lighting up the entire field. There was only a twin row of lights along the runway to guide the Hurricane in. The Hurricane pilot was an experienced airman who had easily landed under such conditions many times before and should have had no trouble doing so again. He was also a practical, unimaginative fellow, not at all the sort that was prone to seeing ghosts. Dozens of airmen on the ground watched the Hurricane come in.

As the pilot almost touched down, he suddenly opened up the engine and with a roar disappeared into the night. The ground crew figured that he had not been aligned correctly and would circle back and try again. Sure enough the Hurricane approached the field once again, this time with his navigation lights on. But the same thing happened; just as he was about to land, he roared away.

The ground crew had no idea what was happening, but they decided that they must take the risk of lighting the entire field. This time the Hurricane made a perfect landing. When the plane stopped, the pilot slid back the hood and shouted, "The fool! Who was the fool who cut me out?" Someone in the ground crew shouted that no one had cut him out. "Of course someone did," shouted the angry pilot. "Why do you think I went round again? Some madman in a biplane balked me just as I was touching down—a thing like a Tiger Moth."

"There's no one else flying," said the flight commander. "Besides, there isn't a biplane on this station."

The only solution, writes ghost hunter Peter Underwood, "seemed to be that the phantom airman was keeping his hand in."

This phantom airman was sighted again during World War II when in the winter of 1940 pilots were sent to Montrose to rest after the Battle of Britain.

World War II produced its own ghost. In 1942 a flight commander was killed in a crash a short distance from the airfield. There seemed no obvious reason for the crash, and it was officially set down to engine failure. But there was another rumor whispered around the base. This particular flight commander was a stern disciplinarian and had made a lot of enemies among the men. About a week before the crash, the flight commander had a tremendous argument with a fitter who was working on a plane he was about to fly. The flight commander had fastened on some trivial offense and was going to report it. The fitter correctly felt that he was being picked on unfairly and was extremely angry. It was assumed that he held a grudge and at the first opportunity he doctored the flight officer's plane, causing it to crash. A routine inquiry was held, but no charges were ever filed.

A little while later some of the men on the base began seeing the ghostly form of the flight commander dressed in full flying suit and goggles. Some thought that he had come back to haunt the fitter who had caused his death. The flight commander became almost a familiar figure around the base, and all new arrivals were warned to watch out for the ghost, especially at night.

One of these arrivals, a tough, skeptical man who had already seen action in Europe, simply scoffed at the story, that is, until he was put on guard duty.

The guards at Montrose patrolled the airfield in pairs at night, generally avoiding the area of a hangar that had been converted into a makeshift morgue. But on this particular night an aircraft had just landed and had been parked close to the morgue. The new arrival, who was on guard duty, was told to keep a close eye on this plane.

All was quiet, so about three in the morning the new arrival and his companion decided that they might just take a quick smoke. The new arrival was to stay on watch while his companion nipped around the corner for a cigarette, and then they would change places. The new man was standing there alone when suddenly the doors of the morgue, which were always kept securely locked, flew open and a man in full flying suit and helmet but with a dead-white face stalked out. The guard dropped his rifle and watched the figure stride across the field and vanish. The doors to the morgue slammed shut, and when the second guard returned, all was as it had been before.

The guard wondered if he was not being made the subject of a practical joke, so he decided to say nothing. No one ever mentioned the subject to him, and it was only after the war when he heard that others at Montrose had similar experiences that he was able to talk about what he had seen.

See also: THE APPEARANCE OF LIEUTENANT MC CONNEL

THE HAUNTED U-BOAT   In 1916 the Germans were building twenty-four U-Boats in the shipyard at Bruges in occupied Belgium. The U-boat had proved to be an enormously successful weapon for Germany during World War I, and the work was being rushed. Construction was normal for twenty-three of the boats, but for the twenty-fourth boat nothing seemed to go right. This submarine was known only by its number, U-65.

Several workers were killed in accidents during the construction. In October of 1916 when U-65 was finally launched, one of its officers either fell or was swept overboard and drowned. The first underwater test was nearly catastrophic, for the U-boat was unable to surface for nearly twelve hours. The crew was badly frightened and didn't know what had happened. When the ship was examined, no reason for the malfunction could be found. The day after this accident there was another; a torpedo exploded on deck and a second lieutenant and five crewmen were killed. Most of the later stories about a haunting center around the second lieutenant killed in that blast.

Ships that have had trouble in construction or seem to have an unusually large number of accidents soon pick up the reputation as a bad luck or jinx ship, and rumors about such a ship quickly spread. The rumor was that several crewmen of U-65 had seen the dead lieutenant. One man said, "We saw him come aboard and walk slowly to the bow. He stood there, staring at us, with his arms folded across his chest."

Even when they are not believed one hundred percent, such tales can seriously demoralize a ship's crew, and the U-boat commander tried to play them down. "I'm sure it's just imagination," he said. "The accident was a sad experience for all of us. Just try and put it out of your minds." But apparently at least one of the men who had reported seeing the ghost could not put the experience out of his mind for he deserted and was never found.

U-65 was repaired and put back out to sea for several uneventful months, and then the crew began seeing the ghost again. This time the captain himself saw it. The ship docked at Bruges for routine maintenance, and captain and crew went ashore. During their stay there was an Allied attack on the port city and the captain was killed in the bombardment.

That only strengthened U-65's reputation as a jinx ship. But the German navy needed every U-boat it had and could not allow the stories to destroy the effectiveness of the ship. The high command ordered that the ship be checked once again. There was a theory that some kind of noxious fumes might be causing hallucinations. But once again nothing out of the ordinary was found. Admiral Schroeder, head of the U-boat command, denounced all the talk of ghosts as "superstitious nonsense." He even spent a night on U-65

Admiral Schroeder

and in the morning announced to the crew that he had slept very well and had not been disturbed by any ghosts. But just in case, the admiral called in a minister to perform an exorcism on the ship.

That was simply window dressing. What Admiral Schroeder really thought the ship needed was the discipline of a tough new commander. For that job he chose Lieutenant Commander Gustav Schelle. The new commander laid down the law that if anyone reported seeing any ghosts, he would be severely punished. And for the next year there were no sightings of the ghost reported on U-65.

When the ghost did come back, it was with a vengeance. One of the most trusted officers on the ship, Master Gunner Erich Eberhardt, rushed into the control room screaming, "I've seen the ghost—an officer standing near the bow torpedo tubes. He brushed past me and disappeared." The master gunner was so hysterical that he had to be locked up. After a few hours he calmed down and seemed to return to normal. But as soon as he had the chance, he grabbed a bayonet and stabbed himself to death.

A short time later another of Captain Schelle's close associates, Chief Petty Officer Richard Meyer, was swept overboard. His body was never recovered.

These two deaths thoroughly demoralized the U-boat crew. Instead of seeking out the enemy, U-65 now tried to avoid all possibility of dangerous contact. But the ship was still struck by shellfire and had to limp back to Bruges for repairs. Admiral Schroeder was enraged. He had Captain Schelle and every other officer of U-65 removed, and when she set to sea again in mid-1918, U-65 had an entirely different staff of officers and a new crew.

The end of U-65 is quite mysterious. On the morning of July 10, 1918, an American submarine patrolling off the southern coast of Ireland saw a U-boat lying on its side on the surface. The ship was identified as U-65.

At first the Americans thought that the ship might be a decoy, so they watched it carefully for a long time. Nothing seemed to be moving on the ship, so the American captain decided to blow it up. As the Americans were preparing to torpedo U-65, the ship was torn apart by a violent explosion.

Was U-65 really a decoy filled with explosives that just went off too soon, or was there some other reason for the explosion? Just before she blew up, the American captain said that he thought he saw someone standing on the ship near the bow. The figure appeared to be that of a German officer wearing a navy overcoat. It stood there unmoving with its arms folded.

The war ended a few months later, and the other German U-boats surrendered peacefully. The case of U-65 has been investigated a number of times by German naval authorities and others. No one has ever been able to come up with a completely satisfactory explanation for all of the strange happenings.

THE HEAD OF A CHILD   The collector of ghostly tales, Lord
Halifax, recorded this statement from an unnamed lady.

"I have had a strange and ghostly experience once in my lifetime. It happened when my mother and my little sister and I were
all staying at Sutton Varney. As the house was very full my hostess
asked if I would mind having my little sister to sleep in my room.
In the middle of the night I woke up with the distinct feeling that
a child's head was resting on my shoulder. I said, as I thought it
was my sister, 'Maudie, why have you come into my bed?' There
was no answer and I struck a light and on looking saw that my sister was fast asleep in her cot beside me. Presently I dropped off to
sleep again only to wake up once more with exactly the same feeling, but when I put my hand out there was no child's head on my
shoulder. After this I could not sleep and on the following day related my experience to my hostess. When the same feeling came
over me the next night I began to feel very nervous and for the rest
of my stay to my great relief I was given another room in which I
had a peaceful night."

It was later learned that others had had similar experiences in
the same room. Indeed it became so troublesome that when new
owners bought Sutton Varney, they had the wing in which that
particular room was situated pulled down. When the workmen
broke through the floor, they found a compartment which contained the skeletons of five children.

THE HOBY GHOSTS   The ghost of poor little William Hoby
has been used to frighten generations of careless scholars. William
was the son of Sir Thomas Hoby, who lived during the time of
King Henry VII.

The boy's parents were both brilliant and energetic, though his mother had always been considered a bit odd. Aside from being a scholar in several languages, Lady Hoby has also been described as a "pest of outstanding quality." Poor William inherited none of his family's intellectual gifts. Not only was he a slow learner, he was sloppy as well. During his lessons he became so nervous that he always made ink blots on his copybook. Lady Hoby was severely disappointed with her son's abilities, and the sight of a blotted copybook absolutely enraged her. William was frequently beaten because of his poor schoolwork. One day, when presented with a blotted copybook, Lady Hoby became so enraged that she completely lost control of herself and beat the boy to death.

The place where William died is called Bisham Abbey. It was said to be haunted not only by the ghost of poor little William but by the ghost of Lady Hoby as well. The ghost of Lady Hoby was seen washing her hands in a basin which floated before her. She was trying to wash off the bloodstains. According to one account, the ghost was seen "in negative," that is, with a black face and hands and wearing a white dress.

In the nineteenth century renovations were made on Bisham Abbey. Behind one of the walls was found a number of badly blotted copybooks. According to tradition, they were the very books which drove Lady Hoby to her murderous fury.

After World War II the abbey was taken over by a sports organization and converted into a gymnasium and hostel for students. The ghosts have not been reported since that time.

THE MAN IN GRAY   Many different ghosts are reputed to haunt the venerable old Drury Lane Theatre in London. The most famous of them is The Man in Gray. This particular spirit is unusual for it is regarded more as a symbol of good luck than a threat or omen of evil. An offer to exorcise this particular ghost was once turned down flat by the theater management.

The Man in Gray is a dignified ghost, a handsome and elegantly

The Drury Lane Theatre

dressed young man, apparently from the eighteenth century. He wears his hair in a powdered wig and carries a three-cornered hat. His most prominent article of clothing and the one that gives him his name is a long gray cloak. The hilt of a sword can be seen protruding from beneath the cloak.

The Man in Gray does not come howling or shrieking through the theater; he does not rattle chains to frighten patrons. He doesn't even appear at night. He is most frequently seen between the hours of 9 A.M. and 6 P.M., before showtime. The figure takes a slow stately walk from one end of the balcony to the other and disappears into the wall; he will also disappear if someone tries to get too close to him.

The Man in Gray has been reported for well over a century, appearing most frequently at rehearsals when the theater is almost empty. On occasion he has been seen during matinees, but he has been reported backstage on only one occasion. This ghost is considered to be part of the audience rather than a performer.

King George VI once went to a matinee at Drury Lane specifically to see the ghost, but The Man in Gray failed to appear on royal command. Some think that it takes a special talent or sensitivity to see the ghost, for one or two people in a group will see him, while others will not. It is also believed that many sightings of The Man in Gray go unreported because people who have never heard the story simply take him for an actor in costume.

No one knows who The Man in Gray is supposed to be, but there is a story that may explain the origin of the figure. A little over a century ago workmen repairing the balcony broke through an old wall and found an unsuspected small chamber. Inside the chamber was the skeleton of a man, with a dagger still sticking between its ribs. A few bits of clothing clung to the bones and allowed the skeleton to be dated as eighteenth century. The remains were removed and buried in a churchyard near the theater.

W. J. Macqueen-Pope, an expert on theater history, advanced a theory about the skeleton. He said that the skeleton was the remains of a young man who had been murdered, perhaps by someone connected with the theater. The body was then walled up and was not discovered until the victim and the crime had been entirely forgotten.

But The Man in Gray is no angry ghost seeking revenge, quite the reverse. He is most often seen during the rehearsals of a play that turns out to be a hit. He is not much interested in attending flops. He was seen during rehearsals of the musicals *Oklahoma, Carousel, South Pacific,* and *The King and I,* all huge successes at Drury Lane.

Oklahoma also attracted the ghost of King Charles II and a group of his attendants. They were seen at a performance in 1948. During his lifetime Charles II had always loved the theater.

The ghosts were active backstage as well at *Oklahoma.* A young American actress named Betty Joe Jones reported getting help from a ghost. She had an important comic part, but her performance was not going as well as it should. People just weren't laughing in the right places. Then during one scene she felt some-

The lobby of the Drury Lane

one or something gently push her into a different position. The unseen hands continued to guide her around the stage. Amazingly the performance got better, and the next night the ghostly hands again pushed her about. As her performance improved, the hands gave her a friendly pat on the back.

During the tryouts for *The King and I* an inexperienced young actress named Doreen Duke felt unseen hands guiding her about. When she became nervous, the hands gave her a pat on the back. She got the part, and the hands continued to guide her during rehearsal and through the tensions of opening night.

Macqueen-Pope thought the unseen ghost was Joe Grimaldi, a celebrated comic and singer who often performed at Drury Lane. He was known for his willingness to aid young performers.

A somewhat less pleasant ghost is that of Charles Macklin, a short-tempered actor who killed fellow-actor Thomas Hallam during a brawl. Macklin was never really punished for his act and lived to the amazing age of 107. After his death his thin, ugly figure was reported stalking the corridors backstage. Perhaps he was doomed to continue to haunt the scene of his unpunished crime.

Macqueen-Pope also had a letter from a woman who said that she and her sister had been sitting in the audience at Drury Lane when they noticed a man in old-fashioned garb sitting at the end of the aisle and watching the play intently. When the lights went on, the figure was gone. In order to leave the theater, the man would have had to pass directly by the two sisters, but he had not; he had simply vanished. Later, when they looked at a book of theater photos, they recognized the man as Charles Keene, a celebrated actor of the nineteenth century.

THE PHANTOM CHILD   A rather pathetic little ghost was reported by Marilis Hornidge in the February 1976 issue of *Fate* magazine. She described how she was helping a friend move into a house in Larchmont, New York, a suburb of New York City. The house was not very old or creepy-looking, not at all the sort of place that one would traditionally find a ghost.

After a day of unpacking, Miss Hornidge and her friend were resting in front of the fire when they heard a strange rhythmic noise coming from one of the upstairs rooms.

The sound was not particularly ominous or ghostly, nothing like the clanking chains of the traditional ghost account. It sounded like a bouncing ball, but still it made them feel uncomfortable, and they decided to go upstairs to investigate. The noise appeared to be coming from a small suite of rooms on the third floor. As they approached the rooms, Miss Hornidge noted something strange. The door to the suite had a hook closure on the outside. All the other bedrooms in the house had latches on the inside and outside, high enough so a child could not reach them.

The suite was filled with half-unpacked boxes but nothing else that they could see. As Miss Hornidge turned to leave, she felt a tug at her skirt. Thinking she had caught the skirt on a nail, she reached down, and suddenly her hand was grasped by what felt like a tiny ice-cold hand. Somehow the icy hold "communicated a feeling of panic and painful loneliness. I wanted to look down—but I couldn't."

She walked straight out of the room and said nothing to her friend. As she left the room, the icy hand loosened its grip and faded away, but Miss Hornidge's own hand remained cold all night.

After that the house was troubled by occasional strange noises but only when Miss Hornidge was a guest. It was much later, after her friend moved from the house, that Miss Hornidge learned that one of the previous owners of the house had a retarded daughter who had died young. Most of the unfortunate child's life had been spent locked in the suite on the third floor. Her favorite toy was a ball which she bounced endlessly against the wall.

THE POLISH MERCENARY   In the early 1940s the Broadway columnist Danton Walker bought a house in Rockland County, New York, about a one-hour drive from New York City. Walker intended using it mainly as a weekend and vacation home. The house itself was very old, parts of it dating back to pre-Revolutionary times, and it was in need of considerable repair. The house was located in a part of New York State that had figured prominently in the Revolutionary War. The headquarters of General "Mad" Anthony Wayne had stood nearby, and the bloody battle of Stony Point was fought just a few miles away. The house itself may have once housed soldiers or been used to store equipment or as a prison, though there was no definite record of any of this.

Walker had heard rumors that the place was "haunted," but all old houses are supposed to be haunted so he didn't pay much attention to that rumor. It wasn't until 1944, when the house was fully restored and Walker began to go there regularly, that he became aware of the ghostly happenings.

There were the familiar ghostly footsteps, mostly the sound of heavy boots tramping around empty rooms. There were unexplained knocks at the door when no one was there. Objects would disappear from one place and turn up in another days or weeks later. People who came to the house were oppressed by the feeling that there was something "unearthly" about the place. Finally Walker himself felt he couldn't even sleep there and put his bed in a studio behind the main house.

Yet oddly, though Walker had a long-standing interest in ghosts, he didn't do anything about his own haunted house for almost ten years. In 1952 rumors of the haunting reached Mrs. Eileen Garrett, an Irish-born medium who lived in New York City. Mrs. Garrett was the most impressive, respected, and responsible medium of the mid–twentieth century. She had made a lot of money from mediumship and from her shrewd business sense, and she put a lot of money back into psychical research when she founded her own research organization, The Parapsychology Foundation.

On a stormy day in November 1952, Mrs. Garrett and a small group from the foundation drove up to Walker's house. They carried with them infrared photographic equipment for taking pictures in the dark and a tape recorder. However, the principal tool with which they hoped to track the ghost was Mrs. Garrett herself.

Mrs. Garrett rarely bothered with the elaborate ritual of the traditional séance. It was the middle of the afternoon when she arrived. After a brief inspection she marched into the living room and sat down in a comfortable chair while the others gathered around her. The tape recorder was switched on, and Mrs. Garrett slipped easily into a trance. Almost immediately her East Indian spirit control, Unvani, began speaking through her. He had said that he was going to allow another spirit, the spirit that presumably had been haunting the Walker house, to take control of the medium. Unvani warned, "Remember that you are dealing with a personality very young, tired, who has been very much hurt in life."

The change from the dignified and calm Unvani control to this new spirit was startling and grotesque to the observers. Mrs. Garrett's eyes popped wide open, and she stared straight ahead in terror, but it also appeared that she was unable to see anything. Her whole body began to tremble violently, and she started moaning and weeping. The medium fell out of her chair and tried to drag herself across the floor to where Walker was seated. When she tried to stand up, her leg gave way as though it was broken. She lay on the floor trembling violently. There were several uncomfortable moments before anyone could make contact with this new spirit that was supposed to be controlling the body of the medium. Even then they could get little information, for the spirit seemed confused, in great pain, and spoke very little English.

What the observers could gather from the garbled dialogue was that they were talking to the spirit of a Polish mercenary named Andreas who had served with the Revolutionary Army. He had been carrying some sort of map when he was trapped by the British soldiers in that very house. They beat him horribly and left him for dead, but he did not die, at least not at once. He lingered on for several terrible, pain-filled days before finally expiring. The Andreas spirit also made some mention of a brother, but at first no one could make head or tail out of this.

After the story had been told, Unvani again resumed control of the medium. She got up off the floor, bowed, sat down in a chair, and with the voice of Unvani explained the situation further. He said that Danton Walker resembled the dead soldier's brother, who had also been killed during the Revolutionary War, and it was this resemblance that had triggered the haunting after Walker purchased the house.

Unvani suggested that all present pray for the repose of the troubled spirit of the Polish mercenary. At that Mrs. Garrett awoke from her trance and said that she was totally unaware of what had been going on. The whole séance had taken an hour and fifteen minutes. A few months after the séance Walker reported that the atmosphere in his house seemed much calmer.

THE TOWER OF LONDON   The Tower of London with its grim and imposing appearance and its long history as a prison and place of execution is a natural gathering place for ghosts, or at least for ghostly legends. The Tower was first built over eight hundred years ago though it has been considerably altered and enlarged over the centuries. It is also the place where the Crown Jewels of England are kept on display, along with a marvelous collection of arms and armor. It is London's number-one tourist attraction. While many come to see the jewels and the armor, most tourists are drawn to the Tower by its bloody and ghostly history.

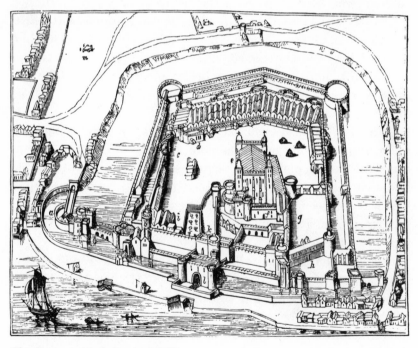

The Tower of London in 1597

The Tower of London in 1833

No one knows how many people have been executed there, probably thousands. The victims have ranged from common thieves to kings and princes. Perhaps the saddest event in the Tower's long sad history was the murder of the two little princes in 1483. Twelve-year-old Edward V and his ten-year-old brother, Richard, Duke of York, were imprisoned in the Tower during a time of political turmoil. The two boys were not officially executed but were secretly murdered in their rooms. Suspicion quite naturally fell on their uncle, the Duke of Gloucester, for with the boys out of the way, he could become king, which he did, assuming the name Richard III. There is no proof that Richard ordered the murder, and he always denied his part in it. But because of Shakespeare's play, which makes Richard the master villain, he has always been blamed for the murder.

For nearly two centuries the Tower was said to have been

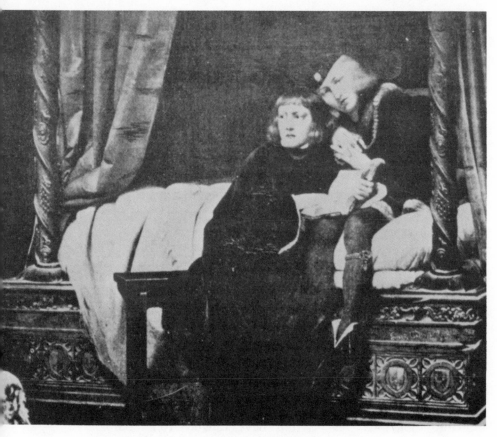

The two princes murdered in the Tower

haunted by the ghosts of the little princes. In 1674 some alterations were being made in the Tower and workmen came upon a
wooden chest containing the skeletons of two young boys. It was
assumed at the time that the skeletons were those of the two
princes, and King Charles II ordered that the remains be given a
royal burial. Since that time the boys' ghosts have not troubled the
Tower.

Sir Walter Raleigh was imprisoned in the Tower for thirteen
years. On some moonlit nights his ghost can be seen walking up
and down along the walls near the room in which he was kept.

In 1605 Guy Fawkes tried unsuccessfully to blow up the Houses of Parliament. He and his fellow conspirators stored a great deal of gunpowder in the cellars of the building, but before they could carry out their plot, they were betrayed and thrown into the Tower. Fawkes was executed, but first he was horribly tortured, and his screams can still be heard echoing through the Tower, according to some stories.

Of all the Tower ghosts surely the most famous is Anne Boleyn, the second wife of Henry VIII. Henry had divorced his first wife to marry Anne, an act that caused him no end of trouble with the Church. But after his struggle to get her, Henry soon tired of Anne, particularly when she did not present him with a son and heir. He didn't want to go through another divorce, so in 1536 he had Anne imprisoned in the Tower and beheaded. Another of

Anne Boleyn

Henry's six wives, Catherine Howard, was also beheaded in the Tower.

Of all Henry's wives Anne Boleyn has always been the most popular, and her execution did most to damage Henry's reputation. Anne's ghost has been spotted frequently in the Tower, both with and without her head.

The best documented sighting came in 1864. While the captain of the guards was making his rounds, he found one of his men unconscious. When the man was awakened, he said he had seen the figure of a woman in a white gown coming out of a room, which just happened to be the room where Anne spent her last night before execution. The figure glided toward the guard. He called for it to stop, but it kept right on coming. So he stabbed at it with his bayonet, and the bayonet went right through it. Then he knew that he was facing a ghost, so he fainted.

The captain of the guards didn't really believe that story and assumed that the man had simply fallen asleep while on duty. The guard was to be court-martialed on that charge, but during the proceedings several other guards said that they had seen the whole thing. They added that the ghost disappeared as soon as the man fainted. Several other guards reported seeing the phantom at other times when they had been on duty near the room. The "ghost defense" worked, and the case against the guard was dismissed.

In addition to the ghosts of royalty, the Tower has been the scene of some other curious ghostly phenomena. Around 1800 a guard near the Jewel Tower, where the Crown Jewels are kept, said that he saw a huge black bear standing on its hind legs. He struck at the thing with his bayonet, but as with the ghost of Anne Boleyn, the bayonet passed right through the figure. This guard also fainted, but he never fully recovered from the experience. He was taken to the hospital, where he regained consciousness long enough to tell his story, then lapsed into a coma and died a few days later.

One of those who had talked to the dying guard was Edmund Swifte, keeper of the Crown Jewels. Swifte had heard many tales of strange and ghostly events at the Tower in which he lived, but it wasn't until a Sunday evening in October 1817 that Swifte had an experience of his own.

He was having supper with his family in a room in the Jewel Tower. This room, like so many others in the tower, had once been used as a prison, though it had served as living quarters for people who worked in the Tower for many years. All the doors in the room were closed, and heavy curtains had been drawn over the windows. The only light came from candles on the table.

Swifte was pouring a glass of wine for his wife when she looked up and shouted, "Good God! What is that!" Swifte turned around and saw what looked like a cylinder filled with a bubbling blue liquid. It was stationary for a few moments; then it began to move. When it got behind Swifte's wife, it paused, and she shouted that it had tried to grab her. Swifte swung at it with a chair, but the chair passed right through the form. It retreated and disappeared. Years later Swifte recalled, "Even now . . . I feel the horror of that moment."

The strange thing was never seen again, and though Swifte had been frightened, he stayed on his job for another quarter century and didn't retire until 1842.

See also: HAMPTON COURT

THE WEIR HOUSE   During the seventeenth century Major Thomas Weir was regarded as one of Edinburgh, Scotland's, most upstanding citizens. To the outside world he seemed a man of undisputed honesty and fierce, almost fanatical religious piety. He was the last person in Edinburg that anyone would have suspected of engaging in evil practices. So one can imagine that the community was shocked when in the year 1670 Major Weir, who was then about seventy years old, suddenly confessed to a long series of crimes, including witchcraft.

For two centuries the Scots had been particularly obsessed with the idea of witchcraft, and people had been tortured and executed with little or no evidence to support the charge. But Major Weir had been such a righteous man that at first no one would believe his confession. It was assumed that he had gone mad, and the assumption is probably correct. But Major Weir was persistent in confessing his crimes, and some doctors examined him and adjudged him to be sane. He was finally brought to trial and executed along with his sister, who was implicated in the crimes.

The case of Major Weir became quite famous, but it arose at a time in history when the witchcraft mania was beginning to die down. That is probably why the major had so much trouble getting people to take his confession seriously. Yet the Weir case remained famous long after people stopped believing in witchcraft. The gloomy Weir house on the street called the Bow in Edinburgh became the center for what came to be regarded as all manner of ghostly rather than diabolical activities.

People reported seeing a spectral coach drive to the door of the house in order to take the major and his sister to hell. No one would live in the place, so it remained vacant for a century. Finally one old couple was induced to move in because of the low rent. The next morning they fled, swearing that a calf had gazed at them through a window while they were in bed. Just why this should have terrified them so is not recorded. The house remained empty and falling down until 1830, when it was finally torn down. During the entire period it may well have been the most celebrated haunted house in the world.

A book called *Traditions of Edinburgh,* published in 1825, states, "His [Major Weir's] house, though known to be deserted by everything human was sometimes observed at midnight to be full of lights and heard to emit strange sounds as if of dancing, howling, and, what is strangest of all, spinning. Some people occasionally saw the major issue forth from the low close [alley] at midnight mounted on a black horse without a head, and gallop in a whirlwind of flame."

Shortly before the house was torn down, the novelist Sir Walter

Scott testified to the hold it retained on the popular imagination: "Bold was the urchin from the high school who dared approach the gloomy ruin at the risk of seeing the Major's enchanted staff parading through the old apartments, or hearing the hum of the necromancer's wheel, which procured for his sister such a character as a spinner."

THE WINCHESTER MYSTERY HOUSE   One of the oddest monuments to a belief in ghosts is a rambling 160-room mansion in California's Santa Clara Valley. It is often referred to as the Winchester Mystery House. The person behind this architectural curiosity was Sara L. Winchester, the eccentric widow of William Winchester, heir to the Winchester arms fortune.

For much of her life Sara Winchester seemed to be a perfectly ordinary individual; then in a single year both her husband and only child died, and the double tragedy may have unhinged her mind. She slipped into a deep depression from which she could not be shaken.

Like so many people in the late nineteenth century, Sara Winchester had an interest in spiritualism, and this grew more pronounced after the death of her husband and son. On one of her rare outings, she attended a séance given by the Boston medium Adam Coons. The medium told her that the spirit of her husband was standing beside her and that he had a task for her to perform. She was to build a house for the spirits of all of those who had been killed by Winchester rifles. Since the Winchester was the most popular rifle in the world, the house would of necessity have to be huge.

Sara Winchester took this instruction from the spirit world very seriously. She sold her house in New Haven, Connecticut, and headed west, fully believing that the spirit of her husband would pick her destination. As she was passing through California's Santa Clara Valley, she saw a large house under construction, and the spirits informed her that this was the place. She immediately arranged to buy the uncompleted house from its owner, a California doctor.

Naturally she required some changes in the building plan, but as the builder discussed these changes with her, he realized that he was not dealing with a normal person and quit the job at once. Sara Winchester didn't have to worry; for the kind of money that she was able to pay she could always find plenty of willing workers who would follow even the maddest of plans.

For the remaining thirty-six years of Sara Winchester's life, she devoted much of her time to building, tearing down, and otherwise altering her "ghost house." Though she was constantly changing her mind, she was also always in a hurry; the building went on seven days a week. Sara believed that she was getting her plans directly from the spirit world and the spirits would not wait.

The final result was what has been described as the largest private home in the world. It could also be described as a mad jumble. There are stairways that lead nowhere. Elevators that go up only one floor. Doors that open onto blank walls or, worse, to sheer drops.

The outside of the house is just as mad as the inside. There are peaks and spires all over the top of the structure. Rooms and whole wings seem to be simply stuck on randomly. One writer aptly compared the whole thing to a crazy house at an amusement park. During Sara Winchester's lifetime the grandiose madness of her project was generally hidden from public view by great hedges and high trees. A crew of gardeners was kept busy tending to the protective greenery, and today only the peaks and spires of the house can be seen on the other side of the green wall.

The widow Winchester was superstitious, but she was not afraid of the number thirteen. It can be found repeated all over the house. Many of the rooms have thirteen windows. Chandeliers have thirteen lights. There are thirteen bathrooms in the house. Most of the stairways have thirteen steps and so on. There is one oddity, a stairway with forty-four steps, but it goes up only one floor, ten feet in all.

The labyrinthine construction of the house had a sort of mad logic behind it, dictated by a fear of evil or vengeful spirits. Sara Winchester may have been trying to confuse them by losing them in the maze of corridors and dead ends. It was said that she would sleep in a different bedroom every night, and when she had slept in every bedroom in the house, she would start the rotation all over again. Rather ghostlike herself, she often wandered the corridors of the house.

The bizarre reputation of the Winchester house was enhanced by secrecy. Sara wasn't a total recluse. Her needs were attended to by a large staff of well-paid and very discreet servants. Generally, however, visitors were discouraged. It was said that she turned away President Theodore Roosevelt. But she did invite in the magician Harry Houdini, who had a deep interest in spiritualism but didn't believe in it. What the ghost-ridden old woman wanted with the skeptical magician is hard to say. Perhaps the meeting never really took place, for the lives of both Mrs. Winchester and Houdini are encrusted with legend.

The strangest room in this very strange house was a small windowless chamber called the Blue Room. It was here that Sara held her regular séances. No one except Sara herself and presumably the ghosts were allowed to enter this room. At midnight a bell would ring, and Sara, wearing a long gown decorated with occult symbols, would enter the Blue Room for her ghostly meetings.

Sara was also said to hold regular banquets. The table was always set for thirteen, but Sara was the only visible guest. The servants doubtless took care of the uneaten food.

In the thirty-six years she lived in the house, Sara is known to have left it only once, and that was in 1906 during the San Francisco earthquake. When the earthquake struck, the old woman was terrified because she thought the evil spirits had finally gotten to her. She was rescued unhurt, but she developed a deep aversion to the bedroom in which she had been sleeping at the time and ordered it boarded up.

Sara Winchester had some other strange ideas. She thought that the world was going to be destroyed in a great flood. She had a large houseboat, a sort of ark, built on her land. After the earthquake she lived in the houseboat for six years before moving back to the house in the Santa Clara Valley.

Sara Winchester died in her ghost house in September 1922 at the age of 85. The house is now run as a tourist attraction and is a very popular one.

See also: HARRY HOUDINI

4

ANIMAL GHOSTS

ANIMAL POLTERGEISTS

ANIMAL POLTERGEISTS The poltergeist phenomena traditionally involves strange noises and objects being moved about. But apparitions, while rare, are not completely unknown, and occasional poltergeist phenomena are accompanied by apparitions of animals, usually strange and unnatural-looking ones.

One of the more celebrated poltergeist cases in the history of psychical research took place during the last century in England at Willington Mill, which was owned by the Proctor family. For over ten years the mill was the scene of all manner of poltergeist manifestations. There were loud and dreadful noises sometimes sounding like a galloping donkey and other times like falling fire irons. Doors creaked and sticks crackled as though burning. At times rappings were almost constant. And there were apparitions, many of an animal shape.

A memorable experience at Willington Mill was related by Thomas Davidson, who was courting a maid in the Proctor household. Davidson was standing by the mill when what looked like a whitish cat came up to him. Davidson, apparently no animal lover, tried to kick it, but his boot went right through the form as if it was not there at all. The cat, or whatever it was, disappeared. It reappeared a few minutes later, this time hopping like a rabbit. Davidson took another kick at it, and again his boot passed right through the figure. The third time it appeared, it was as large as a sheep and quite luminous. By now Davidson was very frightened.

According to an account written by his son:

"All muscle power seemed for the moment paralyzed. It moved

Rabbits or rabbitlike creatures have sometimes been reported during poltergeist outbreaks.

on, disappearing at the same spot as the preceding apparition. My father declared if it was possible for 'hair to stand on end' his did just then. Thinking for once that he had seen sufficient, he went home, keeping the knowledge of the scene to himself."

A man named Wedgewood reported that he had seen a tabby cat in the furnace room of the mill. There was nothing unusual about the cat's appearance. But instead of walking like an ordinary cat, it wriggled along like a snake. He tried to follow, but it passed through a solid stone wall.

One woman was standing in the kitchen when she heard a dog bark; then she felt what seemed to be paws land heavily on her shoulders. There was, of course, no dog to be seen. Children in the area sometimes reported seeing an animal they described as a "funny cat or bonny monkey" during the years of the disturbances at the mill.

A more recent American poltergeist case took place in southern California in the 1930s in the house of a Mrs. James H. Rogers. All the members of the family heard strange noises including clickings and what sounded like footsteps.

One night Mrs. Rogers's daughter was awakened by noises coming from the kitchen. When she went to investigate, she was able to find nothing out of the ordinary. When she returned to her bedroom, she saw a strange dog there. The animal stood silently and stared fixedly at her. She became aware there was something very unusual about the dog because it was semitransparent. As she walked toward it, waving her hand, the dog vanished.

See also: THE EPWORTH POLTERGEIST

THE BLACK CAT OF KILLAKEE   A building at Killakee in southern Ireland that was used as an arts center was assailed by a variety of different ghostly phenomena, the worst of which was a monstrous black cat.

The building, called Dower House, was almost in ruins when it was purchased in 1968 by Mrs. Margaret O'Brien, an artist and poet, and her husband, Nicholas. The house had been deserted for years, and there was so much renovation work to be done that some of the workmen were actually living on the site during the rebuilding. They were first disturbed by strange sounds and doors that seemed to open mysteriously. But it was the sudden appearance and disappearance of a large black cat that most troubled them.

At first Mrs. O'Brien refused to take the stories seriously. "I thought the whole thing was nonsense," she said. "A group of country people sitting alone in an empty house on a lonely hillside at night telling each other stories and frightening themselves. Then I saw the creature myself and I began to understand their fear."

She described the black cat as being about as big as a medium-sized dog. The first time she came across the creature, it was squatting in the hallway. All of the doors of the house had been locked before the black cat appeared, and they remained locked after it disappeared.

The black cat painted by someone who said he had seen it

A painter named Tom McAssey, who was helping to decorate the house, had an even more alarming experience. He was working in a room with two other men when suddenly the room, which had been quite warm, became icy cold. The room had been locked, but now the door stood wide open. "A shadowy figure stood in the darkness beyond," said McAssey. "At first I thought someone was playing a joke and I said; 'Come in, I see you.' Then there was a deep sort of guttural growl and the three of us turned and ran in panic. We slammed the heavy door behind us, and I turned and looked back. The door was open again, and a monstrous black cat with red-flecked amber eyes was crouched there in the half-light. I thought my legs wouldn't take me away from the place. . . . I was really in a bad state."

McAssey also reported seeing a shadowy figure in the hall which said in a deep voice, "You cannot see me. You don't even know who I am."

In 1968 Mrs. O'Brien had an exorcism performed in the house, and that seemed to quiet things down for about a year. But in the fall of 1969, a group of actors who were staying at the arts center decided—half-seriously—to hold a séance, and after that the disturbances started once again.

Next Mrs. O'Brien called in a spirit medium named Sheila St. Clair, who went into a trance and said that she saw the spirits of two women who had helped to serve at Black Masses held by a group of Devil worshipers called the Hell Fire Club in the eighteenth century.

The O'Briens also unearthed some local legends about Thomas "Black" Whaley, the notorious and depraved member of a rich family in the area who had once joined such a society. Furthermore the legend told of how Whaley and some of his friends had killed a deformed boy just for sport at Dower House. It was said that a small deformed skeleton was unearthed on the grounds of Dower House in 1968. A small metal statue of a devil was also dug up near the house.

There were those who suspected that the whole thing was a publicity stunt for the arts center, for the press attention certainly helped to attract larger crowds to exhibitions and boost the sale of paintings.

Mrs. O'Brien, however, insisted that such was not the case and that the disturbances were more of a problem than an aid to the center. "I finally decided to have the house and grounds exorcised once again, and in July 1970 a priest came up from Dublin. Since then we have had very few disturbances, although the priest felt there were still 'emanations' around and we do get the odd bump in the night."

$\mathbb{D}$OGS OF DOOM   Many old families have a tradition which holds that before a member of the family dies some sort of warning specter will appear. There are the traditional ghostly monks and nuns, the white and gray ladies. The Scots are particularly partial to phantom pipers. But in many tales the warning phantom appears in animal form, most frequently in the shape of a dog.

Members of the Vaughn family are supposed to see a black dog before one of them dies. There is a story about one member of the family who did not believe in the tradition, though he didn't exactly disbelieve it either, because he never told his wife about it for fear of frightening her.

Then one of his children fell ill with smallpox. Though the case seemed a relatively mild one, smallpox was a dangerous disease and everyone in the family was worried. One evening the family was just sitting down to dinner when his wife said that she would go upstairs to check on the sick child. A moment later she came running down the stairs and said that the child was asleep, "But please go upstairs, for there is a large black dog lying on his bed. Go drive it out of the house."

The father knew instantly what the appearance of the dog meant. Filled with fear, he rushed upstairs. There was no dog to be seen, but the child was already dead.

A small white dog was said to appear at the gates of the notorious Newgate Prison before every execution. In the famous Sherlock Holmes story *The Hound of the Baskervilles*, the crime is built around a legend which holds that a gigantic hound appears on the moors before the death of a member of the Baskerville family. Though this story was entirely fiction, it was based on an ancient and widespread spectral hound tradition in England.

But not all of the stories of death warnings go back hundreds of years. There is a story connected with the death in 1924 of a popu-

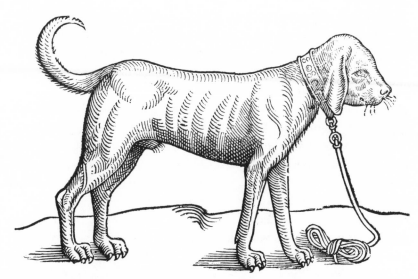

A spectral hound is often regarded as a warning of death.

lar British composer named Lionel Monckton.

One evening a group of Monckton's friends were sitting around their club when one of them, Donald Calthrop, got the feeling that something had happened to Monckton. When he mentioned this feeling to the others, they all laughed it off. Then Calthrop suddenly fixed his eyes on a corner of the room and shouted, "Look! There is his dog." Monckton often took his dog with him to the club. No one else in the room saw the dog, and they decided that Calthrop was joking. Then a few hours later came the news that Monckton had died unexpectedly. The time of his death was fixed at about the time the dog was seen by Calthrop.

See also: THE HOHENZOLLERNS' SPECTER

Ⓖ HOSTLY PETS   People have often felt that pets are quite literally members of the family; therefore it would seem logical that many people have seen or otherwise experienced the presence of their departed pets. However, records of such cases are not nearly as common as they are for cases involving human spirits. This may simply be because psychical researchers have not paid much attention to animal ghosts.

Psychical researcher and writer Raymond Bayless made a special attempt to collect such accounts for his book *Animal Ghosts.* He quickly found that there was no shortage of them.

A typical case was reported by Mrs. Joy Baterski. She said that Red, the family Irish setter, had died on August 27, 1965. The animal had been the family pet for over fourteen years and was greatly missed. Red was buried in the yard.

On the night after Red's death and burial, Mrs. Baterski was awakened by what she was sure was Red's barking. The Irish setter had an unusual and distinctive bark. Mrs. Baterski described it as sounding like a "hoarse seal." It could not, she insisted, be mistaken for the bark of any other dog. Her husband was also awakened by the sounds. These mysterious barkings continued on and off for several weeks, until the Baterski's got a new dog, a German shepherd puppy. "From that day forward," she said, "the mysterious barking was heard no more."

The experience was an emotional one, particularly for Mrs. Baterski. In a letter to Bayless she stated:

"The last and final time [the barking was heard] almost a week later, when I was crying in my sleep, and my husband woke me. Only I heard the barking then. It was becoming more distant. At this point I was so upset that I even insisted that my husband dig the dog up to make certain that he was dead. My husband assured me that he was.

"Who can say that if we had not brought another dog into the house whether or not the phenomenon might have continued?

"I would say that within a period of about four weeks we were awakened by Red's barking at least five times and at least once a week. But the last time only I heard it."

Bayless obtained a statement from Mr. Lawrence Baterski which confirmed his wife's account in every detail. A neighbor of the Baterski's also wrote Bayless. "Red had the most unusual bark I have ever heard and it could not be mistaken. After hearing the dog over thirteen years they [the Baterskis] would surely recognize the bark."

Al H. Morrison of New York supplied Bayless with a very similar story. Late on Sunday afternoon in June of 1966, the dog that he had owned for fourteen years died. Morrison's letter continues:

"In late August of the same year at the same time of day—2 P.M. or so on Sunday—I had a new client sitting there when there came a loud, happy barking from my dog. You don't live with a dog for fourteen years and fail to recognize its voice.

"I would have written it all off as my own wishful thinking but my client heard it at the same time. It was so loud that it frightened her, and she asked, 'Where is the dog?' I thought about it and decided that she couldn't deal with such a story so I just said, 'Oh, she's around here somewhere' and went on working."

Morrison said that he doubted if the incident would recur. "It seemed to me that it took an enormous effort and energy to get back through, and that she wouldn't have the energy again."

Another of Bayless's cases comes from Australia. It was told by William A. Courtney. In 1953 Courtney was living in the small town of Sarina in north Australia. He had a valuable female greyhound named Lady to which he was greatly attached. But the dog contracted distemper and had to be destroyed.

"That night I lay on my bed thinking of her and grieving when suddenly I heard pattering footsteps coming along the passage from the front door. . . . The footsteps entered my room, then I heard a sound of a heavy body dropping to the floor beside my bed.

"I sprang up and turned on the light fully expecting to see Lady stretched out on the floor. But the room was empty, or at least I saw nothing."

Courtney could find nothing unusual in the house or garden to account for the noise. Then he realized that he heard the noise at 10 P.M., the hour when Lady had usually come in for the night.

Bayless found a somewhat older account in the pages of the *Journal of the American Society for Psychical Research*. Mrs. W. E. Dickson recounted how her dog, Butch, died at about noon on Tuesday, March 29, 1949.

That night she thought she heard Butch whining and crying. At first she didn't want to tell her husband about what she heard because she was afraid that he would not believe her. In the morning he said, "I don't know if you will believe this, but I heard Butch crying all night." They decided not to tell anyone else, but one of their neighbors reported dreaming that she heard Butch. The strange whinings and barkings continued for about three months.

Mrs. Dickson added, "And another unusual thing happened about two mornings after he died—I was positive I saw a shadow jump up on the bed where my husband was lying. I cannot define this in any other way except as a shadow."

TERHUNE'S GHOST DOG   Albert Payson Terhune was America's foremost writer of dog stories. In addition to writing about dogs, Terhune was a genuine dog lover, and during his lifetime he owned a great many of them. One of his favorites was a large, fawn-colored, short-haired dog of mixed ancestry, named Rex. Rex's appearance was unmistakable because he had a large scar on his face. Often when the Terhune family sat down to dinner, Rex would come to the window and stare in. The dog also spent a lot of time in the hallway sprawled out next to the author's study.

Rex was killed in 1916. A short time later an old friend of the Terhunes, the Reverend Appleton Grannis, came to stay with the family. The Reverend Grannis had not seen the Terhunes in years and had never seen Rex and knew nothing about him.

Terhune and the Reverend Grannis were sitting in the dining room talking when Grannis suddenly said that he saw a strange dog looking in at the window. Terhune turned, but the dog disap-

The author Albert Payson Terhune and two of his dogs

peared. Grannis said that the animal at the window did not look like any of the dogs he had seen on the Terhune farm, and he described it. The description matched Rex perfectly, down to the scar on his face.

Two years after Rex's death, another friend of the author's family, Henry A. Healy, insisted he had seen the figure of Rex lying at his feet when he visited the Terhune farm.

Terhune himself noticed that for years after Rex's death another one of his dogs refused to walk over a spot that had been favored by the dead dog.

5

POLTERGEISTS

THE AMHERST POLTERGEIST   In general poltergeists are annoying, even frightening. But there are a number of cases on record where the poltergeist activity seems to have taken a particularly nasty turn. One such case took place in the city of Amherst, Nova Scotia, in 1878. The scene of the affliction was a plain two-story cottage inhabited by Daniel Tweed and his family. Along with his wife, Olive, and two very young sons, the house also contained two of Olive's younger sisters, Jeannie and Esther Cox. Jeannie was twenty-one and Esther, around whom the events seemed to center, was nineteen.

The case started with strange noises coming from the room in which the two girls slept. But within two days matters escalated. Esther woke up screaming, "My God, what's wrong with me? I'm dying." Her face and arms had swollen up horribly and she was in great pain. While she was still screaming, a tremendous knocking was heard throughout the house. The family rushed around to see if they could find out what was causing the noise, but they found nothing.

Esther's swelling went down after a few hours, but it flared up again four days later. Along with the noises there was another typical poltergeist activity, covers were torn off the beds, particularly Esther's bed. Small objects were tossed around the house, and most ominously there was a message scratched into the wall: "Esther Cox You Are Mine To Kill."

The news of these goings-on attracted a crowd to the Tweed

house that grew so large the police had to be brought in to control it. There were plenty of skeptics who insisted that Esther herself was creating the disturbances in order to attract attention. But there were also witnesses who claimed that they saw Esther sitting on one side of the room while objects were thrown about on the other side; she could not possibly have been responsible for that.

The strain was too much for Esther, who became very ill, unable even to get out of bed. Tweed thought she might be better off at some other house so she was sent to the home of another sister; while she was gone the poltergeist activity at the Tweed house ceased. But when she came back, so did the poltergeist. Now it had a new trick; it began playing with matches, lighting them and dropping them everywhere. There were a number of small fires in the house, though Tweed managed to put them out before they did much damage.

Esther also said that she was able to communicate with the spirit. She was told that its name was Bob and that it intended to burn the house down, though it never said why. Tweed apparently suspected that Esther was responsible for the trouble. In any event he ordered her out of the house. She got a job in a local restaurant, but the poltergeist began knocking over chairs and tables so she was fired, and Tweed took her back.

A traveling showman named Walter Hubbell got the idea of making some money out of the now-famous Amherst poltergeist. He figured that he could put Esther on the stage and people would pay to see the poltergeist move objects around. In theory it was a good idea. In practice it didn't work. Esther went on the stage but nothing happened and the audience demanded its money back.

Esther spent the rest of her life wandering from place to place. She spent time in prison for arson. The police accused her of burning down her employer's barn. Esther said that the poltergeist did it, but the judge didn't believe her. The unfortunate woman always claimed that the poltergeist had ruined her life.

See also: THE BELL WITCH, THE HYDESVILLE HAUNTING

BEALINGS BELLS   The ghostly bells that "were not rung by any mortal hand" are a standard feature of many supernatural tales. In fact, there are quite a number of cases in which this sort of thing was actually supposed to have happened. The most well documented is the case of the Bealings Bells.

On February 2, 1834, the bells in the house of Major Edward Moore at Great Bealings, Suffolk, began to ring violently without any apparent cause. The bells were in the kitchen, and wires led to bellpulls in different rooms. The purpose of the bells was to alert servants in the kitchen that they were wanted in some other part of the house. The servants knew which room the call had come from by seeing which bell rang. Major Moore, who was retired from the Indian Army, seemed fascinated by, almost obsessed with, the mysterious ringings in his house.

He wrote a long letter to a local newspaper explaining what had occurred and asking for suggestions as to what had caused the phenomena. He got plenty of suggestions, and in addition the paper received other accounts of similar experiences.

The bell ringing continued until March 27, when it quite suddenly stopped forever. No satisfactory explanation for the mysterious bells was ever offered.

Major Moore himself wrote a little book on his investigations. In it he declared:

"I will here note, once and for all—that after much consideration, I cannot reach any procedure by which they [these effects] have been or can be produced.

"If I had a year to devote to such considerations, and the promise of a thousand pounds in the event of discovery, I should despair of success. I would not, indeed, attempt it."

For those interested in psychical research, the Bealings Bells case has been regarded as a sort of classic early poltergeist investigation. Major Moore himself was a member of the prestigious

Royal Society, and the investigations that he conducted were seemingly very thorough—but the investigation as he wrote it up has enormous and very strange gaps in it.

For example, in his book Major Moore gives a very detailed description of the arrangement of the bell system. But there is something seriously flawed about his description, because no one has ever been able to figure out, from the description, how the bells were supposed to work. The confusion seems deliberate rather than the result of careless writing.

The most obvious explanation for the mysteriously ringing bells was that someone rang them. Major Moore made a detailed record of the temperature, barometric pressure, and other conditions during the period of the bell ringing, but he made no attempt to keep track of the people in his house.

One of the responses Major Moore got to his original letter in the newspaper came from a man named Maskelyne, who outlined a very sensible plan of action. Enlist the aid of some trustworthy neighbors and friends, then take everybody in the household and lock them in a room guarded over by a friend. Station other friends at various points in the house so that no one would be able to enter or leave undetected. Then search the house room by room, locking each room as the search continued.

"If this plan be pursued I will . . . make any moderate bet, either that the bells will not ring at all during the search, or that if they do ring, the party searching the house will find some relative or friend, or one of his establishment concealed in some part of the house."

Unfortunately Major Moore dismissed this excellent suggestion out of hand. "I did not in any way, follow the advice therein offered."

Major Moore ends his pamphlet with some scientific-mystical ramblings that are so confusing and jargon-laden as to be totally incomprehensible.

"Who can say, or imagine where they are to end?" he writes.

There is more than a suspicion that the whole episode is nothing more than an elaborate joke, Major Moore's satire on investigations of other odd phenomena. If satire was his aim, Major Moore was a bit too subtle, for many readers failed to see the humor, and even today Bealings Bells is occasionally cited as a classic example of careful poltergeist research.

THE BELL WITCH   Despite the name, the Bell Witch is usually classified as a poltergeist, though it did a lot of unpoltergeistlike things. Most notably it talked, and once the talking began, the "witch" became downright garrulous. It might also be classed as a ghost or haunting, but it was certainly not a witch. However, back in the early nineteenth century, when this series of phenomena took place, all strange and unexplained events of this type were automatically assumed to be the products of demons or witchcraft in rural areas of America.

The tale of the Bell Witch began in 1817 on the farm of John Bell in Robertson County, Tennessee. This part of Tennessee was no longer frontier country in 1817, but families still tended to live in isolated farmhouses—mother, father, four sons, and a daughter lived in a plain two-story farmhouse. A small number of slaves lived in outbuildings. Two older children who had already married had moved away but not very far. The Bells were considered moderately prosperous and as far as can be determined were well liked by their neighbors.

As in so many poltergeist cases, the disturbances began slowly. There were strange noises, the rappings and scratchings so typical of poltergeists. At about the same time John Bell reported seeing a strange animal. It looked like a dog, and yet it didn't look like a dog. He got his gun and took a shot at it but missed. There was also something that looked like a turkey or some other large bird seen near the house. He couldn't shoot it either. The noises got worse.

More ominous manifestations began. The thing was growing physically violent. At first it just pulled covers off beds, then, according to an account written years later by Richard Williams Bell, the youngest member of the family, it began "slapping people on the face, especially those who resisted the action of pulling the cover from the bed and those who came as detectives to expose the trick. The blows were heard distinctly, like the open palm of a heavy hand, while the sting was keenly felt and it did not neglect to pull my hair, and make Joel [another son] squeal as often." But the chief target of the witch seemed (at this stage anyway) to be Betsy—Elizabeth Bell—the one girl in the family. She was about twelve years old at the time.

At first the family tried to keep the strange events secret, not a difficult task since there were no near neighbors. But as the witch's activities continued and grew worse, secrecy became harder to maintain. John Bell was so affected that he began to act strangely when visiting friends. When invited to a friend's house for dinner, he barely spoke or ate. Later he explained, "All of a sudden my tongue became strangely afflicted. Something that felt like a fungus growth came on both sides, pressing against my jaws, filling my mouth so that I could not talk."

Finally the Bells were driven to ask for help. They called in James Johnson, a neighbor, friend, and a man known for his great piety and vigor as a lay preacher. Johnson visited the Bell house, heard the noises, and decided there definitely was some sort of evil presence at work. He returned with a committee of local residents whose job it apparently was to see if one of the Bells was perpetrating a hoax. The committee decided that there was no hoax, but they hadn't the faintest notion as to what was going on. As strict Protestants they didn't believe in ghosts so they called the thing a "witch" and the name stuck.

As news of the Bell Witch spread, more and more people came to help the afflicted family or simply to look just because they were curious. The witch seemed encouraged by all the attention, and its (the witch was always referred to as it) efforts became more vigorous and varied. It began answering questions by means of a rapping code. Then slowly it acquired the ability to speak.

According to the principal account of the Bell Witch phenomenon, "It commenced whistling when spoken to, in a low, broken sound, as if trying to speak in a whistling voice, and in this way progressed developing until the whistling sound was changed to a weak, flattering whisper uttering indistinct words. The voice, however, gradually gained strength in articulating and soon the utterances became distinct in a low whisper so as to be understood in the absence of any other noise."

The witch's voice got louder and more persistent until it could be heard shrieking about the house at practically any time of the day or night.

Naturally the first question that everyone wanted the witch to answer was who or what it was. To this the witch gave several contradictory answers.

"I am a spirit from everywhere, Heaven, Hell and the Earth. I'm in the air, in houses, any place at any time. I've been created millions of years. That is all I will tell you." That was one answer.

Another was, "I am the spirit of a person who was buried in the woods nearby and the grave has been disturbed and my bones scattered, and one of my teeth was lost under the house. I've been looking for that tooth." That is the traditional troubled-spirit type of haunting. The Bells spent a lot of time digging around the house looking for the missing tooth until the witch informed them it was all a joke.

Another explanation given by the witch was "I am the spirit of an early immigrant who brought a large sum of money and buried my treasure for safekeeping until needed. In the meantime I died without divulging the secret and I have returned in the spirit for the purpose of making known the hiding place. I want Betsy Bell to have the money." This sent the Bells off digging once again, but the witch laughed at them for being so easily taken in.

The explanation which most caught the attention of the people of Robertson County was the witch's assertion that "I am nothing more nor less than old Kate Batts, witch." Kate Batts was a local woman with a loud voice, foul temper, and something of a grudge against John Bell. She may have had the reputation of being a witch, though she was also known for her endless quoting of Scripture. Many people began referring to the Bell Witch as Kate. The problem was that Kate Batts was very much alive at the time. While people may have gossiped about how she somehow or other was responsible for the phenomenon, it is doubtful if too many took it seriously. Kate Batts was never attacked by the Bells or their neighbors, and they surely would have done so if they believed that she was responsible for all their troubles.

While the witch was not clear about identity, it was terribly clear about purpose, which was to destroy "Old Jack Bell." Just why it hated Bell so violently was never made entirely clear. On the other hand the witch adored John's wife, Lucy, or Luce, extolling her virtues while threatening and damning John.

The witch also took a new interest in Betsy. Joshua Gardner, a young man who lived nearby, announced that he intended to marry the girl, though in fact, she was still too young to marry. The witch didn't even like the announcement. First it pleaded with Betsy not to marry Gardner, and when that didn't work, it tormented her with punches, slaps, and by giving her fainting fits. When a friend of Gardner's came over, the witch kept screaming at him and threatening him. Betsy never did marry John Gardner.

The witch did not confine its interests to the Bell family alone. It took to gossiping about everyone in the area. No one was safe from the witch's malicious tongue. The pious James Johnson was referred to as "Old Sugar Mouth."

Yet the Bell Witch did not profess to be entirely godless. On a couple of occasions it was reported to have repeated the minister's Sunday sermon word for word after church.

The Bell Witch continued its activities for three years, and the strain began to tell on the family, most particularly on John Bell. His health declined. He visited a doctor who gave him a variety of medicines, but none of them seemed to really help. On the morning of December 19, 1820, Bell lapsed into a coma. One of his sons rushed to the cabinet where the medicines were kept, but instead of the usual bottles he found "a smoky looking vial, which was about one-third full of a dark colored liquid." The doctor was sent for, but the witch announced that it was too late. "It's useless for you to try to revive Old Jack. I've got him this time. He'll never get up from that bed again." When asked about the bottle with the strange-looking liquid, the witch said, "I put it there and gave Old Jack a big dose out of it last night while he was fast asleep, which fixed him."

The liquid in the bottle was tested on a cat, and the cat died instantly. John Bell lingered a bit longer. He died the following day. The witch was exultant. Even during the funeral the air was filled with loud and derisive shouts and songs.

After the death of John Bell, the witch gradually lost interest in the family. One night several months after Bell's funeral, the living room of the Bell house was suddenly filled with smoke. From the midst of the cloud the witch shouted, "I am going and will be gone for seven years. Goodbye to all!"

Seven years later the witch did make a brief return. By that time Betsy was gone, she had married a former schoolmaster turned politician. He was much older than she was and much richer. John Bell, Jr. had also married and moved away. But John Bell's widow and three sons remained in the house. For about two weeks they were plagued with strange noises and something that pulled off bedclothes, but there were no voices. The married son, however, said that he heard a voice announcing that the witch would come again in one hundred and seven years. The prophesied year was 1934, but none of John Bell's living descendants reported any strange incidents that year.

The Bell Witch story is a remarkable one—but how much truth is in the tale? Some twenty-six years after the Bell Witch first made itself known, Richard Williams Bell (usually called Williams) set down his recollections. The book was never intended for publication, but in 1891 Williams's son Allen turned the manuscript over to a writer named M. V. Ingram, who rewrote it and published it as *An Authenticated History of the Famous Bell*

Witch. The Wonder of the 19th Century, an Unexplained Phenomena of the Christian Era. The Mysterious Talking Goblin That Terrorized the West End of Robertson County, Tennessee, Tormenting John Bell to His Death. The Story of Betsy Bell, Her Lover and the Haunting Sphinx, Clarksville, Tenn. As the lengthy title indicates, the book was written in the melodramatic and sensational style that was popular in the penny dreadfuls of the time.

The other source for information on the Bell Witch comes from a pamphlet, *The Bell Witch, A Mysterious Spirit*, written by Charles Bailey Bell, M.D., great-grandson of the unfortunate John Bell. This was published in 1934. Dr. Bell said that he got much of the information from Betsy Bell herself. She lived to the age of eighty-three and was apparently very fond of relating old Bell Witch tales.

The problems of evidence are obvious. Williams would have been only six years old when these events began, and he wrote his memories down many years later. Even then we have his memories filtered through the work of a sensationalist writer. Charles Bell may or may not have been relying on the stories of a very old woman.

Still something probably happened to begin the Bell Witch legend in the first place. Except for the witch's speech, most of the other phenomena attributed to it are typical of the poltergeist.

Another typical feature is that the manifestations seemed to center around a young person, in this case twelve-year-old Betsy. During the manifestations Betsy often appeared to faint. Some of the Bells' neighbors apparently suspected that Betsy was responsible for the phenomena. They tried to test her in a variety of ways. For example, at one point a doctor clamped his hand over Betsy's mouth while the voice of the witch was heard, to make sure Betsy was not "throwing her voice." According to the accounts Betsy passed all of the tests, but the accounts may not be entirely reliable.

Betsy certainly could not have been responsible for all the phenomena if they happened as reported.

Finally, did Betsy Bell actually contrive to kill her own father? She was never prosecuted for it, much less convicted. Possibly John Bell simply died from natural causes during this period and local gossip immediately assumed that the famous witch was responsible.

The case remains an enigma.

See also: THE EPWORTH POLTERGEIST

THE EPWORTH POLTERGEIST   While there have been hundreds and hundreds of poltergeist cases recorded and investigated, the disturbances which took place in the parsonage at Epworth, England, in December and January 1716–17 are among the best known and most thoroughly investigated. The undoubted reason for the attention that has been focused on this particular case is that the parsonage at Epworth was the birthplace of John Wesley, founder of Methodism and one of the most influential religious leaders of the eighteenth century.

John Wesley himself was not a direct witness to the strange phenomena, but many members of his large family were. Wesley retained an interest in the events throughout his life, and he always seemed to believe that some spiritual or diabolical force was involved in them.

Toward the end of 1716, the house was afflicted by a variety of strange and inexplicable noises—knocks and rumblings—which reverberated from cellar to attic.

Writing to her eldest son, Mrs. Wesley described some of the events:

"One night it made such a noise in the room over our heads as if several people were walking; then [it began] running up and down stairs, and was so outrageous that we thought the children would be frightened so your father and I rose and went down in the dark to light a candle. Just as we came to the bedroom at the bottom of the broad stairs, having hold of each other, on my side there seemed as if somebody had emptied a bag of money at my feet, and on his as if all the bottles under the stairs (which were many) had been dashed in a thousand pieces. We passed through the hall into the kitchen, and got a candle and went to see the children. The next night your father got Mr. Hoole [a neighbor] to lie at our house, and we all sat together till one or two o'clock in the morning, and heard the knocking as usual. Sometimes it would make a noise like the winding up of a jack, at other times as the night Mr. Hoole was with us, like a carpenter planing deals, but most commonly it knocked thrice and stopped and then thrice again, and so many hours together."

Often, when Rev. Wesley tapped his stick on the floor, the poltergeist would answer with knocks of its own. The poltergeist even disturbed the pious family at its prayers. It became particularly unruly when the names of King George I and the prince were mentioned in a prayer. Rev. Wesley tried to speak to it but never received any replies. "Only once or twice two or three feeble squeaks, a little louder than the chirping of a bird but not the noise of rats, which I have often heard."

Rev. Wesley remained defiant, calling the poltergeist, "thou deaf and dumb devil."

Sometimes door latches seemed to rise mysteriously, and Wesley recalled, "I have been thrice pushed by an invisible power over against the corner of my desk in the study, a second time against the door of the matted chamber, a third time against the right side of the frame of my study door as I was going in."

Some strange things were seen, but they were certainly not the traditional ghost. Mrs. Wesley reported seeing something under her bed "like a badger only without any head that was discernible." One of the hired men saw something that looked like a white rabbit but not quite.

According to Mrs. Wesley "one night when the noise was great in the kitchen . . . and the door the latch whereof was often lifted up, my daughter Emilia went and held it fast on the inside, but it was lifted up, and the door pushed violently against her, though

The Reverend John Wesley

nothing was to be seen on the outside."

The Wesleys got a dog in an attempt to track down or frighten away whatever it was that was causing all of the disturbances. That didn't work; in fact, the noises frightened the dog. The Wesley children, however, did not seem at all frightened once they got used to the noises. Indeed, they actually seemed to enjoy the excitement created by the poltergeist. They dubbed it "Old Jeffrey" after someone who had died in the house. In their accounts they often speak of Old Jeffery in a most friendly manner.

After about two months the mysterious phenomena simply faded away, though the family continued to discuss and even write about the happenings for many years. As late as the year 1786 John Wesley published an article on the subject. Upon John's death, all of the materials that he had collected—his own father's firsthand account, letters written by family members at the time and later, and statements made by servants or others in the household—were published.

In his book *Ghosts and Hauntings,* author Dennis Bardens declares flatly, "There is absolutely nothing in the lives of this worthy, God-fearing family to support even a suspicion that they could or would be capable of fraud." But others who have examined the case are not quite so sure.

Pioneer psychical researcher Frank Podmore went over the evidence relating to the case. He found that all of the firsthand contemporary accounts, that is, the statements written shortly after the events had taken place by people who had actually been there, concerned strange noises, broken objects, and other relatively unspectacular events.

Secondhand accounts and those taken from witnesses months or years later were generally much more impressive. These accounts were filled with difficult-to-explain events, like doors mysteriously being opened while someone was trying to hold them closed. Podmore concludes that the Wesley family was engaging in the inevitable human tendency to exaggerate.

What may be most significant about the accounts collected by John Wesley is the one that isn't there—a statement by one of the elder Wesley girls, Hetty. Hetty would have been about nineteen at the time and fully capable of writing her experiences, but for some reason she never seemed to, or at least her account has never been made public.

This is all the more curious since many of the disturbances seemed to center about Hetty. Not only was she always on the spot when there were strange noises, she often behaved oddly as well.

Mrs. Wesley wrote:

"All the family, as well as Robin, were asleep when your father and I went downstairs, nor did they wake in the nursery when we held the candle close to them, only we observed that Hetty trembled exceedingly in her sleep, as she always did before the noise awakened her. It commonly was nearer her than the rest."

Then there is the extract from the letter of another Wesley sister, Emily:

"No sooner was I got upstairs and and undressing for bed, but I heard a noise among the many bottles that stand under the stairs just like the throwing of a great stone among them, which had broken them all to pieces. This made me hasten to bed, but my sister Hetty, who sits always to wait on my father going to bed was still sitting on the lowest step of the garret stairs."

Or from another of Emily's letters:

"If [the noise] never followed me as it did my sister Hetty, I have been with her when it has knocked under her, and when she moved it has followed and still kept just under her feet."

There is a good deal more like this in the evidence surrounding the Epworth poltergeist. That is why it is exceptionally unfortunate and frankly suspicious that we do not have Hetty's own description of what happened.

See also: THE BELL WITCH

THE EXORCIST   The story called *The Exorcist* of the demonic possession of a young girl was an extremely popular novel by William Peter Blatty. It was made into an even more popular film—the first of the modern cycle of horror blockbusters. A good part of the appeal of the book and the film was the claim that it was "based on" a real case. The writer and the film's producer acknowledged that certain changes had been made in order to make the story more dramatic and exciting.

The changes were extensive indeed, and in fact, they entirely altered the nature of the original account, and *The Exorcist* book and film must be considered entirely works of fiction with no claim at all to a factual basis.

In the book and film the "possessed" subject was a girl, whereas in the real case it was a boy. Beyond that the available facts on the original case are scanty. Very few accurate records were kept, and not everything about the case has been made public. Some of those who were involved in the events have since died, while others just don't want to talk about it anymore.

Here is what we do know. The case began early in 1949; the "possessed" subject was a fourteen-year-old boy called Douglas Deen who lived with his family in a suburb of Washington, D.C.

The first manifestation the family noticed were strange noises coming from the boy's room. The family suspected mice and called in the exterminator. No mice were found, and the noises continued.

Gradually the disturbances became more violent. Furniture was moved back and forth; a heavy bowl fell off the top of the refrigerator for no apparent reason. A picture seemed to jump off the wall. The disturbances centered in the boy's room, where his bed shook and trembled, sometimes all night long.

The Deens at first tried to ignore the disturbances, but as they continued and got worse, they became worried and began to discuss the situation with their neighbors. Neighbors tried to laugh off the story, but after they spent a night in the Deen house, they stopped laughing and also became convinced that something very strange was going on.

The family then called in the minister of their church, The Reverend Winston. The minister admitted that he was highly skeptical but willing to investigate more closely. He spent the entire night of February 18, 1949, with Douglas Deen. Later the Reverend Winston described what happened that night to a meeting of the Society of Parapsychology in Washington, D.C.

He said that first the boy's bed began to shake. There were scratchings and scraping noises coming from the wall. The minister switched on the light but could see nothing out of the ordinary. He then asked the boy to sit in an armchair, but as soon as he did, the chair began moving around the room slowly. Then it began to rock back and forth and finally tipped over spilling Douglas on the floor.

Next the minister decided it would be best to get the boy away from the furniture. So he told Douglas to take his pillow and blankets and sleep on the floor; that didn't help either. Boy and bedding began sliding around the room. By the next morning the once skeptical minister was convinced that he had witnessed something extraordinary and unexplainable.

The boy was taken to Georgetown hospital for a full mental and physical examination. The tests' revealed no physical abnormalities. Visits to a psychiatrist did not make the disturbances which centered on the fourteen-year-old boy disappear.

The Dean family finally decided on a drastic "cure." They called on a Roman Catholic priest to perform the ancient rite of exorcism to drive out the demons they now feared were afflicting their son. They were desperate and regarded exorcism as their last hope.

The priest who performed the exorcism remained with the boy for over two months. During that period he performed the long ritual some thirty times. While the ritual was going on, the boy would tremble violently and sometimes scream or shout in a voice that did not sound at all like his ordinary voice.

In May 1949 when the priest performed the ritual, the boy did not react violently, as he usually did, and the priest assumed that the exorcism had worked and the demons were driven out. After that the family was no longer troubled by shaking beds and strange noises.

The more spectacular physical effects such as floating through the air which were found in the book and film are absent from the sketchy original report on the case. What we are left with is what sounds like a fairly typical poltergeist case. This family chose to interpret the manifestations as "demonic," but they could just as easily have been called ghostly or "psychic." It should also be remembered that this case was never really investigated by persons who were familiar with poltergeist cases. All along it was assumed that the phenomena were "real," that is, not produced either consciously or unconsciously by the boy himself. Psychical researchers are well aware of the long history of childish trickery in poltergeist cases and usually try to take pains to guard against being taken in by it. This does not seem to have been done in *The Exorcist* case.

So what *The Exorcist* really is is a piece of imaginative fiction inspired by an incomplete report of a poltergeist case.

See also: THE AMITYVILLE HORROR, THE SEAFORD POLTERGEIST

6

Revenge, Warnings, and Crisis Apparitions

THE APPEARANCE OF LIEUTENANT McCONNELL   One

of the best and most well documented ghost or "crisis apparition" stories of modern times took place at the end of World War I.

Lieutenant David McConnell was an eighteen-year-old British trainee pilot. On the morning of December 7, 1918, his commanding officer unexpectedly asked him to fly a small plane to a field at Tadcaster, some sixty miles from his home base at Scampton. Another pilot was to accompany McConnell in a two-seater plane. McConnell was to leave his plane at Tadcaster, and it was the second pilot's job to bring McConnell back to his home base as soon as he had accomplished the mission.

At 11:30 A.M. McConnell told his roommate, Lieutenant Larkin that he had to deliver an airplane to Tadcaster but that he expected to be back that same afternoon.

The sixty-mile flight from Scampton to Tadcaster was a routine one under normal conditions, but along the way the two planes ran into a heavy fog. The pilots landed and telephoned their home base for instructions. McConnell was told to use his own discretion, so they took off again for Tadcaster. The fog got worse and McConnell's companion in the two-seater made a forced landing. McConnell, however, continued the flight to Tadcaster. Upon reaching the field, he started his approach for landing at a bad angle and crashed. McConnell was thrown violently forward and smashed his head on the gun mounted in front of him. A witness to the crash rushed to the plane and found the pilot dead. His watch had been broken in the crash and was stopped at exactly 3:25 P.M.

173

At the same time that McConnell crashed at Tadcaster, his roommate, Larkin, was sitting in the room they shared at Scampton reading and smoking. He heard footsteps coming up the corridor and heard the door behind him open. Then he heard the familiar words, "Hullo, boy!" This was McConnell's customary greeting. Larkin turned around and saw McConnell—or what looked like McConnell—standing in the doorway, about eight feet from him. He was dressed in the standard flying outfit, but instead of a flying helmet he was wearing a naval cap. McConnell often wore a naval cap because he had served in the naval air service and was very proud of that.

To Larkin there seemed nothing odd about McConnell's coming in at that moment. He said "Hullo! Back already?" The figure replied, "Yes. Got there all right. Had a good trip." The figure then said, "Well, cheerio!" and went out, closing the door behind him.

A little while later—the time was approximately a quarter to four—another officer, Lieutenant Garner Smith, came into the room. Garner Smith said that he hoped that McConnell would be back early so that the three of them could go out that evening. Larkin said that McConnell was already back and that he had been in the room less than half an hour ago. Thus McConnell, or something that looked like McConnell, had appeared to Larkin between 3:15 and 3:30. McConnell, we know, was killed at 3:25.

Larkin didn't even hear of McConnell's death until that evening. At first he assumed that McConnell had returned at about three that afternoon and then gone out on another flight during which he was killed. Only hours later did Larkin realize that McConnell had been killed almost exactly at the moment that he had seen the figure of McConnell standing in the door and had talked to that figure. The next morning Larkin related the incident to other officers on the base. Garner Smith confirmed his part in the story.

Despite what he saw, Larkin remained skeptical about ghosts and other psychical matters. But he had no other explanation to offer. The strange story got around the base, and when McCon-

The type of plane McConnell was flying when he crashed

nell's family came to claim the body of their son, they heard of it and wrote to Larkin immediately. He replied on December 22 and set down a clear matter-of-fact account of the experience.

Eventually the McConnell case came to the attention of the Society for Psychical Research. The SPR investigated, and though it happened nearly three quarters of a century ago, the McConnell case is still generally considered one of the best, if not the best, story of this type in the SPR files, and those files contain many stories of this type.

There are several reasons why this particular incident, though it is not an exceptionally dramatic one, is considered to be so good. First is the quality of the witness, a reliable, level-headed individual, not the sort likely to make up stories or who habitually "sees things."

Secondly, the witness wrote down his version of the event just about two weeks after it took place. So often in cases of this type the written account is not produced until months or even years after the event, and in that time the mind can alter a story beyond recognition, without any effort at conscious fakery. It would have been better if Larkin had written of his experience immediately after hearing of McConnell's death; the details would have been fresher in his mind. But Larkin certainly did not know at the time that his experience would become a psychical research classic. Considering that he was not interested in psychic matters, he may not have cared very much either. Larkin did tell his story to others the day after McConnell's death. Those who heard the story and read the written report confirmed that both were the same; Larkin had changed nothing.

Another thing that makes this case most impressive is that there was a confirming witness—not to the reality of the apparition itself, but to Larkin's belief that he had seen his roommate when in fact the man was dead or about to die sixty miles away. There is no way Larkin could have known of McConnell's death when he talked to Garner Smith. All the times are well established. The time of McConnell's death was established dramatically by his smashed wristwatch.

When SPR investigators looked into the case, they quickly ruled out the possibility of a hoax, because it would have required collusion between Larkin and Garner Smith in order to fool the parents of a dead comrade. That the investigators found unthinkable.

Though the figure never gave its name as McConnell, the possibility of mistaken identity was also ruled out because of the naval cap—McConnell was the only man on the base to wear such a cap. Besides, Larkin said that he knew what his roommate looked like and had an excellent view of him.

It was possible that Larkin had fallen asleep in the chair and then dreamed that he had seen McConnell. However, Larkin insisted that he was wide-awake at the time. He was also wide-awake when Garner Smith entered the room. Even if he had fallen asleep, dreaming of McConnell at the moment that he was killed would be an extraordinary coincidence.

The figure of McConnell may have been a hallucination. Some psychical researchers think that hallucinations are merely waking dreams, while others insist that hallucinations, apparitions, and ghosts are pretty much the same thing. They theorize that McConnell's death released some sort of "psychic energy," and that this created the hallucination or apparition in the mind of his friend, who may have been thinking about him at that moment.

See also: WORLD WAR I APPARITIONS

THE BLACK VELVET RIBBON   The story of Lady Beresford and the black velvet ribbon that she wore around her wrist has been handed down in the family since the eighteenth century. Though it has been retold in many versions, this account is based on what appears to be the first written account of the story set down by Lady Charles Somerset in about 1827.

Lady Beresford and Lord Tyrone were born in Ireland and orphaned while they were still infants. They were placed under the care of a guardian who happened to be a Deist rather than an orthodox Christian. The children both strongly adopted their guardian's somewhat unusual and often unpopular views. The guardian died when they were about fourteen, and those who took over caring for the children tried to break them of their Deistic ideas and bring them back to orthodox Christianity but without success. The two children were very close, and the fact that they shared unpopular religious views brought them closer still.

Some years later they made a solemn pact that whichever one of them should die first would, if possible, appear to the other and declare the true religion.

Even after Lady Beresford was married, she continued to see a good deal of her brother.

One morning, shortly after a visit from her brother, Lady Beresford came down to breakfast looking very pale and drawn. Clearly she had spent a sleepless night. Her husband asked her if she were ill, but she insisted that she was quite well.

"Have you hurt your wrist?" he asked, for he noticed that her wrist was bound by a black ribbon.

She said that nothing had happened, but then after a moment she continued. "Let me beg you, sir, never to ask about this ribbon again. From this day forward you will not see me without it. If it concerned you as a husband, I would tell you at once. I have never denied you any request, but about this ribbon I can say nothing and I beg you never to bring up the subject again."

Her husband was puzzled, but since that is what she so strongly desired, he agreed.

For the rest of breakfast Lady Beresford was very nervous, and she asked the servant if the morning post had arrived. She was told that it had not. A few moments later she rang the bell and once again asked the servant about the post. Once again she was told that it had not yet arrived.

"Do you expect any letters," her husband asked, "that you are so anxious about the arrival of the post."

"I do," she answered. "I expect to hear that Lord Tyrone is dead, that he died last Tuesday at four o'clock."

Her husband was astonished; he had never known his wife to be superstitious or prey to gloomy thoughts of death. He thought that she must have had some dream or nightmare. But at that moment the servant entered and handed Lady Beresford a letter sealed in black. She opened it and only glanced at the contents. "It is as I expected," she said. "He is dead."

Her husband looked at the letter. It contained the news of Lord Tyrone's death, which had occurred just exactly as his wife said it had on the previous Tuesday at four o'clock. Since he knew how close she had been to her brother, he expected that the news would upset her very much. But Lady Beresford surprised her husband by saying that she felt easier in her mind than she had for some time. She also told him that she could give him some news that would be very welcome to him. "I can assure you without the possibility of doubt that I am now with child and the child will be a son." Since they already had two daughters they had longed for a son.

Some seven months after she made her announcement, Lady Beresford was indeed delivered of a son. Her husband lived only a very few years longer, and after his death, she retired to a small house and became, as far as the world at large was concerned, a recluse. Her only company was a clergyman, his wife and young son. She lived this way for several years but one day astonished and shocked the neighborhood by marrying the clergyman's son despite the great difference in their ages and social positions.

The marriage was a disaster almost from the start. Though they had two daughters, the young man turned out to be "an abandoned libertine, destructive of every virtue and human feeling." After a few years of mistreatment, Lady Beresford demanded a separation. Afterward the young man appeared very sorry for the way he had acted. He insisted that he had changed and pleaded to be taken back, but Lady Beresford resisted all the pleas. Then one day quite suddenly she agreed to take him back, and nine months later she bore him a son.

A few weeks after the birth of the boy, Lady Beresford had invited a few friends over for a visit. One of them was an elderly clergyman from Ireland who had known Lady Beresford's family.

Lady Beresford seemed to be in especially good spirits because, she said, "I am forty-eight today."

"No, my lady," said the clergyman, "you are mistaken. Your mother and I had many disputes about your age, and recently I was in the parish where you were born. I searched the register and find that you are only forty-seven today."

The clergyman assumed that Lady Beresford would be delighted to discover that she was a year younger than she had imagined. Her reaction, however, was quite the reverse. She turned deathly pale for a moment and then she gasped, "You have signed my death warrant." She then excused herself from her guests saying that she had not much longer to live and had some important arrangements to make.

She called for her eldest son, then about twelve years of age and her closest friend, Lady Betty Cobb, to come to her. She said that she had something of the utmost confidence to tell them.

She started by reminding them of her brother, Lord Tyrone, and of the close relationship they had. She told them of the pledge to return after death if possible and reveal the true religion. Then she told them of the night many years ago when she awoke to find Lord Tyrone standing by her bedside. She was startled by his sudden appearance.

"Have you forgotten our promise?" he said. "I died last Tuesday at four o'clock and have been permitted to appear to you to assure you that revealed religion is the only true religion."

The specter of Lord Tyrone also said that he was permitted to tell his sister that she was pregnant and would have a son. He then went on to foretell the future in greater detail. Her husband would die within a few years, but she would marry again and her second husband would make her miserable. "You will bring him two daughters and a son, and you will die in the forty-seventh year of your age."

Lady Beresford was horrified by the future that was laid out for her and asked if there was any way that it could be prevented.

"Undoubtedly," he replied, "for you are a free agent and may prevent all of it by resisting the temptation to a second marriage. But your passions are strong, and they have not yet been tested. More than this I am not permitted to tell you."

Lady Beresford then said, "When morning comes, I shall believe that all of this was a dream, an invention of my imagination."

"Will not the news of my death convince you?"

"No, I might have had such a dream that had accidentally come true. I will need stronger proof."

"You are hard on belief," he said. "I must not touch you or I would injure you irreparably."

"I do not mind."

"You are a woman of courage," the phantom said. "Hold out your hand."

"He then touched my wrist with a hand that was as cold as marble. In an instant all of the nerves and sinews were shrunken. 'Now,' he said, 'let no one see your wrist while you live, for to see it would be a sacrilege.' Then the phantom was gone. In the morning I found a piece of black ribbon and bound up my wrist."

Events proceeded as Lord Tyrone had foretold. After the death of her husband, Lady Beresford tried to escape her fate by living in seclusion, seeing only a clergyman and his family. "Little did I imagine that their son, then a mere youth, was the person destined by Fate to prove my undoing.

"The conduct of my husband after a few years had passed amply warranted my demand for a separation, but I was prevailed upon to pardon him and live with him once again. But this was not until I imagined that I had passed my forty-seventh birthday. But today I heard that I am mistaken about my age and that I am now only forty-seven. I therefore have no doubt that my death is at hand."

She stated that once she was dead, the need to conceal her wrist was over, and she asked Lady Betty to take the ribbon from her wrist, "So that you and my son may witness the truth of what I have related."

Before midnight Lady Beresford was indeed dead. Lady Betty ordered the servants to leave the room, and she and the boy unbound the ribbon that the woman had worn around her wrist for so many years. They found her wrist exactly as she had described it, with every nerve and sinew shrunk.

COMMANDER POTTER'S VISION   A dramatic tale of a portent of death was told by Commander George Potter of the RAF. During World War II Commander Potter was a squadron leader at an RAF base in Egypt. Bombers from the base flew out over the Mediterranean, planting torpedoes and mines in the path of General Rommel's supply ships. The bombers usually operated at night, during the full moon, so that they could use the moon's bright reflection off the water as an aid in navigation. Such periods of full moon were referred to as "bomber's moon."

The missions were extremely dangerous, and in the periods between bombing missions, tension at the base was high. The men often tried to overcome the anxiety with an air of fatalistic gaiety.

One evening just before the "bomber's moon," Commander Potter and Flying Officer Reg Lamb were in the officers' mess having a drink. Also in the room at that time was a wing commander whom Potter called Roy. Roy was sitting with a group of his friends, and as Potter and Lamb finished their drinks, there was a burst of laughter from the group around Roy that caused Potter to look in their direction.

It was then that Potter had his vision of death. "I turned and saw the head and shoulders of the wing commander moving ever so slowly in a bottomless depth of blue-blackness. His lips were drawn back from his teeth in a dreadful grin; he had eye-sockets but no eyes; the remaining flesh of his face was dully blotched in greenish purplish shadows, with shreds peeling off near his left ear.

"I gasped. It seemed that my heart had swollen and stopped. I experienced all the storybook sensations of utter horror. The hair on my temples and the back of my neck felt like wire, icy sweat trickled down my spine and I trembled slightly all over. I was vaguely aware of faces nearby, but the horrible death mask dominated the lot."

Potter had no idea how long this vision lasted, but he eventually became aware of Lamb tugging at his sleeve and saying, "What the hell's the matter? You've gone white as a sheet . . . as if you've seen a ghost."

"I have seen a ghost," said Potter, "Roy. Roy has the mark of death on him."

Lamb looked over to where Roy and his friends were sitting, but he saw nothing unusual. Potter was still white-faced and trembling. Both officers knew that Roy was scheduled to be flying the next night, but neither knew what to do about it.

In the end Commander Potter did nothing. He thought of going to the group captain with the story and asking that Roy be withdrawn from the mission. But Roy would certainly have objected and would have refused to be kept from his crew for such a reason. The request to ground Roy would almost certainly have been denied. Potter believed that his final decision not to interfere was a correct one and part of "a preordained sequence of events."

The following night Potter was extremely tense. Finally he got the message that he had been expecting. Roy and his crew had been shot down and forced to ditch in the ocean. But the ditching apparently had gone well, for another plane in the squadron had seen the men in the water climbing into a life raft.

Potter was very relieved and convinced that the men would soon be rescued and that his vision had been a false one. But as the hours dragged on, no sign of Roy and his crew could be found.

"And then I knew what I had seen," said Potter. "The blue-black nothingness was the Mediterranean at night and he was floating somewhere in it dead, with just his head and shoulders held up by the Mae West."

DEATH FORESEEN

Is it possible for a person to see the "ghost" of someone not yet dead? Is such an apparition really a ghost? That is a matter of opinion and definition. However, there are many cases in which individuals are reported to have foreseen the death of another. Here is a striking case that was recorded by the British Society for Psychical Research.

All the names are fictitious, a common SPR practice to protect the privacy of witnesses, but the events are set down exactly as they are supposed to have happened.

A man named Jones who was taking a long walk became fatigued and sat down to rest by the side of a river. At first he felt calm and at peace but soon he began to feel nervous and frightened for no discernible reason. He tried to leave but felt unable to rise from the ground. Then what appeared to be a black cloud or fog rose up in front of him, and in the middle of the cloud was a man in a brown suit. Suddenly the man in the brown suit jumped into the water and sank out of sight.

Jones was horrified by his vision. After a few minutes the shock wore off, and he found that he was able to move once again. There had been no man in a brown suit—it had all been some sort of hallucination; nothing had really happened. Still Jones was very upset by what he had experienced, and when he got home he told his sister all about it. She thought that to dwell upon such a subject was morbid and told him to forget it. He couldn't; the image of the man in the brown suit jumping into the water was too solid to forget easily.

The next week a man named Espie drowned himself in the river at the very spot where Jones had seen his vision of the man in the brown suit. Espie left a note saying that he had been thinking about killing himself for a long time. However, Jones had never met Espie and had no way of knowing what he planned to do.

What was it? Coincidence? Telepathy? Precognition? Or seeing a ghost-to-be?

THE EVIL RETURN   Generally it is assumed that a person who has lived an evil life will return as an evil ghost. But some stories indicate that the evil in a person's life may not be revealed until after the person's death and return as a ghost.

A case in point is the story about a Mrs. Leaky, the much-respected mother of a prominent British shipowner of the seventeenth century. One day an acquaintance remarked to Mrs. Leaky that it was terrible that one day death would separate them from their friends. Mrs. Leaky replied, rather enigmatically, that if her friends met her after her death, they would wish that they had not.

The old lady died in 1636, but shortly after her burial people began reporting that she had been seen near her son's house. Perhaps the strangest story was told by a doctor who didn't know Mrs. Leaky by sight but told of meeting an old woman whom he helped to cross the street. The woman's touch seemed unnaturally cold, so the doctor took a closer look at her and found, to his horror, that she appeared to talk without moving her lips. In response to the kindness he had shown in getting her across the road, the old lady tried to bar his way, and when he finally managed to get past her, she gave him a good hard kick in the pants.

Then she really turned nasty. She began haunting her son's ships and frightening the crews. Her appearance caused several ships to run aground. She would sit atop the masthead and whistle in an eerie and blood-chilling manner. This would cause a storm that would wreck the ship. She became known as "the whistling ghost." Her son's business began to suffer badly.

Mrs. Leaky never appeared directly to her son, but her daughter-in-law often saw the ghost. The terrible climax came when the Leaky's five-year-old daughter was heard screaming from her bedroom: "Help! Help! Father, Father, Grandmother is choking me." Before the parents could reach the child she was dead.

Shortly after the funeral the ghost appeared again to the murdered girl's mother. She turned and faced the ghost and asked it why it was tormenting the family. The ghost told her to go to Ireland to visit her uncle the lord bishop of Waterford, and she was to tell him that unless he repented of his sin, he would be hanged. The sin was that he had once married the sister of the ghostly Mrs. Leaky and had a child by her. But he killed the child and had it buried secretly. All this turned out to be true, and when the bishop confessed, the ghost was seen no more.

Another more subtle tale of an evil return comes from Ireland. It concerns a priest named Father McSweeney. Father McSweeney had returned as parish priest to the town of his birth. He was conscientious and hardworking, performing all his duties correctly and exactly. Yet for some unknown reason no one liked him. People who had known him since birth felt uncomfortable in his presence.

Long after others in town had retired, a light could be seen burning in Father McSweeney's study. For some people this would have been taken as a sign that they were working late at their duties, but in the case of Father McSweeney people wondered if there might not be something sinister going on. Of course, the subject was never discussed openly. One reason was that Father McSweeney's widowed mother adored her son and would never hear a word against him.

While he was still a fairly young man, Father McSweeney suddenly took ill. The nature of his illness was a mystery, and different doctors offered different opinions. The only thing that they all agreed on was that the illness was extremely serious and that no treatment seemed to help. Father McSweeney accepted his fate silently. He seemed to know all along that he would die, and die he did within a few weeks of falling ill. He just seemed to waste away.

The town decided to give Father McSweeney a big funeral. He had, after all, been the priest for years, and he still had many relatives in the area. But the townsfolk may also have felt a little guilty about the secret thoughts they had harbored about the priest and perhaps about the feeling of relief that he would no longer be among them.

The cemetery was in the hills several miles outside of town. The priest's mother was too old and frail to attend the graveside services, but practically everyone else in town was there. The services went on a long time, and when they were over, everyone got into cars for the ride back to town and to pay a courtesy call on the priest's mother.

It was growing dark by the time the procession of cars left the cemetery. A mile or so from the cemetery, the driver of the lead car noticed a figure walking up the road toward them. Walkers were rare in this part of the country, so the passengers were anxious to see who this individual might be. As the figure was illuminated in the car's headlights, its face could be seen.

"Lord have mercy upon us!" gasped the driver. "It's himself!"

The figure on the road was indeed a familiar one; it was the man they had just buried, Father McSweeney. There could be no doubt about that. And yet he had been horribly changed. His always pale skin was an ashen white. His eyes were wide open and unblinking, and they glittered with an unnatural brightness. His lips were drawn back exposing strong white teeth and bloodless gums.

The terrifying figure walked the entire length of the funeral procession but gave no sign of recognition. Everyone, except for a few who were dozing, saw it, but not a single car would stop. Indeed they began to drive faster, and the passengers began to whisper to one another.

"Did you see him?"

"Yes, I saw him too. I thought I was dreaming—or having a nightmare."

The badly shaken mourners arrived at the house of Mrs. McSweeney, and they all agreed to say nothing of what they had seen, for the poor woman had enough grief and did not need this horrible story.

There was no reply when they knocked at the door, and when one of the women looked through the window, she saw the old woman lying facedown on the floor.

They broke down the door and found that the old woman was not dead, as they had feared, but merely unconscious. When she revived, she told them that a short time ago she had heard a knock at the door. Knowing that everyone in town was at the funeral, she peered through the window first to see who her visitor might be—and she saw her son.

"You saw his face?" someone asked.

The old woman hesitated and then began to cry. "Yes, I saw his face. It was my son but he had changed. He looked different—so fierce and wild. His eyes were wide open and his lips drawn back. And his skin—he was as white as . . ."

"As a ghost."

"Yes, I believe I saw the ghost of my son."

The old woman said that she wanted to open the door for him, but the sight made her feel so weak that she fainted.

Father McSweeney was never seen again, but for years people talked about that night. The ghost wore an expression of inhuman cruelty. Perhaps this was something in his character that he had been able to disguise during his lifetime, and that may have been why he had always made people uncomfortable and a little fearful.

THE HOHENZOLLERNS' SPECTER   The Hohenzollerns, the ruling family of Prussia, were said to be plagued by the specter of a lady in white. She would appear to members of the family shortly before they were to die or suffer a family disaster.

At one point the tale is given a rather curious twist when it is said that the ghost of Frederick the Great appeared to his nephew Frederick William. Frederick William had sent his armies to invade France, but apparently his famous uncle's ghost did not approve of the invasion.

"Unless you call off the Prussian army from Paris, nephew," said the spirit, "you may expect to see someone who will not be welcome to you."

Frederick William was more frightened of the message than of the ghost itself. "What do you mean?" he asked.

"I mean," said the great Frederick, "the White Lady of the Old Palace. I'm sure you know what happens to those who see her." With that ominous warning the ghost faded.

No one seems to be sure whose ghost the White Lady of the Old Palace was. Several ladies who had died there in the fifteenth or sixteenth centuries were suspected. How or why she became connected with the Hohenzollerns is also not clear, but she is reputed to have appeared first in 1619 during the reign of John Sigismund. The day after she was seen, John Sigismund died.

Frederick the Great

Frederick the Great never saw her; as a rationalist and skeptic he didn't even believe in ghosts, but according to legend he changed his mind about ghosts after he became one. The White Lady of the Old Palace was seen in 1806 a few days before Prince Louis of Prussia was killed in a battle with Napoleon's army.

There was also a reported sighting of the White Lady in June 1914. The ruler at that time was Kaiser Wilhelm II; the kaiser didn't die, but his relative Archduke Francis Ferdinand was assassinated late in June. That was the spark which started World War I. The kaiser survived the war, but Germany was defeated, and the German monarchy was destroyed forever.

LIEUTENANT SUTTON'S RETURN   In the history of ghosts there are many tales of the ghost returning in order to accuse some living person of murder. Most of these cases are purely legendary or anecdotal. In a few cases actual fraud appears to have been involved. But the facts in the case of Lieutenant James Sutton were carefully investigated by the American Society for Psychical Research.

On October 12, 1907, James Sutton, a lieutenant at the naval academy at Annapolis, Maryland, was shot. According to the official investigation Lieutenant Sutton had attended a navy dance where he had quite a bit to drink. During a drive back to camp with some of his buddies, a fight broke out during which the lieutenant was thrown to the ground. He became almost insanely enraged and threatened to kill the others. When he got back to camp, he went to his tent and got two pistols, but he was spotted carrying the weapons and was arrested. Before the authorities could lay their hands on him Lieutenant Sutton, who was now completely out of control, began to fire. There was another fight, and then suddenly and deliberately the lieutenant put a pistol to his head and pulled the trigger.

The lieutenant's family lived all the way across the country in Portland, Oregon, and even before they heard of his death, his mother had been assailed by a sense of dread that something terrible had happened to her son. When she heard the news that her son was dead by his own hand, she could not believe it. She had a vision of her son standing in front of her. "At that instant," she wrote, "Jimmie stood right before me and said, 'Momma, I never killed myself. . . . My hands are as free from blood as when I was five years old.'" He insisted that others had shot him and then tried to make the killing look like a suicide.

This "ghost" or "vision" continued to appear before Mrs. Sutton for several months. That is not too surprising considering the tragic nature of the mother's loss and the fact that she had previously reported several "psychic" experiences. What makes the case interesting is that the ghost reported several details of the fight and of Lieutenant Sutton's wounds before his mother could possibly have known of them.

Mrs. Sutton was finally moved to contact the American Society for Psychical Research, and an investigator confirmed that the apparition had indeed provided details that would probably not have been obtainable through any normal source.

In 1909 the Suttons actually had the body, which had been buried in Arlington National Cemetery, exhumed. An examination revealed that many of the wounds that had been spoken of by the apparition but not mentioned in the navy doctor's report did indeed exist.

Professor James Hyslop, head of the ASPR, also investigated the details of Lieutenant Sutton's death and the circumstances surrounding the navy's handling of the case and found that there were a large number of unanswered questions. There was no reason given for the initial fight, and there seemed no reason for the lieutenant to have killed himself because of a drunken brawl. The testimonies of the various witnesses were highly inconsistent, and the investigators had never even considered the possibility of murder.

No final resolution to this case has ever been agreed upon, and after the exhumation the appearances of the apparition became less frequent until they stopped entirely. But unlike many of the tales of ghosts out to avenge their murders, this one has an air of reality and genuine mystery about it.

See also: RICHARD TARWELL

R ICHARD TARWELL   Court records from the early eighteenth century in the city of Exeter, capital city of the county of Devon in England, contain an extremely interesting account of a ghostly return. The central figure in this tale was a fourteen-year-old boy named Richard Tarwell, who worked for the Harrises, a wealthy Devon family.

The head of the family, George Harris, held an important position in the king's court. He was often required to spend long periods of time in London away from his estates in Devon. The country property was left in the care of his butler, Richard Morris, who had been with the family for many years and was regarded as completely trustworthy by them.

In 1730 George Harris was in London when he received an urgent letter from Morris asking him to return at once. Harris managed to break off his government business and rush back to Devon, where Morris met him and told him what had happened.

A few days earlier, Morris said, he had been awakened from a sound sleep by unexplained noises. He crept down the stairs and heard through the closed door of the butler's pantry the sound of snapping wood, as if someone were breaking into the boxes which held the Harris family's valuable silverware. He also heard the voices of two men. At first Morris thought the robbers must be two of the footmen for he was sure that no one could have gotten into the house without breaking down a door, and that would have made a great deal of noise and awakened the entire household.

Morris was so enraged by the thought that these two men had betrayed their employer that he burst into the butler's pantry without a thought for his own safety. Much to his surprise, Morris found that the two men breaking into the silver box were not footmen but two rough-looking men whom he had never seen before. And with the robbers was fourteen-year-old Richard Tarwell.

Tarwell was a lad whom Morris had hired just a few weeks earlier to help with the kitchen work. The boy's family lived in the area, and he seemed reliable enough when he began the job. He also appeared to enjoy his work. At night he slept in a small cubbyhole near the butler's pantry. Morris theorized that he had let the robbers in.

The robbers immediately turned on the butler, beat him, and

tied and gagged him, then ran off. Morris was not discovered until the following morning when other servants wondered why the butler, habitually the most punctual of men, had not appeared at breakfast.

The butler was greatly upset by what had happened but was not seriously injured. It was at this point that Morris sent the letter to his employer which brought Harris running home from London.

After the robbery no trace of the silver, the two robbers, or Richard Tarwell could be found. Tarwell's father proclaimed the boy's innocence, but without the boy there to tell his own story, his guilt was presumed.

George Harris took the loss philosophically, saying that his was not the first family to be robbed nor would it be the last. He returned to London to continue his work for the king, and it was several months before he could again go to his Devon estates.

No progress had been made in finding either the missing silver or those who had taken it. Harris tried to dismiss the whole matter from his mind, but still he had some anxiety about the robbery. On his first night back he followed the butler around the house as the servant locked up. Harris marveled at the extraordinary care this trusted man took in locking and securing all the doors and windows. He had never before noticed how careful Morris was. He told his wife that Morris must be taking unusual precautions since the robbery. His wife, who had always been more attentive to domestic affairs, assured him that Morris habitually took such care.

As Harris retired that night, something, he wasn't quite sure what, began to bother him. He tossed and turned for a while, trying to give the thought words, but finally he gave up and fell asleep.

He was sleeping soundly, yet in the middle of the night for a reason he was unable to explain, George Harris was suddenly fully awake. By the light of a small lamp that he always kept burning in his bedroom, he saw a young boy standing at the foot of his bed. Though he had never seen the boy before, somehow he knew that this was the missing Richard Tarwell.

Harris's first thought was that the boy had somehow been hiding in the house for the months since the robbery. Harris asked him what he was doing, but the boy said nothing; he only beckoned. Harris then thought that the boy might have received an injury to the throat or perhaps a fright that had deprived him of the ability to speak.

The figure of Richard Tarwell moved toward the door, beckoning Harris to follow. For some reason he felt almost compelled to do so. He pulled on his boots, threw a cloak over his shoulders, and picked up his sword. Then he followed the boy.

As they crossed the hall, Harris saw that the figure moved without making a sound. For the first time he began to realize that the Richard Tarwell that stood in front of him was not a living boy but a ghost. Yet strangely he felt no fear. As he later stated, he was sure that the ghost meant him no harm.

The pair went downstairs and out a side door, which Harris saw to his amazement was unlocked. Yet he had watched Morris lock the door that very evening.

Once out of the house the figure led Harris about one hundred yards toward a large oak, the trunk of which was surrounded and almost hidden by a thick growth of low shrubs and bushes. At the tree the boy stopped and pointed to the ground. Then he walked around the far side of the tree and disappeared from view.

Harris waited for the ghost to reappear, but it didn't. So he went back to the house determined to find out what the ghost had wanted of him. Very early the next morning Harris quietly went to the room where the two footmen slept. He roused them and told them to get dressed, find some spades, and meet him near the large oak tree.

Shortly after the footmen started digging, they discovered the decaying remains of the boy's body. Harris was now sure of what he had already begun to suspect, that his trusted butler, Morris, had committed the crime and that the boy had been an innocent victim. Harris had remembered what was bothering him on the previous night. When Morris locked up the house, he kept all the keys with him. In order for Richard Tarwell to have let anyone in the house, he would have to have taken the keys from Morris's bedroom without waking the butler. This would have been difficult, for Morris must have been a light sleeper if he was able to hear wood splintering in the butler's pantry some distance from his bedroom.

The constables were sent for, and after Morris was confronted with the missing boy's remains, he broke down and confessed. The two robbers were his accomplices. He had let them in, but when they were breaking into the silver boxes they had awakened Richard Tarwell, who slept nearby and walked in and surprised them. One of the robbers attacked the boy and killed him. They then buried his body near the oak. Murder had not been part of the original plan, but after it happened, the men dreamed up the idea of pinning the crime on the boy.

Morris's accomplices were to have taken the silver to Plymouth, sold it, and sent the butler his share. But they double-crossed him and they were never heard from again. Nor was the silver ever found.

Morris alone suffered for the crime. He was hanged. At least he is the only one that we know of who suffered for it. Perhaps Richard Tarwell's ghost tracked down the other two as well.

See also: LIEUTENANT SUTTON'S RETURN

THE RIVER GHOST   This odd tale of a ghostly warning comes from eighteenth century England. In 1777 Rev. James Crawford was out for a ride. Seated behind him on his horse was his sister-in-law, Miss Hannah Wilson. When they came to the river, Miss Wilson became frightened. She thought that the water was too high and the current too swift and that they might be swept away if they tried to cross.

Rev. Crawford, however, was of a different opinion. "I do not think there can be any danger," he said. "I see another horseman crossing just twenty yards in front of us." Miss Crawford also saw the second horseman. Rev. Crawford called out to the rider to ask if there was any danger.

The rider stopped and turned around, and as he did so, Rev. Crawford and Miss Wilson realized that it was a face that was no longer human. The face of the rider was ghostly white and fairly glowed with hate and evil. Rev. Crawford was astonished and terrified at the sight. Miss Wilson was simply terrified and began screaming. Rev. Crawford turned his horse and got out of the river and rode home as quickly as he possibly could.

He discovered that local folklore held that the spirit of this ghostly rider appeared in the river every time someone was about to drown. Though Rev. Crawford was badly frightened by what he had seen, he felt it his religious duty not to give in to such superstitions. So he declared that he didn't believe in warning spirits. However, when he tried to cross the river again on September 27, 1777, he was drowned in the attempt.

See also: THE HOHENZOLLERNS' SPECTER

WORLD WAR I APPARITIONS

World War I, with its great slaughter of young men, was a breeding ground for a particular type of ghost or apparition account. These were collected in large numbers by the Society for Psychical Research. Here are some typical examples:

A letter from a Mrs. E. S. Russell to the SPR said that her husband was killed in France on November 6, 1917. Communications being what they were, she did not learn of the death for another ten days. At about the time he was killed (she was not sure of the exact date or time), she was sitting with her son, Dicky, aged about three-and-a-half years. They were talking when "he sat up rather suddenly and said 'Daddy is dead.' I said 'Oh no, dear, he's not and I expect he'll come back to us someday,' but Dicky looked very upset and said again, 'No he won't. Dick knows he's dead.' I just

The slaughter of World War I brought forth many ghostly tales.

said 'No dear, I don't think he is' but Dicky seemed so distressed and repeated, 'No, no, Dick knows it,' so emphatically that I thought best to leave the subject alone. He never referred to it again and had never said anything of the sort before."

Mrs. Russell insisted that at that time she had no particular anxiety about her husband's safety. He had been through a number of difficult engagements without a scratch, and she had gotten used to the idea of danger.

More dramatic was the case of Captain Eldred Bowyer-Bower, a twenty-two-year-old pilot killed in action on March 19, 1917. Three persons in three widely scattered places appear to have received a strong intimation of his death at about the time it occurred and long before they could have known of it through natural means.

The most remarkable of these experiences was reported by Captain Bowyer-Bower's half-sister, Mrs. Spearman, who was in India when he died. She was sitting with her newborn baby on the morning of March 19 when:

"I had a great feeling I must turn around and did to see Eldred;

he looked so happy and [had] that dear mischievous look. I was so glad to see him and told him I would just put baby in a safer place, then we could talk. 'Fancy coming out here,' I said turning round again and was just putting my hands out to give him a hug and a kiss but Eldred had gone. I called and looked for him. I never saw him again."

At about the same time an apparition of Captain Bowyer-Bower was seen by his niece, a child of about three years of age. This incident was described in a letter to the SPR by Mrs. Cecily Chater, the girl's mother.

"One morning while I was still in bed, about 9:15, she came into my room and said, 'Uncle Alley Boy is downstairs' (Alley Boy was a familiar pet name for the captain) and although I told her he was in France, she insisted that she had seen him. Later in the day I happened to be writing to my mother and mentioned this, not because I thought much about it, but to show that Betty still thought and spoke of her uncle of whom she was very fond. A few days afterwards we found that the date my brother was missing was the date on the letter. . . . The child was a little under three years old at the time.

The third experience does not involve an actual sighting but rather a feeling of doom. The captain's mother received a letter from a Mrs. Watson, an elderly lady whom she had known for many years. Mrs. Watson had not written for about eighteen months, and then quite unexpectedly came a letter saying, "Something tells me you are having great anxiety about Eldred. Will you let me know?" The letter was dated March 19, 1917, the day the captain was killed. But at the time his mother knew nothing of this. Mrs. Watson later reported that on the day she wrote her letter, she had an awful feeling that he had been killed.

The image of Captain Bowyer-Bower was also reported to have appeared to several other people. But this was after his death was known to them. His spirit was also reported to have been contacted by several spirit mediums.

See also: THE APPEARANCE OF LIEUTENANT MC CONNELL

7

GHOSTLY

PHENOMENA

THE AMITYVILLE HORROR   Whether the Amityville Horror can properly be called a haunting is open to question. However, practically every modern discussion of the subject of ghosts and hauntings will sooner or later touch upon this sensational and very well known case. Here is how it began:

In November, 1974, a twenty-four-year-old man named Ronald DeFeo shot his parents, two brothers, and two sisters to death in their home in Amityville, Long Island. It was the most horrifying crime the affluent suburb of Amityville had ever witnessed. DeFeo pleaded insanity but was found guilty and sentenced to six consecutive life terms. During the trial DeFeo claimed that for months before he committed the crimes he had heard "voices" ordering him to kill.

A little over a year later, the house that was the scene of the murders was purchased by George and Kathy Lutz. Probably because of its ghastly history, the house was selling for less than comparable houses, but the price was still a hefty eighty thousand dollars, far above what the Lutzes had expected to pay for a home and more than they could really afford.

A month after they moved in, the Lutzes abruptly abandoned the place and moved in with friends at a location they refused to disclose. Rapidly word leaked out that they had been driven from the Amityville house by a series of strange and terrifying events.

A month later the Lutzes's story was featured on a New York television news show that was doing a series on ESP and haunted houses. According to the TV program, "They reportedly told of

201

strange voices seeming to come from within themselves, of a power charge which actually lifted Mrs. Lutz off her feet toward a closet behind which was a room not noted on any blueprints."

There were hints that the police had confirmed some of the story, that the place was being investigated by leading parapsychologists, and that the Catholic Church was also involved in its own investigation. The TV report also hinted that others who had owned the house before the murders were committed had strange experiences there and that well before the present house was built that particular site had a bad and "haunted" reputation. Ronald DeFeo's lawyer seized upon this information and said that it might constitute sufficient evidence to get a new trial for his client. It didn't.

The story, however, got quite a bit of publicity, as "haunted house" tales of this type so often do. But unlike most haunted house stories, this one did not fade in a few weeks. The Lutzes got a professional writer named Jay Anson to prepare a book-length account of what had happened during the month they had spent in the house. The book that resulted called *The Amityville Horror* recounted a ghostly tale of diabolical voices, visions of the face of the mass murderer, and everything from a plague of flies to a plague of demons. This highly sensationalized account was published in 1977 and became an instant and enormous best-seller. It was later made into a movie of the same name which sensationalized the events even further and was also a great success. Both book and film sequels were less successful.

The great appeal of the Amityville Horror story is that it is supposed to be true. It is not only a good horror story but solid proof of direct demonic influence on this world. But is it really true?

The answer to that has to be no. Every independent investigation of the case has found that all the evidence of the sensational events cited in the book and movie depends solely on the word of the Lutzes. A large portion of what could be checked out proved to be dead wrong. Even the writer Jay Anson admitted that he didn't know whether what he was writing was true or not; he just put down what the Lutzes told him. The present owners of the house insist they have had no strange experiences.

Among those who are seriously interested in the subject of psychical research, the Amityville Horror is universally regarded as an audacious and profitable hoax.

See also: THE EXORCIST, FLIGHT 401

T**HE ANNAN ROAD APPEARANCES**   Stories of ghostly figures seen along the side of the road are fairly common. But the account given by the brothers Dereck and Norman Ferguson, then aged twenty-two and fourteen, is among the most complete, bizarre, and most terrifying on record.

The brothers had been taking a brief driving vacation in Scotland in April 1962 and were returning to their home in Annan. They had stopped for gas in the town of Dumfries shortly before midnight. Annan lay about fifteen miles away.

As they headed down the moonlit road, it seemed quite deserted, not particularly unusual at that hour of the night. Then quite suddenly something—it looked like a large white bird—flew directly at the windshield. Dereck, who was driving, swerved to avoid hitting the thing, but there was no impact, for it seemed to disappear before it reached the car.

The next appearance was more alarming. It looked like an old woman rushing madly down the middle of the road. She seemed to be screaming and waving her arms; a crash was inevitable, but this figure too disappeared just before hitting the car.

Then things really got bad. There was a stream of figures. Gigantic cats, wild-looking dogs, birds, and some human or vaguely human shapes looming up and hurtling themselves at the car. All disappeared just before the moment of impact. Even though the forms were obviously nonmaterial in nature, Dereck still zigzagged and swerved along the road in an attempt to avoid them.

The temperature inside the car seemed to drop, though both of the Fergusons were drenched in perspiration from their ordeal.

Later Dereck reported, "My hands seemed to become very heavy, and it was as if some force were trying to gain control of the steering wheel; the control of the car became increasingly difficult. We seemed to be suffocating and I opened the window to get some fresh air but it was bitterly cold outside and I just hung on to the wheel as screaming, high-pitched laughter and cackling noises seemed to mark our predicament. I was absolutely certain at the time that an attempt was being made to force us off the road and I was equally certain that a fatal accident would result."

Finally Dereck stopped the car, and immediately the brothers were buffeted by a powerful force that rocked the car. Dereck opened the door and jumped out. Once outside of the car all seemed quiet and peaceful. But as soon as he got back in the car the rocking and shaking began again, and there was the sound of horrible ghostly laughter. Outside it sounded as though fists were striking the car.

Dereck decided that the best course of action was to drive on to Annan, slowly and carefully. And so the car inched down a road seemingly filled with terrifying figures that loomed up on all sides.

Finally the brothers noticed a pair of glowing red lights up ahead, and they saw to their relief that it was a large truck. It was the first normal-looking object that they had seen on the road in quite some time. But relief soon turned to fear when Dereck realized that he was approaching the truck much too quickly and was unable to stop, slow, or swerve the car. A crash was unavoidable, but just before it happened, the truck vanished. It had been just another of the phantoms on the road.

The brothers reached Annan exhausted but safe. The entire experience had taken about half an hour.

Dereck was convinced that if he had swerved off the road or had stopped for any length of time, he and his brother might not have survived the experience.

Later Dereck Ferguson was told that witchcraft had once been practiced in the area he had driven through, and others said that a phantom truck like the one he and his brother had seen was sometimes reported in the vicinity.

This experience is faintly reminiscent of the account of Betty and Barney Hill, an American couple who said that they were stopped on a road one night by strange creatures that had come from a UFO. Like the experience of the Fergusons, the Hill account has a nightmarelike quality. There are, in addition, numerous reports of monstrous creatures, often of the Bigfoot type, that seem to loom up along the side of the road late at night only to disappear when the observer gets too near.

"**B**LACK AGGIE"   The scene is practically a cliché in Hollywood ghost films. We see a graveyard, a mist is rising, and we hear the clock strike twelve. The camera pans over the tombstones and lingers on one monument, a tombstone with a carved angel on top. Suddenly the eyes of the statue begin to glow and its head moves!

Cinematic cliché or not, this is the sort of thing that is supposed to happen in Pikeville's Druid Ridge Cemetery outside of Baltimore, Maryland. The "haunted tombstone" marks the grave of newspaper publisher General Felix Angus, who died in the 1920s. Upon his death the family commissioned a well-known monument sculptor to design the tombstone. The sculptor designed a stone with a rather curious-looking small black angel perched on top.

The monument acquired the name "Black Aggie" and a sinister reputation. The newspapers reported the belief that at the stroke of midnight Black Aggie's eyes would glow. As the legend grew, it was said that all of the ghosts in the graveyard would gather around her at midnight and that any living person who was struck by her glowing gaze would immediately become blind. Pregnant women who passed under her shadow, where no grass would grow, would have miscarriages.

Another tale was that part of the initiation rites of a local college fraternity required that the prospective member had to spend the entire night sitting beneath (or on) Black Aggie. But the first candidate to try was found dead at the base of the tombstone the following morning. A medical exmaination determined that he had died of fright.

Unfortunately this sort of reputation rarely does a monument any good. In 1962 one of Black Aggie's arms was found missing. The arm later turned up in the trunk of a car owned by a sheet metal worker. Also in the trunk was a stout saw. At his trial the metal worker claimed that Black Aggie had sawed off her own arm and given it to him. That ingenious defense did not save him from a term in jail.

By that time Black Aggie had become so infamous that tourists would gather in the cemetery at midnight to see if they could catch a glimpse of her glowing eyes. Apparently the fear of blindness didn't worry them. However the Angus family began to worry about further desecration of the grave, and they decided that the only way to prevent it was to remove Black Aggie entirely. In 1967 she was donated to the Smithsonian Institution, where she is gathering dust in some storeroom. There seems little chance that she will ever be put on display. One *Baltimore Sun* reporter quipped that perhaps the Smithsonian just wasn't taking any chances.

BURIED ALIVE   The fear of being buried alive is an ancient and deep-seated one. Today with modern medical technology the possibility of being prematurely buried is virtually nonexistent. But in past centuries the possibility of falling into an unconscious and deathlike state and being buried or placed in a crypt only to revive when it was too late, while remote, at least existed. This would be particularly true during times of epidemic when diagnosis would be hurried and burial quick. The fear certainly haunted the nightmares of many writers, in particular Edgar Allan Poe, who never wrote a ghost story but wrote several on the theme of being buried alive.

A late nineteenth-century physician and occultist Dr. Franz Hartmann estimated that there were thousands of premature burials every year in Germany alone. He thought that this might have helped to give rise to the vampire legend, for when certain coffins were dug up, the corpse showed evidence of having been moved about. Rather than indicating that the corpse may really be one of the undead, Hartmann said that it more likely indicated it was the victim of premature burial. The motion was the still-living person's final agonizing struggles to get out of the coffin. Hartmann's conclusions appear to have been based more on imaginative speculation than any kind of sound research. It is yet another reflection of the fear of premature burial that once gripped so many.

Some enterprising entrepeneurs profited from people's fears by selling a variety of coffins that would give a person who had been buried alive a way to signal those on the surface that the burial had taken place too quickly. In one a bell could be rung from inside the coffin. Another was actually equipped with a periscope-like device. There is no authenticated case of such a coffin ever being successfully used by someone who had been buried alive. And it seems fairly safe to conclude that the whole fear of being buried alive was an exaggerated and irrational one. Yet it is reflected in scores of anecdotes which were and still are widely told and widely believed.

Fairly typical of these stories is one of the young woman who had become ill with typhoid fever. Her condition rapidly became so grave that the physicians were sure she was going to die and the members of her family were sent for. However, her oldest brother, and the member of the family to whom she was closest was off on a business trip when he received word of his sister's illness. He returned home as quickly as he could, but by the time he arrived, he was told that his sister had already died and that he had even missed the funeral which had taken place just a few hours earlier.

The grief-stricken brother rushed to the cemetery, where he found the gravediggers just putting the last shovelful of earth in his sister's grave. He pleaded with them to dig up the coffin and

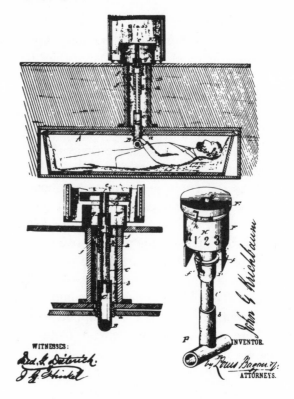

WITNESSES:

INVENTOR.

ATTORNEYS.

A patented device to prevent people
from being buried alive

open it so that he could take one last look at his beloved sister, but the gravediggers refused. The brother continued pleading and begging so loudly that soon a crowd gathered, and many who came to watch were deeply moved by the young man's grief. Finally a couple of the men said that they would dig up the grave themselves so the young man could have his wish.

Since the earth was still soft, the digging went quickly, and within half an hour the coffin was uncovered and opened. The mourning brother looked down upon what he assumed to be the corpse of his sister. One of the members of the crowd thought he saw the "corpse" move. Others also noticed a slight motion, and

soon whispering began among the onlookers. The "corpse" became more agitated and finally sat up in her coffin. The young
woman had not been dead after all. She had merely been unconscious, but fear of the spread of deadly typhoid had caused people
to bury her too quickly.

According to the story the young woman recovered, lived on for
many years after her "death" and raised a large family.

Other buried-alive tales have a more ghostly element. A man
named Samuel Jocelyn of North Carolina was thrown from his
horse, struck his head on a rock, and was pronounced dead by the
local doctor and quickly buried.

A few nights after the funeral, Jocelyn's old friend Alexander
Hostler was troubled by a bad dream in which the form of his
friend Jocelyn appeared before him.

"How could you let me be buried when I was not dead?" said
the shade of Jocelyn.

"But you were dead," answered Hostler.

"No, I wasn't," replied the form. "Open my coffin and you will
see that I am not lying the way that I was buried."

Hostler tried to ignore the dream, but it was repeated on the
next night and the night after, and it seemed that he would continue to have the terrible dream until he did something about it.
He persuaded a friend to go with him at night to the graveyard to
dig up Jocelyn's grave. When they opened the coffin lid, they
found that though Jocelyn had been buried face up just like everyone else, the corpse was now face down. Somehow it had turned
over.

Somewhere on the border between the buried-alive story and
the more traditional ghost story is this tale:

A girl from a wealthy family fell in love with the son of a local
handyman. Her parents were not at all pleased and tried to break
up the relationship but without success. Finally they sent her off to
a strict boarding school in a different state. The girl was extremely
unhappy, but the boy fared even worse. Cut off from his love, he
seemed to lose all interest in living. He became ill, and his condi-

tion worsened rapidly. The doctors didn't know what was wrong with him except that he no longer possessed the will to live. Within a few weeks he was dead. The girl's parents were overcome with remorse, but they could not bring themselves to tell the girl of his death.

A few days after the funeral, the girl was returning to her dormitory when she saw one of her family's cars on the campus, and most astonishingly sitting behind the wheel was the boy she loved. She was overjoyed to see him but alarmed because he looked so pale and ill. "My God, what's wrong?" she said. "What's happened?"

"Your family has asked me to come and get you," he replied. "I don't know why."

Without bothering to get permission or even tell school authorities that she was leaving, she jumped into the car. During the long drive back the boy said practically nothing, and the girl became more worried. She reached over and touched his forehead—it was cold and clammy.

"Are you sick?" she asked.

"I'm all right."

"You must be cold. Here take my scarf." She carefully wound her long woolen muffler around his neck.

When the car pulled up in front of the house, the girl rushed inside, where her parents were surprised—shocked would be more accurate—to see her. They were even more shocked when she told them why she had come and who brought her.

Her father then explained that the boy had died, but she refused to believe him. If the boy was dead, who had driven her home? When they went outside, the car was there, the engine was still warm, but there was no sign of the driver.

The girl and her parents went to the boy's house, and his parents sadly confirmed that he was indeed dead. But when they heard the girl's story, they were shocked and frightened as well. They decided that the only thing that they could do would be open the grave, which they did the very next morning. The boy's body was in the coffin, just as it should have been, but wrapped around the corpse's neck was the girl's long woolen muffler.

See also: WINTERTON'S DISAPPEARANCE

CH'IANG SHICH   In China an unburied corpse was regarded as a potential danger, for the corpse was like an empty house. The air was thought to be full of invisible and mostly evil spirits or demons that might take possession of the corpse and turn it into a monstrous being called a *Ch'iang Shich.* This popular tale of such a being is typical of many.

Very late one night four exhausted travelers arrived at an inn near Shantung. The innkeeper told them that there was no room available, but the travelers pleaded that they were too weary to go on. Finally the innkeeper agreed to put them up in a little shack some distance from the inn. The innkeeper failed to inform them that his daughter-in-law had died just that day and her unburied corpse was stretched out on a plank just behind a curtain in the shack.

Three of the travelers fell asleep immediately, but the fourth, sensing some unknown danger, remained awake. To his horror he saw a bony hand pull the curtain aside, and he watched the greenish, glowing-eyed corpse emerge. The creature bent down over the sleeping men one by one and breathed on them. The foul breath from such a monster causes instant death. When the creature approached the only traveler who was awake, he was paralyzed with fear. Pretending to be asleep, he held his breath while the thing bent over him, and thus his life was saved. When it had returned to its place behind the curtain, the man bolted for the door and ran out into the night. The *Ch'iang Shich* heard the door open and ran after him.

The fleeing man could see the blazing eyes of the corpse behind him, and he knew it was gaining on him. He ducked behind a huge willow tree to hide, and as he peered cautiously around the trunk of the tree, he found himself staring directly into the burning eyes of the creature—no more than a few feet away. The thing let out a hideous shriek and made a leap toward him. This was just too much for the poor man, who fell into a dead faint. In his doing so, his life was spared, for the corpse missed him completely, and it plunged forward with such force that it hit the tree and buried its long nails deep into the wood.

The next morning the corpse, no longer animated, was found with its nails still stuck in the tree trunk. The intended victim was on the ground, still unconscious but alive.

See also: WALKING CORPSES

THE CHILD'S RETURN   In the late nineteenth century the *Illustrated Police News* of London printed this very strange tale. It said that in 1878 the daughter of a D. J. Demarest, a grocer of Paterson, New Jersey, died suddenly. The death took place on a Tuesday, and as was the custom at that time, the body was dressed for burial and laid out in a small coffin in the living room of the house.

On Friday the grieving father, who had been praying and weeping by the coffin, finally became so exhausted that he went into the next room, collapsed into an armchair, and dozed off for the first time in days.

He was roused from a light sleep by the sound of footsteps. Then he saw the door open, and standing in the doorway was his daughter, still dressed in her shroud. She walked unsteadily across the room to where her father sat, threw herself into his lap, and clasped her arms around his neck. Then, abruptly, her grasp loosened, and she fell backward. The father tried to raise her up, but her body was now completely limp and apparently lifeless.

The doctor was called, and the child was indeed dead. It was decided that her first "death" was merely a coma and that she really was dead this time. She was buried that same day.

See also: BURIED ALIVE, WINTERTON'S DISAPPEARANCE

ᏨORDER'S SKULL   In 1826 an English countryman named
William Corder decided that he wished to be free of his intended
bride, Maria Marten. He told Maria that they were to run off together, but they got no farther than a place called the Red Barn.
There William shot Maria and buried her body beneath the dirt
floor of the barn.

It was a tawdry crime, and Corder was a stupid and essentially
uninteresting murderer. He acted so suspiciously after Maria's disappearance that he practically put the noose around his own neck.
Finally the floor of the Red Barn was dug up, and Maria's body
was discovered. Corder was brought to trial, and since the evidence against him was overwhelming, he was found guilty and
sentenced to be hanged.

A common crime, yet for some reason the Murder in the Red
Barn, as the case came to be called, attracted an enormous amount
of attention, and when Corder was hanged outside the gates of the
Bury St. Edmunds jail on August 11, 1828, there was a huge crowd
on hand to witness the spectacle. After the hanging the executioner picked up a little extra money by selling pieces of rope to
members of the crowd.

Corder's body was sent to a medical school for dissection, a
common fate for the corpses of the condemned. Before the remains were given over to the medical students, they were put on
public display, and some five thousand people paid to see them.
After dissection the murderer's skin was tanned and made into a
book cover for a volume which contained a complete account of
his trial.

Corder's skeleton was used for teaching anatomy, but after a
few years a member of the hospital staff, one Dr. Kilner, stole the
murderer's skull and put a spare skull from the anatomy lab in its
place atop the skeleton. Dr. Kilner had Corder's skull polished and
placed in a fancy wooden box which he put on display in his

drawing room. But Corder's skull had its revenge.

At first people just felt uncomfortable when they entered Dr. Kilner's drawing room, then they began hearing strange noises. Doors opened and slammed violently without apparent reason. Hammering and sobbing sounds were reported coming from the box where the skull was kept. The servants said that a man dressed in strangely old-fashioned clothes was waiting to see the doctor, but by the time the doctor arrived, the man had vanished. The strange man was reported around the house several times, always disappearing before anyone got a good look at him.

At first Dr. Kilner insisted that nothing out of the ordinary had happened, but the servants reports began to make him very nervous. One night he was awakened by a loud noise. He ran into the hall in time to see the drawing room door being opened by a white hand—just a hand. Suddenly the door was nearly blown off its hinges by an explosion. The doctor rushed into the drawing room and was met with a blast of icy air. The candle he was carrying went out, and when he finally managed to light a match, the first thing he saw was the skull on the floor grinning at him. Around the grisly relic lay the fragments of the box in which it had been kept. The skull itself was undamaged. And that was just about enough for Dr. Kilner.

He wanted to get rid of the skull. At first he thought of returning it to the hospital and reattaching it to the rest of the skeleton, but the skull was so highly polished now that it would stand out, and everyone would notice and wonder why the skull had been polished. Ultimately the truth of Dr. Kilner's theft would come out, so that idea was abandoned. He couldn't just throw the thing away, for there was no telling what sort of revenge it might take. So he decided to give the trophy to Mr. F. C. Hopkins, a retired official of the prison commission. He thought Hopkins would appreciate the present since he had already bought the old Bury St. Edmunds jail where Corder had been hanged. Dr. Kilner turned over the skull with these words: "Take it as a present; as you already own Corder's condemned cell, and the gallows where they hanged him, perhaps it won't harm you to look after his skull."

So the retired prison official wrapped the skull in a silk hand-kerchief and started home. On the way he tripped and sprained his ankle. The skull rolled out of the handkerchief and past a lady who was walking down the road. She promptly fainted.

After that both Hopkins and Dr. Kilner had nothing but bad luck, and in a few months both of them were bankrupt. Naturally they blamed the evil influence of Corder's skull. Finally Hopkins hit upon a plan of action. He took the skull to an isolated grave-yard and bribed a gravedigger to bury it in consecrated ground. After that the run of bad luck ceased, for the murderer's skull was apparently satisfied at last.

See also: THE MUMMY'S BONE, SCREAMING SKULLS

DOPPELGÄNGER   The Doppelgänger, or "double," is a common belief in Europe, particularly in Germany. The dop-pelgänger figures prominently in folklore, but there are also a large number of firsthand accounts of this phenomena, some from well-known people. The great German writer Goethe recorded this experience:

"I rode on horseback over the footpath Drusenheim, when one of the strangest experiences befell me. Not with the eyes of the body, but with those of the spirit, I saw myself on horseback com-ing toward me on the same path dressed in a suit such as I had never worn, pale-grey with some gold. As soon as I had shaken myself out of this reverie the form vanished. It is strange, however, that I found myself returning on the same path eight years after-ward . . . and that I then wore the suit I had dreamt of, and not by design but chance."

Goethe's experience seems more a hallucination or possibly precognitive vision than a ghost. But often the doppelgänger is as-sociated with impending death or illness or appears to be a warn-ing figure.

Probably the most celebrated doppelgänger story concerns the French writer Guy de Maupassant. In 1885 De Maupassant was at work on his masterful horror story "The Horla." Quite unexpectedly a figure appeared at the door of his study, walked across the room, and sat down in front of him. The figure then began dictating the words of the story to De Maupassant.

The writer was astounded. How could this person have gotten into his study? How could he know the very words that De Maupassant intended to write? Who was he? It was then that he realized that the figure sitting across from him was no stranger at all but his exact double. The figure disappeared quickly, but the incident left De Maupassant a thoroughly shaken man.

The figure may have been the first warning of a disease that was to overtake the writer and quickly lead to insanity and death.

British psychologist Graham Reed has noted that while the doppelgänger phenomena has been largely ignored by British and American scientists, it has been the subject of serious scientific study on the European continent. From the European studies Reed has drawn this picture of the doppelgänger.

"Usually the doppelgänger appears without warning and takes the form of a mirror-image of the viewer, facing him and just beyond arm's reach. It is life-sized but very often only the face or the head and trunk are 'seen.' Details are very clear, but the colors are either dull or absent. Generally the image is transparent; some people have described it as being 'jelly-like' or as though projected onto glass. In most cases the double imitates the subject's movements and facial expressions in mirror imagery, as though it were his reflection in glass."

A couple of American cases collected by the writer John Goodwin show the doppelgänger usurping the ghost's traditional role as a warning apparition. In one case a California artist named Catherine Reinhardt had repeated doppelgänger experiences. But instead of being a mirror image, the figure always looked about five years older than she did at the moment.

The most striking experience came when she was twenty-eight.

She saw her double at a cocktail party. The double looked a little older and walked with a slight limp. Four years later Catherine Reinhardt was in a serious auto accident. Her husband was killed, and her leg was badly injured. She never fully recovered from the injury and continued to walk with a slight limp, just as her double had done.

Goodwin also recounted the story of Alex B. Griffith, who received two timely warnings from the doppelgänger.

In the summer of 1944 Griffith was an infantry sergeant, leading a patrol in France. Though the part of the country through which Griffith and his men were passing was known to be infested with the enemy, there was no sign of danger, and everyone felt quite relaxed.

Then Griffith saw a figure on the road ahead of him. The figure was the double of Griffith, and it was waving its arms and appeared to be shouting, though no words could be heard. The figure was obviously trying to make Griffith and his men stop. No one else in the patrol had seen the figure, and therefore they were quite surprised when the sergeant told them to turn back. He didn't explain why; he just knew that if they went any farther they would be killed.

As he sat on the ground trying to figure out what to do next, an American supply vehicle passed the foot soldiers and headed down the road toward the spot where the doppelgänger had given its warning. There was a sudden burst of machine-gun fire, and the jeep careened wildly out of control, its driver killed in the blast. Somewhere up ahead a German machine gun was hidden to guard the road, and if Griffith and his men had gone any farther, they would have been gunned down.

Twenty years later Griffith saw the doppelgänger again. It wasn't Griffith as he was then but Sergeant Griffith, as he had been in France. This time Griffith was again on a trail, but he was leading his family on a hike. There had been a tremendous storm and the winds were still gusty.

Once again the figure was waving its arms and appeared to be shouting a warning. No one else saw the figure, but Griffith instantly told his family to turn back. A few seconds later a huge tree weakened by the storm came crashing down into the clearing where Griffith and his family would have been had they not stopped.

Ⓖ HOSTLY FOOTSTEPS   Often a ghost is not seen but makes its presence known in other ways. A commonly reported phenomena are footsteps, usually heard in a darkened corridor at night. But a Captain A. W. Monckton had a more unusual experience with ghostly footsteps. When Monckton was a magistrate in New Guinea he was staying alone in the house of a friend, working on his official business, when suddenly he realized that the doors leading to a veranda which had been closed were now standing open. In his book *Some Experiences of a New Guinea Resident Magistrate,* he recounted:

"I became conscious that both doors were wide open and—hardly thinking what I was doing—I got up, closed them both and went on writing. A few minutes later I heard footsteps upon the coral path leading up to the house; they came across the squeaky palm veranda, my door opened, and the footsteps went across the room and—as I raised my eyes from my dispatch—the other door opened, and the footsteps passed across the veranda and down again on to the coral."

A short time later the experience was repeated. ". . . the squeak changed to the tramp of booted feet on the boarded floor. As I looked to see who it was, the tramp passed close behind my chair and across the room to the door, which opened, and then the tramp changed to the squeak and the squeak to the crash of the coral."

The most remarkable part of Monckton's experience came the third time the footsteps were heard. Monckton had brought in several of the servants in a futile attempt to locate the source of the sounds. They were all in the room when the footsteps passed through. "Precisely in the same manner came the tread of a heavily booted man, and then went out on to the palm veranda where—in the now brilliant illumination—we could see the depressing at the spots from which the sound came, as though a man were stepping there."

THE MOVING COFFINS OF BARBADOS   Ghosts? A poltergeist? Or some natural phenomenon? Whatever the cause, the moving coffins of Barbados is one of those mysteries that has continued to fascinate lovers of the odd and unusual for well over one hundred fifty years. And it is quite ghostly enough to warrant being included in a book on ghosts.

The mystery took place on the West Indian island of Barbados. About seven miles from the capital of Bridgetown is the graveyard of Christ Church. In the graveyard is a massive vault built partly above and partly below the ground. It's empty today and has been for a very long time, and the reasons why it is empty constitute the mystery.

Just exactly who had the vault constructed is unknown today. The church records refer to it as the Chase Vault, and the majority of people buried in it were Chases, but there were others. The first coffin to be placed in the vault contained the mortal remains of Mrs. Thomasina Goddard. Her simple wooden coffin was interred in the underground chamber in July 1807. In 1808 the coffin of little Mary Ann Chase, aged two, was put in the vault, followed on July 6, 1812 by that of Dorcas Chase, an older sister of Mary Ann. Rumor had it that Dorcas had starved herself to death after being driven to despair by a cruel and tyrannical father.

A few weeks later it was the father's turn. He was the Honorable Thomas Chase, who had the reputation of being one of the most hated men on the island. When the chamber was opened, members of the funeral party entered with their lights and found to their surprise that not one of the coffins was in its original place.

Entrance to the Chase vault in Barbados

The coffin of the Chase child had been moved all the way to the opposite wall.

The first reaction of the funeral party was one of anger, for it was assumed that the coffins had been thrown about by tomb robbers. But as the anger subsided, the members of the funeral party realized that ordinary tomb robbers could not have been the culprits. There was nothing in the vault to steal, but more significantly there was only one entrance and it was covered by a heavy marble slab. After each interment the slab was cemented in place, and the cement had to be chipped away so that the slab could be moved before the next burial. Before the vault had been opened, the slab had been in place, and the cement that held it was hard as a rock. It could, of course, have been chipped open and then recemented—but why would anyone want to go through all that trouble?

No one could quite figure out what had happened, but most of the mourners assumed that somehow or other the gravediggers had been responsible, though no one knew quite how or why. The coffins were put back in place, and the immensely heavy lead coffin of the Honorable Mr. Chase was heaved and shoved with great difficulty into the spot assigned to it. The vault was then sealed once again.

It was four years before another burial took place in the Chase Vault. On September 25, 1816, the vault was again opened to receive the body of eleven-year-old Charles Brewster Ames. And once again the funeral party found that the coffins inside had been tumbled about.

Now the mystery was greater than ever. Of the first three coffins, one was wooden and the other two relatively small children's coffins. But the Honorable Mr. Chase's had weighed 240 pounds, and his lead coffin was so heavy that it had taken eight men to get it into the vault in the first place. This time the disorder would have required not a lone vandal but a small gang of them. Why would anyone have wanted to go through all the trouble and face the danger, for punishment would have been severe for anyone found defiling a tomb.

The next burial was a mere fifty-two days later. This time it was Samuel Brewster, father of the boy who had been so recently buried. The elder Brewster had been buried elsewhere, and his remains were moved to the Chase Vault. The funeral procession was now swelled by the curious, who wanted to know if the coffins had been moved once again. The slab covering the vault entrance was carefully examined. It appeared to be completely untouched. But when the vault was opened, it was obvious that the coffins had been tossed about once again. Mrs. Goddard's coffin, the only wooden one in the vault, had been badly damaged—whether from being moved about or from natural causes is unknown. It had to be wrapped with wire so it would hold together. The other four coffins, all lead, had been scattered about.

The Reverend Thomas Oderson, rector of Christ Church, and several other prominent persons investigated the Chase Vault thoroughly but could not find a clue as to why or how the coffins were being moved. All they could do was order that the coffins be properly stacked and seal the vault once again.

By now the moving coffins were a subject of speculation for everyone on the island, and they waited anxiously to see what would happen next time the vault was opened. They had to wait three years, until July 17, 1819. It was hard work chipping the cement from around the marble slab. But when the vault was opened, the onlookers found that the coffins were again in disarray. Oddly, only the fragile and light wooden coffin of Thomasina Goddard was still where it had been set before.

The governor of the island, Lord Combermere, ordered his own investigation. Every inch of the vault was gone over. The sealed coffins were minutely examined, but not a clue was found.

Once again the coffins were placed with the largest ones on the ground and those of the two small children on top. The wooden coffin remained propped up against a wall. The governor had sand sprinkled on the vault floor. The sand would show the footprints of anyone inside the vault. Then the vault was closed and the private seals of the governor and two other men were pressed into the wet cement that sealed the stone slab into the vault door. Whoever tampered with the coffins this time would have to break these imprints.

And so everyone retired to wait for the next funeral. But the governor couldn't wait. On April 18, 1820, he and a party of curious friends went to Christ Church and examined the vault. The seals had not been disturbed, but when the vault was opened, the coffins were found in worse disarray than ever, some had even been turned over. The wooden coffin, however, had not moved. The sand on the floor showed no footprints.

At that point the thoroughly puzzled and exasperated governor ordered the coffins taken out of the Chase Vault and buried elsewhere. The Chase Vault has remained open and unused to this day.

The reasons for the disturbances in the Chase Vault have been

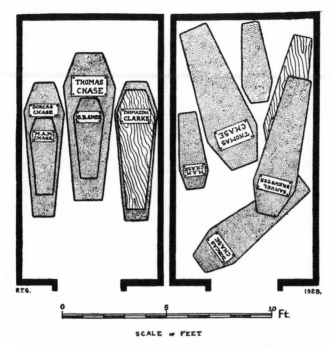

SCALE of FEET

Sketch showing how the coffins were moved between
July 17, 1819 and April 18, 1820

the subject of lively speculation since they were first noticed. Unfortunately the information on the events is not as complete or accurate as we might hope. The Reverend Oderson's original records were destroyed either in a hurricane in 1831 or in a fire in 1935. What remains are copies and recollections, which do not make the best evidence. But obvious explanations such as earth tremors and flooding seem to be eliminated. Why would an earth tremor affect only this one spot on the island? No water was ever found in the vault, and besides, Mrs. Goddard's wooden coffin was the one that wasn't moved, while the heavy lead coffins were.

More exciting speculation has focused on possible "psychic" explanations. Many have pointed out that the disturbances began only after the interment of Dorcas Chase, a probable suicide. Suicides are, of course, the origin of many of the traditional "restless spirit" accounts. The Honorable Thomas Chase himself had an evil reputation, another popular feature of the "restless spirit" story.

The fact is that the mystery of the moving coffins of Barbados is unsolved and likely to remain so.

THE MUMMY'S BONE   In 1936 Sir Alexander Hay Seton and his first wife, Zeyla, visited Egypt. One of the local guides offered to take them to the site of a tomb that was just then being excavated near the Pyramids. They were led down a stone staircase into an underground chamber. There on a stone slab lay a crumbling and obviously very ancient skeleton. Sir Alexander was told that this was the unwrapped remains of the mummy of an aristocratic young woman, one of hundreds of such mummies that were interred near the pyramids.

Zeyla was fascinated by what she saw and determined to bring back an unusual souvenir. After the others left, she sneaked back into the chamber and took a bone from the skeleton. She showed it to her husband back in the hotel room that night.

"It looked," he wrote, "like a digestive biscuit, slightly convex and shaped like a heart." Later he discovered it was a triangular bone from the base of the spine linking it with the pelvis.

When the couple returned home from their trip, they put the ancient bone on display in their house in Edinburgh, Scotland. Almost immediately strange things began to happen. The very evening that he put the bone in a glass case in his dining room, Sir Alexander stepped outside and was almost struck by a large piece of roofing tile that had been blown from his house.

For the next few nights strange sounds were heard coming from the dining room, and the table which contained the glass case was mysteriously overturned during the night. A young nephew, Alexander Black, came for a visit and one morning announced that he had seen a "funnily dressed person going up the stairs." Other

A mummy partially unwrapped

visitors and servants also claimed to have seen a spectral robed figure wandering the halls of the house at night.

The bone was moved to an upstairs drawing room, and Sir Alexander decided that he was going to spend one entire night just watching it to see what happened. He locked all the doors and windows and sat there, but nothing happened, and finally he decided that nothing would, so he went to bed. After he left, things did begin to happen. His wife shouted that she could hear someone moving around in the room with the bone. He unlocked the door and found the room looking "as if a battle royal had taken place!" Chairs and tables were thrown about, but in the middle of it all stood the bone in its glass case, completely untouched. No matter what room the bone was moved into, chaos and destruction seemed to follow.

The newspapers got wind of the affair, and it was the subject of a number of sensational stories. One reporter asked to borrow the bone, and Sir Alexander gratefully lent it to him. A week later the reporter returned it and said that nothing had happened. Shortly thereafter the reporter, who had been in excellent health, was rushed to the hospital for an emergency operation.

Not only was the bone making a mess out of his house, Sir Alexander began blaming it for a host of other problems he was having, including financial setbacks and serious marriage problems. He decided that he would just have to get rid of the thing. He discussed all sorts of possibilities including taking it back to Egypt and returning it to the tomb from which it had been stolen. His wife, however, would not hear of disposing of her ancient treasure, and the subject became another matter of controversy between them.

One evening, when his wife was away from home, Sir Alexander arranged to have his uncle who was a monk at the abbey at Fort Augustus on Loch Ness come to the house to perform an exorcism on the bone. It was then burned to ashes in the stove.

With the destruction of the bone, the noises ended, but it did not help the rest of Sir Alexander's life. He wrote, "The curse did not end with the destruction of the Bone. From 1936 onwards trouble always seemed to beset me. Zeyla never forgave me for destroying the Bone and it did not help our already rocky marriage."

Until the day of his death, Sir Alexander insisted that the bone had a malevolent influence on his life.

See also: CORDER'S SKULL

MUSIC FROM THE DEAD

Rosemary Brown is a British medium who claims that she has not only been in contact with long-gone composers such as Liszt, Chopin, Beethoven, and Rachmaninoff but that she has received musical compositions from them. Her claims have attracted an extraordinary amount of attention, she has been the subject of many articles and at least one book, and a record, *A Musical Séance,* has been made from the compositions that she has allegedly received from the composers.

Mrs. Brown herself had some limited musical training but had never tried to write music until the spirits of the composers began dictating the music to her. However, she also says that she has been "psychic" since childhood and has often seen and heard things that others were unable to see and hear. She had been seeing the spirit of Liszt since she was seven, and he had predicted that he would make her a famous musician.

After Liszt came Chopin, and he was followed by Schubert and Beethoven all the way up to the more modern composers like Debussy.

"Liszt began simply by guiding my hands at the piano," she says. "This is rather like the technique of automatic writing. I almost felt as if somebody was putting my hands on like gloves, then playing through them.

"I didn't understand what the music was; I wouldn't know what key it was in. I used to learn through the pattern of notes on the keyboard. I simply knew whereabouts I'd put my hands next."

Gradually the composers switched to dictating the music, giving their earthly collaborator the key, the timing, the left hand, the right hand.

"I graduated from where my hands were guided at the piano to the system of oral dictation we use now most of the time.

"When I get to the final score, Beethoven, who's very fussy, will go through it in detail. Liszt doesn't seem to worry as long as I have got it down. Bach is usually so clear and sure that I get it right the first time. It's a mathematical process almost with him."

Mrs. Brown's music has impressed a few critics who have said that it would be impossible, or at least highly unlikely, for a person of her limited musical education to produce imitations of the works of the great composers. Other critics have been less kind and not nearly so impressed. They say that the music of Rosemary Brown is exactly the sort of poor imitations of composers' styles that one might expect from a poorly trained amateur. Mrs. Brown, however, is unmoved by her harsh critics. She says that the quality of the music is not what is really important anyway.

"I think the quality of the music varies according to the quality of the communicating. I think, as I've mentioned, that the composers are interested in primarily communicating the fact of survival rather than in getting some of the great pieces of music across. I don't think they worry about criticism."

See also: PATIENCE WORTH

N EAR-DEATH EXPERIENCES   Though death is supposed to be "the land from which there is no return," from time to time throughout history there have been stories from people who have nearly died about what it felt like to be "dead." Modern medical science has made it possible to revive people who in past ages would certainly have been considered clinically dead and past any possibility of revival. Thus accounts of these "near death experiences" have become much more common, and interest in them has risen accordingly.

There was a great outpouring of interest in the subject after the publication of a book called *Life After Life* by Dr. Raymond Moody in 1975.

The book was widely reputed to present "scientific proof" of life after death, though Dr. Moody's own assessment of his work was considerably more modest. He became interested in the subject of life after death and was able to interview a large number of people who had "died" and "been brought back" to life. Death is not a single instant when the heart stops or breathing ceases, it is a complex phenomena, and the moment when a person is considered truly dead is still a matter of great debate in the medical and legal profession.

Dr. Moody found that many of the "dead" people to whom he talked experienced similar feelings. First they felt that they were outside of their own bodies, then had a feeling of passing through a long dark tunnel and then of being "on the other side," where they often glimpsed dead friends and relatives, and finally of encountering a very bright light which someone referred to as a "being of light," which talked to the newly dead person.

Life after Life stimulated a good deal of research in the near-death experience. Many researchers confirmed Dr. Moody's findings about the feelings and experiences of those who had been near death. But other researchers found that similar feelings and experiences were recorded by those who had any form of traumatic shock but had not actually been near death. The bulk of medical opinion now favors the theory that the "near-death" experience is a psychological one that can be triggered by a number of different powerful stimuli.

THE PALATINE LIGHT   In the winter of 1752 a Dutch ship, *The Palatine*, set sail for Philadelphia. Most of the passengers on the ship were Dutch immigrants bound for the New World. Off the coast of North America the ship was struck by a series of storms. The crew of the badly damaged *Palatine* then mutinied, murdered the captain, stole all of the passengers' valuables, and took off in the lifeboats, leaving the luckless passengers to their fate.

The foundering ship ran aground on Block Island off the coast of Rhode Island and fell into the clutches of the notorious Block Island Wreckers, who made their living by salvaging wrecks. In this case, however, the wreckers behaved with uncharacteristic humanity. They took most of the survivors off of the ship. But there was one woman who had been driven mad by the hardships she had already suffered. She refused to leave the ship even after the wreckers set it afire. The blazing hulk was taken out to the sea with the tide, and the madwoman could still be heard screaming from the burning deck.

How much if any of this story is true is impossible to determine. Block Island historian Ethel Colt Ritchie says it is composed of "little truth and much fanciful fiction." But it has become one of the most widely known tales of the North Atlantic islands.

The ghostly part of the story holds that the light from the burning ship can still often be seen at night. The Palatine Light is from time to time still reported today.

A long poem on the subject by John Greenleaf Whittier contains these verses:

> For still, on many a moonless night,
> From Kingston Head and from Montauk Light
> The spectre kindles and burns in sight.
>
> Now low and dim, now clear and higher,
> Leaps up the terrible Ghost of Fire,
> Then, slowly sinking, the flames expire.
>
> And the wise Sound skippers, though skies be fine
> Reef their sails when they see the sign
> Of the blazing wreck of the Palatine!

See also: SPOOK LIGHTS

THE PHANTOM FACES   In December 1924 there was an accident aboard the SS *Watertown*, a large oil tanker owned by the Cities Service Company. The ship was en route to the Panama Canal from the Pacific Coast. Two merchant seamen, James Courtney and Thomas Meehan, were cleaning one of the cargo tanks when they apparently were overcome by fumes and died. As is usual in such cases, the bodies were buried at sea, on December 4, 1924.

The very next day the first mate reported to the captain that the faces of the two dead men could be seen in the water and apparently were following the ship. Captain Keith Tracy looked out into the water, and sure enough there were the faces of the dead men. The faces followed the ship for days and were seen by all of the officers and members of the crew repeatedly and for long periods of time. After the ship made its way through the Panama Canal and docked at New Orleans, the captain made a full report of the strange occurrence to officials of the Cities Service Company. One company official, S. J. Patton, suggested that if the faces should appear again they should be photographed, so he gave Captain Tracy a roll of sealed film and watched while it was loaded into the first mate's camera. This was a precaution to prevent fraud.

All too often in similar cases, the phantom fails to appear when someone has a camera, but in this case the faces appeared again, and six photographs were taken. The film was not developed until the ship had once again returned to New Orleans. The film was turned over to Patton, who sent it to a commercial developer. Five of the photographs showed nothing, but the sixth showed the faces in the water very clearly.

The story made the rounds of the Cities Service Company, which was apparently quite unafraid of having one of its tankers get the reputation of being "haunted." A blowup of the photograph was on display in the Cities Service New York office. The first published account of the case was in the Cities Service magazine *Service,* but that unfortunately was not until 1934, for it was the publication of the article that first drew the attention of psychical researchers like Hereward Carrington. Carrington tried to dig up additional facts on the case, but ten years had passed, and Patton and the *Watertown's* first mate had died by that time, and the captain and most of the crew had dispersed and were impossible to locate so further investigation was next to impossible.

The details of how the photographs were taken and developed remained completely unknown. Carrington wasn't even able to get a copy of the original photograph. However, one copy did turn up in 1957. Michael Mann, who had been intrigued by the phantom faces story, spent five years looking for a copy of the photo. He also found that the authenticity of the photograph had been sworn to by Captain Tracy and his assistant engineer and that the film and photo had been checked for fakery by a detective agency. The original negatives were returned to Cities Service and apparently lost.

A great many questions remain about the *Watertown's* phantom faces. One is why the faces were clear enough to be seen yet could be recorded on film only one out of six times. Still the case remains a unique and an intriguing one.

PROPHETIC CORPSES   Necromancy, consulting the dead for the purpose of foretelling the future, has long been regarded as the most dangerous magical operation, the blackest of the black arts. Indeed, the word necromancy has become synonymous with the practice of black magic even when calling up the dead is not involved.

The most complete and oldest account of the act of necromancy was set down by the Roman writer Lucian, who lived during the second century of the Christian era. Lucian described the visit of

The necromancer in action

Sextus Pompey, son of Julius Caesar's chief adversary, Pompey the Great, to a particularly horrid Thessalian witch named Erichtho. Sextus wanted the witch to find out what the future held for him. Erichtho warned him that despite her powers she could not break the chains of fate but that she could see the future through the use of necromancy. Sextus was satisfied. "Though it may be well enough for the oracles and prophets who serve the Olympians to give riddling responses, a man who dares consult the dead deserves to be told the truth!"

For Erichtho's magic to be successful, she had to invoke the aura of death. She lived in an open grave surrounded by bones and pieces of corpses. To perform the ghastly ceremony she asked for a fresh dead body "whose flexible organs shall yet be capable of speech, not with lineaments already hardened by the sun." Old corpses, she complained, "only squeak incoherently."

When a proper corpse was chosen, "she passed a hook beneath the jaw of the selected one, and fastening it to a cord, dragged him along over rocks and stones until she reached a cave overhung by a projecting ridge. A gloomy fissure in the ground was there of a depth almost reaching to the Infernal Gods, where the yew tree spread thick its horizontal branches of all times excluding the light of the sun."

Erichtho put on a colored robe, combed her hair over her face, and adjusted her wreath of vipers. She then cut a hole in the dead man's chest and poured in a concoction of the most revolting imaginable ingredients such as froth from the jaws of a mad dog, marrow of a stag fed on serpents, and hump of corpse-fed hyena. Next she began to chant an incantation which "seemed to mingle the barking of dogs and howling of wolves, the screech of an owl, the roaring of wild beasts and hissing of snakes, the crash of waves on rocks, the murmur of forest trees and the bellow of thunder." All the gods of darkness were appealed to. Finally a ghost appeared but refused at first to enter the corpse. So Erichtho threatened it with a long list of infernal powers and also promised that when the ceremony was over the corpse would be burned so that it could never again be used for such a purpose. The ghost then agreed and entered the corpse.

"The body raises itself, not by degrees, but at a single impulse, and stands erect. The eyelids unclose, the countenance is not that of a living subject, but of the dead. The paleness of the complexion, the rigidity of the lines remain. And he looks about with an unswerving stare."

When the corpse answers the desired questions, "The sorceress constructs a funeral pyre; the dead man places himself thereon; Erichtho applies the torch, and the charm is forever at an end."

The response the corpse gave to Sextus's questions is unrecorded, but his life was not a successful one. He opposed the power of Julius Caesar's successor, Augustus, and was ultimately reduced to an outlaw's life.

Lucian was a poet writing long after the event he described was supposed to have taken place. The scene may be entirely fictional, and if not it is certainly exaggerated. Yet from what we know of the practice of necromancy, ceremonies of the sort must have been attempted from time to time. The belief that the dead can foresee the future is an ancient and persistent one. In order to magically raise the dead, the witch had to use the symbols of death, the open grave, the gloomy places, and other reminders of death.

See also: THE SPIRIT OF SAMUEL

*S*CREAMING SKULLS   Scattered throughout the British Isles there are several "screaming skulls." That is, skulls that, according to tradition, protest loudly if they are moved from their accustomed place. At a farmhouse in Dorsetshire there is a skull that is supposed to scream when anyone tries to bury it.

As is common in such cases, there is considerable confusion as to the origins of the skull. According to the most widely repeated tale, the skull belonged to a black servant who declared while dying that his spirit would never rest until his body was taken back

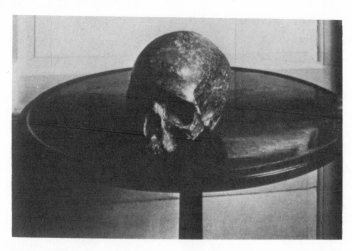

The screaming skull of Bettiscombe Manor

to his native Africa. This was not done, instead the body was buried in the local churchyard.

After this unwanted burial there was no end of trouble. Terrible screams issued from the grave, and the house in which the servant had lived rattled and creaked incessantly. Finally the restless corpse was dug up and placed in the house. That stopped the noises, but residents of the house didn't like sharing it with an unburied body, so there were persistent attempts to rebury the remains with the same results. Every time they were buried, the noises started all over again. After three attempts the owners of the house gave up and kept the body, now reduced to a skeleton, in the house. Over the years bits and pieces of the skeleton disappeared until only the skull remained.

A woman named Garnett left an account of seeing this particular skull on a visit to the house in 1863. She did not hear it scream, for this happened only when an attempt was made to bury it in the churchyard, and the owners of the house were not about to allow anyone to try that just to find out if the skull really screamed.

Another English farmhouse, this one in Derbyshire, is the reputed repository of yet another screaming skull. The origins of this skull are even more obscure. A local tradition holds that the skull was that of a wealthy young woman who had been murdered in the house some centuries ago. While dying, she declared that her remains should never be removed from that spot. Yet the very same local tradition also holds that the skull is nicknamed Dickie.

The powers of the skull are explained in this nineteenth century account:

"It is believed that if the skull is removed everything on the farm will go wrong; the cows will be dry and barren, the sheep will have the rot, the horses will fall down and break their knees and other misfortunes will happen. . . .

"I had been informed by a credible person, a Mr. Adam Fox, who was brought up in the house, that he had not only repeatedly heard singular noises and observed extraordinary circumstances, but can produce fifty persons within the parish who have seen an apparition at this place. He has often found the doors opening to his hand. The servants have been repeatedly called up in the morning and many good offices have been done by the apparition at different times. It is indeed looked upon more as a guardian spirit than a terror to the family.

"Twice within the memory of man, the skull has been taken from the premises; once on building the present house on the site of the old one, and another time, when an attempt was made to bury it in the Chapel churchyard. But there was no peace, no rest! It had to be replaced."

Local legend holds that Dickie's powers caused an entire rail line to be relocated. A bridge for a rail line between London and Manchester was being built in what was considered to be Dickie's Territory, that is, near the farmhouse in which the skull resided. But the foundations for the bridge could never be properly laid owing to the boggy nature of the soil, and the line had to be diverted. The locals assumed that Dickie just didn't want those noisy trains rumbling by and disturbing "him."

Samuel Laycock, a Lancashire poet, even penned a few lines of dialect verse on the subject:

An unburied skull in a window at Turnsead Farm, said to be opposed
to the new line of railway from Waley Bridge, to Brunton, 1863.

> New, Dickie, be quiet wi'thee lad,
>   An 'let Navvies and railway be;
> Mon, tha shouldn't do soa—it's t'bad,
>   Whar harm are they doin' to thee?
> Dead folk shouldn't meddle at o'
>   But leov o' these matters to their wick
> They'll see they're done gradely aw know—
>   Dos't t' year what aw say to that, Dick?

See also: CORDER'S SKULL, THE SKULL OF WARDLEY HALL

THE SKULL OF WARDLEY HALL   The most celebrated of the
so-called screaming skulls is the one that allegedly belonged to a
seventeenth century rake by the name of Roger Downes. Downes
lived during the reign of Charles II and was such an enthusiastic
participant in the revels that marked the "merry monarch's" reign
that he was killed one night in a drunken brawl on London Bridge.
During the fight he had been beheaded by a watchman and his
body was thrown into the Thames. His head, however, was packed
up and sent, a grisly memento mori to his sister, who lived on the
family estate of Wardley Hall in Manchester. His sister kept the
head at the hall, and though it has now been reduced to a skull, it's
still there and stoutly resists any efforts to move it elsewhere.

In a book called *Traditions of Lancashire,* the author states,
"The skull was removed secretly at first, but it invariably returned
to the Hall and no human power could drive it hence. It has been
riven to pieces, burnt and otherwise destroyed but on the subsequent day it was seen filling its wonted place."

It's "wonted place" was a little locked recess behind the main

The screaming skull of Wardley Hall

stairs or on the stairs themselves—the stories differ. Though Roger Downes's relatives had long since ceased to live at Wardley Hall, new owners found the skull so difficult to get rid of that they decided that it was best just to leave it where it was.

Thomas Barritt, an antiquary who visited Wardley Hall, described the skull thus:

"A human skull which time out of mind hath had a superstitious veneration paid to it, the occupiers of the Hall not permitting it to be removed from its situation which is on the topmost step of a staircase. There is a tradition that if removed or ill-used some uncommon noise or disturbance always follows to the terror of the whole house.

"Some years ago, I and three of my acquaintances went to view it and found it bleached white with weather that beats on it from a four-square window in the hall. The tenants never permit it to be glazed or filled up. However, one of us who was last in company with the skull removed it from its place into a dark part of the room and then left it and returned home.

"The night but one following, such a storm arose about the house of wind and lightning as tore down some trees. When hearing of this my father went over to witness the wreckage the storm had made. Yet all this might have happened had the skull never been removed."

That is, of course, a rational view, and in such matters people have rarely been rational.

While there is no doubt that a skull with allegedly supernatural properties has been kept at Wardley Hall, there is some doubt as to whether the owner of the skull was Roger Downes. According to one history of the Hall, all of Roger Downes is properly buried in the family vault. Vaughan Hart-Davis, author of *History of Wardley Hall*, writes that Roger's coffin was opened at the end of the eighteenth century just to see if he was all there. He was, though oddly, the skull had been sawed off just above the eyes and the top was missing.

No reason for this peculiar mutilation could be given, but if this account is accurate, then it cannot be Roger's skull that is kept in the hall.

According to Hart-Davis the skull belonged to Ambrose Barlow, a monk who was executed during the anti-Catholic hysteria of the seventeenth century. The owner of the hall, who was a secret Catholic sympathizer, was said to have obtained the monk's head from the old church at Manchester, where it had been impaled on a pike as a display. Not wishing to reveal his religious sympathies, he kept the skull hidden in a box sealed in a wall. Many years later the box was discovered, and the skull was simply kept around the hall as a curious relic.

According to this version the legend grew when a careless servant, thinking the skull to be that of some animal, threw it out of a window and into the moat. That night there was a terrible storm, and the owner of Wardley Hall assumed that it was caused by the wrath of the skull. So he had the moat drained and the skull was recovered. From that time onward it was considered extremely unwise to move the skull, no matter whose it was.

See also: CORDER'S SKULL, SCREAMING SKULLS

*S*PIRIT PHOTOGRAPHY   Spiritualism and photography became popular at about the same time. This helps to explain the enormous interest that once existed in spirit photography. Spiritualism was often linked to new technological developments. In the early years of spiritualism the spirits were supposed to communicate via a rapping code which sounded very much like the newly developed telegraphic code. Indeed this phenomena was often called the "spiritual telegraph." It is not surprising therefore that many who were interested in spiritualism believed that the images of the dead might be captured on photographic film.

The first well-known instance of spirit photography took place in Boston in 1862. A professional photographer named Mumler said that he had taken his own self-portrait. When he developed

Above and opposite: *Early examples of spirit photography*

the picture, he found that it contained the image of a cousin who had been dead for twelve years.

When the news of this marvel got around in spiritualist circles, they flocked to Mumler's studio to have their pictures taken with dead friends and relatives. Mumler began turning out spirit photographs by the bushel. Most of the "spirits" in these photographs were heavily draped and in such poor focus that it was impossible to make out any of the features clearly. Yet many of those who got photographs from Mumler unhesitatingly identified the indistinct figures as being the images of dead friends and relatives. Some of Mumler's photos must have been a little too clear, however, because the spirits were recognized as living people who happened to work for the photographer. Mumler left Boston in a hurry, and he turned up a few years later in New York City doing exactly the same thing. The city tried to prosecute Mumler for fraud, but numerous witnesses who appeared said that he was not a faker because he had provided them with genuine photographs of their departed loved ones. The charges against the photographer were dismissed.

Most spirit photographs were remarkably easy to fake. The photographer took a picture of the subject who wished to receive a "spirit photograph." He then took another picture on the same piece of film of the "spirit," usually a heavily draped assistant, though some photographers cut costs by using draped dummies. Thus the spirit photographs were simply double exposures.

Some spirit photographers used even cruder methods. They just cut out the faces of famous people and superimposed them on another photograph they had taken. Occasionally they painted in some swirls of clouds around the floating face to make it look more "spiritual" and to hide the sharp outlines of the cutouts. There were scores of "spirit photographs" that contained the face of Abraham Lincoln.

Most of the spirit photographs that were taken during this period look to the modern observer so obviously fake that one wonders how anyone but an idiot could have been taken in by them. Yet there were thousands of nonidiots who took them very seriously indeed. There are two basic reasons: First people were not at all sophisticated about photography. The mere appearance of an image on film seemed quite miraculous; that the picture also contained the image of a ghost seemed just another miracle. Even more important was the will to believe. People wanted to believe that their dead loved ones were somehow still with them, and they would grasp at any bit of evidence, no matter how flimsy or fraudulent. Exposure of fraud would not shake the belief of many in the least.

Take the case of the French "spirit photographer" named Buget, who operated in London and Paris during the 1870s. Buget did a booming business in double-exposure spirit photographs, which were endorsed by many of the leading spiritualists of the time as genuine.

At first Buget used assistants to pose as spirits, but later he started using a dummy which had a number of interchangeable heads. An assistant would ask the sitter what spirit he or she would like to have in the picture, and Buget would choose the proper

A medium surrounded by "spirits"

Medium with a "spirit" on her shoulder

head accordingly. Sometimes Buget was able to obtain a picture of the person whose "spirit" he was to photograph. He would then try to make his dummy appear as true-to-life as possible, but such elaborate lengths were not usually necessary.

In 1875 Buget was arrested by the French government for selling fraudulent photos. The police seized the dummy with the extra heads. Buget himself made a full confession to the charge. Yet at his trial witness after witness stepped forward to say that the photograph they had received from the photographer could not possibly have been faked. Many refused to believe Buget's own confession and rejected the evidence of the dummy and the photographer's other trick apparatus which was on display in the courtroom.

Here is a bit of typical testimony from the trial. The witness was a man named Dessenon, a picture seller aged fifty-five. He explained that he had first received several spirit photographs which he had not recognized but then:

"The portrait of my wife, which I had specially asked for, is so like her that when I showed it to one of my relatives he exclaimed, 'It's my cousin.' "

THE COURT: Was that chance, Buget?

BUGET: Yes, pure chance. I had no photograph of Madame Dessenon.

THE WITNESS: My children, like myself, thought the likeness perfect. When I showed them the picture they cried, "It's mama."

THE COURT: You see this doll and all the rest of these things?

THE WITNESS: There is nothing there in the least like the photograph which I obtained.

THE COURT: You may stand down.

There is something genuinely pathetic about such testimony. Many spiritualists refused to admit they were taken in by a faker. Some asserted that Buget was a genuine medium and said that he had been bribed or terrorized into making a false confession and fabricating the dummy and all the other apparatus for faking photos in order to discredit spiritualism.

How some spirit photographs were taken

Repeated exposures of fake spirit photography plus increasing sophistication about photography in general have virtually eliminated this type of spirit photography today.

There are, however, other types of "spirit photographs." During the late nineteenth and early twentieth centuries, some perfectly honest photographers would develop their pictures and find faint and ghostly images in the scene when none should have been there. Occasionally the image would be identified as being someone who had recently died.

In the early 1900s an English photographer was taking a picture inside a chapel. When he developed the photograph, he observed a faintly discernible human face in one of the panels. He recognized the face as that of a young friend who had recently died tragically. The photographer showed the photograph to psychical

Above and on next page: *Twentieth-century spirit photographs taken by a psychical researcher to show what can be done with trick photography*

researcher Frank Podmore. Podmore was thoroughly skeptical about spirit photography. Yet Podmore said, "When he told me the story and showed me the picture I could easily see the faint but well-marked features of a handsome, melancholy lad of eighteen."

Podmore then showed the photograph to another friend of his but did not tell him the story about the boy who had died. Podmore's friend at once identified the face in the picture as belonging to a woman of about thirty. Podmore commented, "The outlines are in reality so indistinct as to leave ample room for the imagination to work in."

How was such a spirit photograph produced in the first place? The answer lies in the way photographs were taken at that time. The film was very slow, and it took a long time to make a picture, especially in poor light—and this particular photo was taken inside a chapel. In such a case the film would have to be exposed for an hour or more. The photographer would set up his camera on a tripod, open the lens, and then walk away from it. If, during that

period, someone walked into the scene that was being photographed and paused for a few seconds to look at the camera, that
person's face and form would register as a faint and ghostly image
on the film. If the photographer did not know that someone had
walked into the scene, he might indeed believe that he had photographed a ghost.

Many more modern spirit photographs seem to be little more
than the result of an imperfection in the film or camera. While
there still are a few spirit photographs that are taken seriously or
at least considered unexplained by responsible psychical researchers, photography is no longer thought to be a particularly
effective way of "trapping" a ghost.

See also: THE BROWN LADY OF RAYNHAM HALL, TAPES FROM THE
DEAD, THE TULIP STAIRCASE

$\mathcal{S}$POOK LIGHTS   Throughout the United States there are
various spots where mysterious lights appear regularly. Generally
local tradition gives these lights a ghostly origin. One of the best
known of the United States "spook lights" is in the West Mountain
Valley area of Colorado, where the lights appear, appropriately
enough, over a graveyard. The graveyard is just outside of the
town of Silver Cliff, once a prosperous mining town but now—
again appropriately—a ghost town, with a population of only one
hundred.

The strange phenomena of the lights were first observed in
about 1880 when Silver Cliff was at its boomtown height, with a
population of five thousand. A group of drunken miners returning
from their diggings reported seeing eerie lights hovering over each
grave in the local graveyard. Drunken miners do not make the best
witnesses, but other more reliable and completely sober observers
began seeing the lights too. The lights continued to be seen over
the years, and in 1967 a story about them appeared in *The New
York Times*. The lights became something of a tourist attraction.

The most complete written account of these lights appeared in the *National Geographic* magazine in 1969.

Edward J. Linehan from *National Geographic* drove out to the graveyard accompanied by local resident Bill Kleine. They arrived at dark, and when Linehan turned off the car's headlights and got out of the car, Kleine pointed and shouted: "There! See them? And over there."

There they were, "dim round spots of blue-white light" glowing over the graves. As Linehan approached to get a better look at one of the lights, it vanished, then slowly reappeared. Linehan pointed his flashlight at the hovering light, but the beam revealed only a tombstone. He pursued the lights for about fifteen minutes without ever being able to figure out what was causing them.

One popular theory was that the lights were merely a reflection of lights from Silver Cliff and Westcliff, another small town nearby. Linehan thought that the lights from the towns were too faint to cause such an effect, and he noted they were often seen when the fog was so thick that you couldn't see the town at all. Another theory is that they are caused by radioactive ore, but a check of the area with a Geiger counter showed no evidence of a high level of radioactivity.

Linehan cited the theory of anthropologist and folklorist Dale Ferguson that the Cheyenne and other Plains Indians buried their dead on "hilltops sacred to the spirits." A number of Indian legends speak of "dancing blue spirits" on such sites.

Old-timers in the Silver Cliff area have quite another explanation; they will tell you that the lights are the helmet lamps of long-dead miners still searching for silver on the hilltops.

"No doubt someone, someday, will prove there's nothing at all supernatural in the luminous manifestations at Silver Cliff's cemetery," Linehan concludes. "And I will feel a tinge of disappointment."

See also: THE PALATINE LIGHT

$\mathcal{S}$UMMONING A SPIRIT   Calling up a spirit of the dead is a
traditional magical operation. The best and most complete modern description of how this is to be done comes from the nineteenth century French magician and occultist Eliphas Levi.

In 1854, when Levi was in London, he attempted to summon
the spirit of the ancient magician Apollonius of Tyana. Levi prepared himself by fasting for twenty-one days. This is numerologi-
cally significant for both seven and three are powerful magic
numbers and seven times three is twenty-one. Levi was alone
when the ceremony was performed so we have only his word for
what happened.

The ceremonial room had four concave mirrors and an altar
covered with white lambskin. A pentagram (five-pointed star) was
carved on the top of the altar. There were two chafing dishes, one
on the altar, the other on a tripod. Levi wore a white robe. All of
this white was to indicate that the magician was practicing white
as opposed to black magic. On the magician's head was a wreath
of vervain leaves, useful in warding off any demons that might accidentally be called up. In one hand the magician held a sword, in
the other a copy of the ritual.

Fires were lit in the chafing dishes, and Levi began a long incantation: "In unison the demons chant the praises of God; they
lose their malace and fury. . . . Cerberus opens his triple jaw and
fire chants the praises of God with three tongues of their lightning.
. . . the soul revists the tombs; the magical lamps are lighted." As
the chant rose in pitch, Levi felt the ground shake and he thought
he saw a figure of a man standing before the altar, but the figure
vanished.

The magician repeated the incantations, and this time something seemed to stir in the depths of the mirrors. Levi closed his
eyes and summoned three times for the ghost to appear. "When I
again looked forth there was a man in front of me, wrapped from

head to foot in a species of shroud, which seemed more grey than white, he was lean, melancholy and beardless."

Levi suddenly felt abnormally cold and badly frightened. He tried to command the spirit but was unable to speak properly. Something touched his sword arm, which went numb at the elbow. He was overcome by intense weakness, and he fainted.

For several days after the ceremony, Levi's arm was sore. The questions he had intended to ask the ghost had never been asked, though Levi felt that they had been answered in his mind. The answers were "death" and "dead." The magician did not reveal the questions.

When it came to explaining what had happened, Eliphas Levi was obscure and even contradictory. He did not believe that he had really seen the ghost of Apollonius but rather that the intense strain of the ceremony had produced "an actual drunkenness of the imagination." Yet he would not say that what he had experienced was a hallucination. "I do not explain the physical laws by which I saw and touched. I affirm solely that I did see and that I did touch, that I saw clearly and distinctly, apart from dreaming, and this is sufficient to establish the real efficacy of magical ceremonies. . . . I commend the greatest caution to those who propose devoting themselves to similar experiences; their result is intense exhaustion and frequently a shock sufficient to occasion illness."

See also: PROPHETIC CORPSES

TAPES FROM THE DEAD   In the summer of 1959 Friedrich Jurgenson, a Swedish painter and film producer, set out a tape recorder to record bird songs near his home in Sweden. When he played the recording back, he thought that he could hear on the tape a male voice discussing "nocturnal bird songs" in Norwegian. Jurgenson's first thought was that his tape recorder had somehow picked up some Norwegian radio broadcast and the fact that the broadcast was about bird songs when he was recording bird songs was just a coincidence.

He tried several more recordings, and he continued to pick up voices of some kind. But now the voices seemed more personal and directed at him. Moreover many of the voices claimed to be dead friends or relatives. Jurgenson continued his recordings, and the voices on the tapes began giving him advice on how to improve the quality of the recordings. His work came to the attention of parapsychologists in various parts of the world, and eventually he wrote several books on the subject.

Most English-speaking readers learned of the "tapes from the dead" from a book called *Breakthrough* by Dr. Konstantin Raudive, a psychologist who met Jurgenson in 1965, became fascinated by his work, and began making recordings on his own. Raudive believes that Jurgenson had recorded over one hundred thousand phrases spoken by the enigmatic voices. He has carefully classified and cataloged these recordings. The phrases are usually very short—never more than about twelve words. The messages are an ungrammatical collection of languages. A "telegraphic word salad," Raudive has called them.

In their *Handbook of Psi Discoveries*, authors Sheila Ostrander and Lynn Schroeder write:

"The voices sound a little like the early radio transmissions of the astronauts from the moon. The voices are audible over tremendous background noise and a rushing sound. It's a little like trying to hear someone on a terribly bad phone connection from a foreign country. Raudive and Jurgenson both emphasize it's a question of training the ear. Raudive feels the skill develops gradually. If a person has fine hearing and perfect pitch he or she has a big advantage."

There have been a number of theories about the origins of these voices. Some have suggested that they come from outer space, that they are transmissions from secret space projects or even from some sort of extraterrestrial civilizations. But by far the most popular hypothesis has always been that these are recordings of voices from beyond the grave. In addition to Raudive and Jurgenson, people all over the world who have become aware of their work have begun making their own recordings with similar results. Say Ostrander and Schroeder:

"Probably the most urgent, constant theme in all voice tape messages received from all parts of the world is—there's life after death. 'We are dead—we live.'"

Unfortunately these messages do not come through loud and clear, and many who have heard fragments of the "tapes from the dead" hear nothing but noise and contend that the "voices" are a combination of a peculiarity of the recording method and wishful thinking. People expecting to hear voices tend to hear voices when in reality all they are hearing is noise. Skeptics point to the many "spirit photographs" during the early days of photography which turned out to be nothing more than artifacts of the photographic process.

While interest in the tapes continues in some quarters, it has not produced the type of parapsychological breakthrough that was first predicted.

See also: SPIRIT PHOTOGRAPHY

THE TULIP STAIRCASE   In 1966 two Canadian tourists, the Reverend Ralph Hardy, a retired clergyman, and his wife, were visiting the National Maritime Museum in Greenwich, England. One of the buildings on the museum grounds is the Queen's House, built for Anne of Denmark, wife of King James I.

Inside the Queen's House is a fine spiral staircase called the Tulip Staircase. It attracted the Reverend Hardy's attention, and he decided to take a picture of it. The staircase looked empty when the shot was taken.

After the Reverend Hardy returned to Canada and developed the picture, he found that it contained an image of what appeared to be a robed figure climbing the stairs. His (her?) left hand with a ring was clearly seen holding the handrail. Some people also think that they can see a second or even a third robed figure in the picture, but these images are very faint and difficult if not impossible to see in black-and-white reproductions of the original photo.

The Tulip Staircase

The Reverend Hardy and his wife were not at all interested in ghosts, but they did send the photo on to some psychical researchers who had it examined by photography experts. The experts could find no evidence that the picture had been altered in any way. The Hardys themselves were interviewed by psychical researchers who were convinced that the couple had no reason for taking fake ghost photographs.

An odd thing about the picture is that the Queen's House and the Tulip Staircase never had a reputation for being haunted before the photograph was taken and given wide publicity. Afterwards, of course, a number of people said that they too had seen ghostly robed figures on or near the staircase, but such stories are not taken seriously.

See also: THE BROWN LADY OF RAYNHAM HALL, SPIRIT PHOTOGRAPHY

WALKING CORPSES   In modern times it is usually the
ghost—the spirit of the dead—that is feared. But there have been
times and places where an animated corpse, the body itself which
is able to get up and walk around, was the primary object of fear.

A twelfth-century English chronicle by a writer known as William of Newburgh contains several stories labeled "Of the Extraordinary Happening When a Dead Man Wandered Abroad out of
His Grave." Here is one of his stories:

An exceedingly evil man who had lived in the vicinity of Aln-
wick Castle died without confessing his numerous sins. He was
nevertheless given a good Christian burial which, William notes:
". . . he did not deserve and which profited him nothing."

This evil man could not be held in his grave. "For by the power
of Satan in the dark hours, he was wont to come forth from his
tomb and to wander about through the streets, prowling round the
houses, whilst on every side dogs were howling and yelping the
whole night long."

People were afraid to go out at night because anyone who met
the unnatural creature would be attacked and severely beaten by
it. Worse yet, the walking body was beginning to rot. "The air became foul and tainted as the fetid and corrupting body wandered
abroad, so that a terrible plague broke out and there was hardly a
house that did not mourn its dead."

Finally two brothers whose father had died in the plague decided on a bold scheme: They would dig up the body and burn it.
This took considerable courage since the corpse could move about
and there was no telling what it might do. In addition digging up a
body, even in such an obviously good cause, was a profoundly sin-
ful act. But they went ahead anyway.

"And whilst they yet thought they would have to dig much
deeper, suddenly they came upon the body, covered with a thin
layer of earth. It was gorged and swollen with a frightful corpu-

lence, and its face was florid and chubby, with huge red puffed cheeks, and the shroud in which it had been wrapped was all soiled and torn."

One of the young men struck the corpse with a spade, "and there immediately gushed out such a stream of warm red gore that they realized that the creature had fattened upon the blood of many poor folk." They burned the body and the plague ended. "Just as if the polluted air was cleansed by the fire that burned up the hellish brute who had infected the whole atmosphere."

This story gets fairly close to what we now regard as traditional vampire lore. However, in the twelfth century the word vampire was unknown in England. Vampire lore reached England from Central Europe, but it merged with the older tales of walking corpses which were already well known.

William has several walking corpse tales which he relates with an air of absolute sincerity. Yet some of his accounts are so wildly extravagant that it is reasonable to suspect that he is repeating a tall tale and knows it. In one of his stories a monk chases a walking (or in this case running) corpse around a deserted castle with a spade. The corpse escapes by jumping into the moat.

In Russia there were many tales of walking corpses. The famed occultist Helena Petrovena Blavatsky told a story of an evil old Russian governor who married a young and unwilling bride. He was insanely jealous of her, and as he lay dying, he warned her that if she remarried he would return from the grave to torment her.

But she was still a young woman, and desire overcame fear, so after a few months she announced her plans to marry the man she had loved before she was forced to marry the old governor. That very evening a coach was seen rumbling out of the graveyard where the governor's body was buried. It approached the residence where the governor's widow lived, and as it did so, everyone in the house was overcome with a feeling of lethargy and quickly fell asleep. The governor's corpse then got out of the carriage, went up to the room that his widow was occupying, and proceeded to beat and pinch her until she was black-and-blue.

This same treatment was repeated every night for several weeks until the poor woman was near death. Neither soldiers nor the intervention of a priest were able to stop the dead governor's carriage. Those who tried to block it were knocked aside by an invisible force. Finally both civil and religious authorities agreed to have the old governor's corpse dug up and burned. Only then did the widow's torments come to an end.

A walking corpse of this type, which rises from the grave because of its own evil, is not to be confused with a zombie, which is a corpse reanimated by magic.

See also: BURIED ALIVE, CH'IANG SHICH

WINTERTON'S DISAPPEARANCE

WINTERTON'S DISAPPEARANCE   Ghosts, fear of being buried alive, and psychic phenomena all merge in this curious tale about an expatriate Englishman named Winterton. Winterton had been an army man and had traveled widely. After he was discharged, he continued to travel and used up what little money he had saved. Finally he wound up living in cheap lodgings in Damascus, Syria, where he was barely able to support himself as a tourist guide.

Winterton's best, indeed his only, friend was an Arab shopkeeper named Hassan. The two men shared a serious interest in psychic phenomena and the possibility of life after death. They were both aware of many tales of "crisis apparitions," where a person at the point of death or recently dead appears to a friend or relative many miles away. Like so many others have done, Winterton and his friend made a pact that whoever should die first would try to contact the other.

Shortly after they made the pact, it looked very much as if Winterton was going to have a chance to see if he could come back because a severe cholera epidemic swept through Damascus and Winterton fell victim to the disease. He was taken to the hospital, but he was already in such a weakened condition that there seemed little chance he would survive.

Hassan did not try to visit his friend for he knew that during an epidemic no visits were allowed; besides, he was afraid that he might catch the disease. In a few days he heard that Winterton was dead.

Hassan was saddened by the news, and he thought to the pact that he had made. For that reason he was not totally surprised to see the form of Winterton appear in his room at about seven that evening. Winterton looked very much the same as he always had.

"I'm sorry that you are dead, my friend," said Hassan. "When I heard the terrible news, I didn't want to believe it."

"But I'm not dead," said the form of Winterton. "That's why I have come to you. They only think I'm dead, but I'm sure I will recover, if they don't bury me first. You must stop them."

Hassan knew what hospital conditions were like, particularly during an epidemic. The doctors and nurses were badly over-worked; they didn't have the time to examine each patient care-fully. They knew that most of the patients were going to die no matter what they did, and this knowledge led to callousness. Under such conditions it was possible that an unconscious but still-living person might indeed be pronounced dead.

The form of Winterton described how he had been taken for dead, then loaded onto a cart with a lot of bodies and taken to a mortuary. "Can you imagine what it is like to lie among all those bodies?" he said. "I must get out of that place; if I don't they will bury me alive."

As Winterton talked, his form began to fade and soon disap-peared completely. Poor Hassan didn't know what to think—the story had shaken him severely. He began to wonder if perhaps the figure he had seen was telling the truth. He certainly believed in the possibility of such appearances, so Winterton might really be still alive but in grave danger. What was he to do?

Early the next morning Hassan went to the hospital. The doctor didn't specifically recall Winterton, but he did think that an Englishman had been among those who had died on the previous day and been taken to the mortuary. Bodies were only to remain in the mortuary overnight, for it was dangerous to keep the corpses of cholera victims around for long. If he were in the mortuary, Winterton was sure to be buried that very day.

Hassan hurried to the mortuary and found the caretaker, an old man who was all alone. Hassan described his friend, and the old man said that he did recall such a body. Hassan knew that there was danger of infection if he entered the mortuary, but he became convinced that the apparition he had seen was telling the truth and that Winterton really wasn't dead. He felt he had no choice.

The old mortuary keeper, however, didn't want to let him in. He even refused a bribe, which was very unusual. "It is forbidden to enter," he said. Finally Hassan was forced to push the old man aside to get into the mortuary.

"It's not against the law," Hassan insisted. "All I wish to do is see the body. It has not yet been taken for burial, has it?"

The mortuary caretaker looked extremely uncomfortable and answered, "To tell you the truth, I'm not sure."

"What do you mean you're not sure? It's your job to know these things. Don't you keep any records here!"

"The body has disappeared. I saw it brought in yesterday and put on a table just like all the others. But during the evening I stepped out for a little drink. It's against the rules, I know, but this is such a hard job, a man needs a drink now and then. I locked the door of course, but when I came back the body was gone. No one could have gotten in; no one would have wanted to. Why steal a body? There was nothing of value on it."

"About what time did this happen?" asked Hassan.

"I went out at about seven," said the caretaker.

Hassan recalled that was about the time when the figure of Winterton had appeared to him. He was upset and angry:

"Do you mean to tell me that a corpse just got up and walked out?"

"Oh no," said the caretaker, "I told you the door was locked. But there is a ventilator. When I left it was closed and when I came back it was open."

Hassan examined the ventilator. It was just large enough for a thin man to have squeezed through. Winterton had always been thin.

"Please don't tell anyone what has happened," pleaded the caretaker. "If the authorities find out I'll lose my job, and where will I ever find another at my age?"

Hassan was deep in his own thoughts. If he had come at the time the form of Winterton appeared in his room, he might have been able to save his old friend. Now there was no way of telling what had happened. If Winterton had escaped the mortuary, he would still be a very sick man. Wandering the streets in an advanced stage of cholera, he would probably not last very long; indeed he was probably dead already.

Hassan assured the old man that he would tell no one. "It's not really your fault," he said. "If anyone is to blame it's me. I should have come sooner."

Winterton's corpse was never found, nor did the spirit appear again to Hassan.

See also: BURIED ALIVE

8

GHOSTLY
LEGENDS

THE ANGELS OF MONS   Tales of phantom armies haunting battlefields are common, though such reports are rarely more than vague folklore. Sometimes, however, the folklore is persistent enough to gain a degree of credence. Soon after the first major battle of the English Civil War, called Edge Hill, in 1642, in which some four thousand men were killed, there were reports of ghostly armies reenacting the slaughter.

These tales were apparently so convincing that King Charles I sent a group of three officers and three private gentlemen to conduct an investigation. The group stated that not only were the reports true but that they had recognized among the ghosts several men they had known who were killed at Edge Hill.

Such tales of ghostly battles have declined in modern times, though they made a brief and curious reappearance during World War I. Arthur Machen, a journalist and a writer of supernatural fiction, wrote an imaginary first-person account of the retreat of the British Army from Mons in 1914. In the story ghostly archers from the past appear among the ranks of the British Army. Though the account was clearly fiction, it was widely accepted as fact in the emotion-charged atmosphere that the war had generated. The specters, which acquired the popular name of the Angels of Mons, were seriously discussed in letters to the editor, and sermons were preached on the supernatural appearance throughout the nation.

Machen was surprised, even shocked, by the reaction to his little story. He tried valiantly but unsuccessfully to make people re-

The Battle of Edge Hill

alize that he had really made the whole thing up. Indeed, he was denounced by some for denying the reality of the ghosts that he had invented. In those grim days of World War I, many in Britain were looking for hope and comfort from any source. The tale of the Angels of Mons filled a need, and thus they were given a reality that their creator had never intended.

CHRISTMAS GHOSTS   Today ghosts are most closely associated with the night before All Saints' Day, All Hallows' Eve, or Halloween. This is the time when, according to legend, the spirits of the dead and other supernatural or diabolical creatures are free to roam the earth until sunrise of the holy day.

But traditionally ghosts were most closely associated with a very different holiday—Christmas. Indeed, Christmas is the only holiday which has its own separate literary genre—the Christmas ghost story. The most famous of all Christmas stories, *A Christmas Carol* by Charles Dickens is a ghost story. Dickens even subtitled his famous tale *A Ghost Story of Christmas* so that everybody would know just what he was writing.

"There is probably a smell of roasted chestnuts and other good comfortable things all the time, for we are telling Winter stories—Ghost stories, or more shame for us—round the Christmas fire; and we have never stirred except to draw a little nearer to it."

Just how the tradition of Christmas ghosts got started is difficult to determine, like many traditions its origins are lost in the mists of unwritten history.

We do know that many Christian holidays replaced older pagan festivals and that Christmas seems to have replaced an ancient winter solstice celebration marking the shortest day of the year. Both the use of evergreens and the use of lights, symbols of hope and of the return of longer days, hark back to this ancient festival. The date for the birth of Christ is not given in the Bible and was not fixed by tradition until about the fourth century.

Christianity rarely purged all of the pagan elements from any festival—the egg and the rabbit, both fertility symbols, are still prominent at Easter time. And there seems to have been a generalized feeling that on the night before any holy day, the old gods and the old spirits still held power—hence All Hallows' Eve as the time of ghosts and demons. So from ancient times Christmas Eve may have retained some pagan and thus diabolical and ghostly associations.

But that certainly was not all. Christmas does come at the darkest time of the year. In the centuries before television people had to make their own entertainment during the long winter evenings. Sitting around telling stories is one of mankind's oldest forms of entertainment. And when people sit around and tell stories at night, these, as often as not, turn out to be ghost stories.

This in theory is how the tradition of Christmas ghosts began. But the tradition is hard to trace historically until relatively recent times.

In the late eighteenth century American author Washington Irving was traveling in England and recorded the events which surrounded a traditional English Christmas. Prominent among these activities was the telling of ghost stories round the fire.

But it appears that it was Dickens who really gave renewed life to the Christmas ghost tradition (along with a lot of other Christmas traditions) with his enormously popular story *A Christmas Carol* published in 1843. The story was instantly and phenomenally successful, and it has retained its high position ever since.

Other writers soon began producing Christmas ghost stories, and though they did not necessarily concern Christmas, they were most certainly ghost stories, and they appeared in magazines around Christmastime presumably for reading and retelling during the holiday season.

By about 1860 the Christmas ghost story became a regular feature of that curious British, and later American, publishing phenomenon known as the Christmas Annual. These were large

Marley's ghost

elaborately printed issues put out by most of the leading magazines at Christmastime. These publications were expensive and
were often given as gifts.

E. F. Bleiler, an expert on Victorian fiction, has written:

"It [The Christmas Annual] offered things to do. It entertained
the adults both individually and in groups. It gave ways to keep

under control the children who were home for the holidays—
games, charades, plays, songs, thrillers. Such was the heart of the
Victorian Christmas situation; the great family was to gather as a
social sacrament, once a year and everyone was to be merry or be
damned."

One of the entertainments contained in these Christmas An-
nuals was a ghost story, sometimes several of them. Much of the
best supernatural fiction of the era came from these Christmas an-
nuals. The tone of these tales can be discerned from this opening
passage of "The Last of Squire Ennismore" by Mrs. J. H. Riddell,
one of the most popular writers of Christmas ghost stories of the
last century:

"Did I see it myself? No sir; I did not see it, and my father before me did not see it, and his father before him, and he was Phil
Regan just the same as myself. But it is true, for all that; just as
true as you are looking at the very place where the whole thing
happened. My great-grandfather (and he did not die till he was
ninety-eight) used to tell, many and many's the time, how he met
the stranger, night after night, walking lonesome-like about the
sands where most of the wreckage came ashore."

Traditionally the Christmas ghost story started out with a statement that what was to follow was an absolutely true experience.

Not all Christmas ghost stories appeared in magazines. Many
families had their own tales and collections. One of the most celebrated personal collections was kept by Lord Halifax. Years later
his son wrote of what Christmastime was like at his home:

"As long as I can remember, my father's Ghost Book was one of
the most distinctive associations of Hickleton. He kept it always
with great care himself, from time to time making additions to it
in his own hand-writing and bringing it out on special occasions
such as Christmas to read some of the particular favorites aloud
before we all went to bed. Many's the time that after such an evening we children would hurry upstairs, feeling that the distance
between the library and our nurseries dimly lit by oil lamps and
full of shadows was a danger area where we would not willingly go

alone, and where it was unwise to dawdle.

"Such treatment of young nerves, even in those days, would not have been everybody's prescription; and I well recollect my mother protesting—though I believe almost inevitably to no effect—against 'the children being frightened too much.' . . . The victims themselves, fascinated and spell-bound by a sense of delicious terror, never failed to ask for more."

During the twentieth century the popularity of the Christmas Annual has faded, as has the custom of telling or reading ghost stories at Christmas—except of course *A Christmas Carol.* The specters of Christmas even have been almost entirely replaced by the jolly fat man in the red suit. But the era did leave behind a fine body of supernatural tales.

THE FLYING DUTCHMAN   There are countless legends of ghost and phantom ships, but certainly the most famous is the one about the ship called the *Flying Dutchman.* No one seems to know where or when this particular legend began. An early version of it appeared in a British magazine in 1821, and that version formed the basis for a short story, a play, and a well-known opera.

In the 1821 version of the legend there is a ship sailing around the Cape of Good Hope, the southern tip of Africa, when suddenly it encounters a terrible storm. The crew begs the captain to put into a safe harbor. Not only does the captain refuse, he laughs at their fears and tells them that he is afraid of nothing on earth or in Heaven. The captain then shuts himself up in his cabin drinking and smoking his pipe.

As the storm grows worse, the captain challenges God to sink his ship. At that a glowing form appears on the deck. The crew is terrified, but as usual the captain shows neither fear nor respect. He says to it, "Who wants a peaceful passage? I don't, I'm asking nothing from you. Clear out unless you want your brains blown out."

The ghost ship

The captain then draws his pistol and fires at the form, but the pistol explodes in his hand. Then the form pronounces a curse on the captain. He is doomed to sail forever, without rest. "And since it is your delight to torment sailors you shall torment them, for you shall be the evil spirit of the sea. Your ship shall bring misfortune to all who sight it."

That is the most widely known version of the legend of the *Flying Dutchman*. Oddly, though sailors were known to be immensely superstitious, this particular legend doesn't appear to have been widely believed by them.

One possible origin for the *Flying Dutchman* legend may be in the exploits of a seventeenth-century Dutch sea captain named

Bernard Fokke. Fokke was a daring and skilled mariner, and some of the voyages that he made were so remarkable that it was rumored that he had supernatural aid. Fokke's ship disappeared without a trace during a voyage, and this strengthened the rumor.

Legends of phantom ships were not only attached to the Cape of Good Hope. Captain Kidd's ship is said to sail around the New England coast with the old pirate still looking for his lost buried treasure. Another pirate ship, that of Jean Laffite, has been reported off Galveston, Texas. That is where Laffite's ship is believed to have sunk in the 1820s. In the nineteenth century an American ship named *Dash* vanished at sea. The ghost of that ship is supposed to return to port every so often in order to pick up the souls of crew member's families after they have died.

Ghost ship tales are not limited to the sea either. The Great Lakes, which are notoriously stormy and treacherous, have more

The captain of the
Flying Dutchman

than their share of vanished ships—and their attendant ghost tales. The best known of the Great Lakes phantom ships is the *Griffin*, property of the great French explorer Robert Cavelier de LaSalle. It was built at Niagara and first set sail on August 7, 1679. The *Griffin* was almost certainly the largest ship to sail the Great Lakes up to that time.

La Salle left the *Griffin* at Green Bay at the end of the first leg of its journey. He set out by canoe down the St. Joseph River searching for a river route to the Mississippi. The *Griffin* without La Salle set sail from Green Bay on September 18, 1679 bound back for Niagara. She never made it. She simply "sailed through a crack in the ice"—or so the legend goes. But on some nights lake men have reported seeing the ghostly *Griffin* looming out of the fog.

See also: THE GHOSTLY WANDERER

THE GREEN LADY   There is a valley in Banffshire, Scotland, said to once have been haunted by a Green Lady.

The wife of the local laird had died, and about six months later a ploughman on the laird's land was riding home one evening when he was stopped by a strange lady, clad from head to foot in green. She wore a large hood over her head so that he could not even see her face. She asked the ploughman to give her a ride across a small stream.

Collector of ghostly lore Peter Underwood writes:

"There was something in the tone of her voice that chilled the hearer and as he afterwards said, seemed to insinuate itself in the form of an icy fluid between his skull and his scalp. The request itself was odd for the stream was little more than a rivulet, small and slight presenting no problem to the most timid traveler."

But the man invited her to climb up on the horse, and she sprang up behind him with remarkable agility. As she sat behind him, she felt more like a "half-filled sack of wool" than a living human being.

When they reached the other side of the stream, the woman in green sprang down from the horse and pulled back her hood, revealing the face of the laird's dead wife. She told the ploughman to ride home and said that they would be better acquainted before long.

After this initial encounter the Green Lady appeared regularly to the servants of the house, though never to her husband. She always seemed to be interested in the welfare of the servants and in the running of the house. Indeed, she became such a regular visitor that while the servants first feared her, in time they remarked when she appeared that it was "only the Green Lady."

She looked pale and miserable—very ghostlike indeed, but she tried to keep up an appearance of cheerfulness and was often seen to laugh. Her laugh could sometimes be heard when she was not visible. Occasionally she was even playful. When a servant girl refused to answer her questions, the Green Lady playfully threw a pillow at her.

About a year after she first was seen, the Green Lady intervened dramatically in the affairs of the household. She appeared to the old family nurse and said that two of the children were in great danger at the seashore. The nurse alerted the laird, who rushed to the shore and found the two children clinging to a rock, just about to be swept away by the angry sea. He was able to save them.

When the nurse returned to her room, she found the Green Lady sitting by the fire. The ghost then told her the story of why she had come back from the grave. Two years before she died, a traveling peddler had broken into the fruit garden. She sent one of the servants to drive him away, but there was a fight and the peddler was killed. At first she wanted to tell the laird what had happened, but she saw that the dead man's pack as filled with lovely silks and velvets and one particularly beautiful piece of green satin. His purse also contained a large number of gold coins. So she and the servant buried the body and divided the goods and the gold between them. The gold was hidden behind a tapestry in her room, and the green satin was made into the dress that she continued to wear after death.

That was the last time that the Green Lady ever appeared to anyone in the house. When the place behind the tapestry in her room was examined, a small cache of gold coins was discovered. Later the remains of the peddler were also found, thus confirming the Green Lady's story.

GHOSTS OF FAIRYLAND   The lore of the "little people" or the "fairy folk" is enormously complex and involves a blending of many different traditions and beliefs, among them beliefs about the spirits of the dead.

According to the eminent British folklorist and expert on fairy lore Katherine Briggs:

"Sometimes the particular class of the dead is specified. The *Slaugh* or fairy hosts are the evil dead, according to Highland belief. *Finvarras* in Ireland seem to comprise the dead who have recently died as well as the ancient dead; but they are almost as sinister as the *Slaugh*. In Cornwall the Small People are the souls of the heathen dead, who died before Christianity and were not good enough for Heaven nor bad enough for Hell, and therefore lingered on, gradually shrinking until they became as small as ants, and disappeared altogether out of the world. . . . In Cornwall and Devon too the souls of unchristened babies were called Piskies and appeared at twilight in the form of little white moths. The Knockers in the mines were the souls of the dead too, but of the Jews who had been transported there for their part in the crucifixion."

During the eighteenth and nineteenth centuries, folklorists collected many statements from people who insisted that they had actually seen the fairy folk or at least knew someone who had. Such statements often indicated that the witness had recognized the forms of people who had recently died among the fairy folk.

In many stories mortals who enter fairyland are in fact entering a ghostlike state. The fairy folk and ghosts often cannot be seen or heard by other mortals except by those who possess special powers or second sight. In fairyland time is suspended so if a mortal is released by magic from fairyland, he may age suddenly, and if his captivity has been a long one, he will die of old age within a few minutes. However, for all the dancing and singing, fairyland is not considered to be a truly jolly place, and to enter it is not believed to be any more desirable than it is to enter the state of death.

Often people who died mysteriously or whose bodies were never found were said to be "taken by the fairies," and sometimes anciet burial mounds were thought of as "fairy hills."

See also: THE SLEEPING KNIGHTS

THE GHOSTLY PASSENGER   Lord Halifax, the celebrated British collector of ghostly accounts, considered this one of his favorite tales, and he always insisted that it was true and that he had heard it from the nephew of the man who actually had the experience.

Colonel Ewart was not at all the sort of person who would make up stories or start "seeing things." He was hardheaded and down-to-earth to the point of being downright stuffy. He wasn't very sociable either, and for that reason he hated traveling on trains, because he sometimes was forced to share his compartment with a total stranger.

However, travel was sometimes unavoidable, and one day the colonel had to take a train from the city of Carlisle, where he lived, to London. When he got to the station he was very relieved to see that the train was not at all crowded, and without any trouble he was able to secure a compartment for himself.

Now happy and relaxed, he took off his coat and boots in order to be more comfortable. Then he opened up a copy of the *Times* and prepared to read the day's news. But the train was warm and rocked gently as it sped toward London. The colonel found himself dozing over his newspaper, and it was not long before he had fallen deeply asleep and the paper slipped from his hand to the floor.

When Colonel Ewart awoke, he felt rather fuzzy-headed. He was not at all sure how long he had been asleep, but he assumed it must have been at least an hour, for his back and neck felt stiff and his mouth was very dry. He began to look around for his newspaper, and it was then that he realized that he was no longer alone in the compartment.

Sitting across from him was a woman in a black dress, her face almost completely hidden by a thick black veil.

The colonel was extremely embarrassed, for he was a very proper man and he felt that it was totally inappropriate for him to share a compartment with a lady while he was not wearing his coat and boots. He didn't know how long the woman had been sitting there, she must have come in quietly while he was asleep.

He quickly pulled on his boots and put on his coat and began to make his apologies. "I'm so sorry, madam, I didn't realize you had come in. I was asleep and thought I was alone!"

The woman said nothing; she did not even look up to acknowledge his presence.

Thinking that his fellow passenger might be a trifle deaf, the colonel repeated his apology more loudly. She still did not reply or look up. She was staring into her lap as though she were looking at something hidden in the folds of her skirt, but Colonel Ewart could not see what it might be, and he was of course far too polite to stand up and stare.

After a short time the woman began rocking back and forth and singing softly to herself. The tune sounded vaguely familiar to the colonel. He could not quite make it out, but it seemed like some sort of lullaby. The colonel was suddenly struck by the fear that the woman had a baby with her. Colonel Ewart could not abide children of any kind, and babies were the worst of all. He had a horrible vision of the infant screaming and crying all the way to London.

Then he thought if the woman were traveling with a baby she

must have some equipment for it. Babies always seemed to require trunkloads of paraphernalia for even the shortest trip. Yet the woman did not seem to have brought any luggage at all into the compartment.

Colonel Ewart was not normally a curious man, but the strange woman in black who now shared his compartment had aroused his curiosity. He really did want to get a look at what she had in her lap.

Suddenly all such thoughts were wiped from his mind, for there was a screech of metal wheels against metal rails; then came a crashing sound and a terrible jolt. Colonel Ewart was thrown foward, then pitched sharply backward. His suitcase which had been placed in the rack above his head went flying and struck him on the head. The blow was not a serious one, but it was enough to render him momentarily unconscious.

As a military man the colonel had faced danger and emergency situations many times. When he awoke, he did not panic. He got up slowly to make sure that he was not badly hurt. The only damage was a nasty bump on the head where the suitcase had hit him. Then he carefully left the train to see what had happened.

Outside there was mass confusion. People were running about shouting, but fortunately the accident had not been as bad as he first feared, although there were some injuries at the front end of the train. The colonel went forward to see if he could help. Only then did he remember his fellow passenger, the woman in the black dress. He realized he had left the train without checking on her condition. He rushed back to the compartment where he had been sitting, but it was empty. Was she there after the crash? He couldn't recall. The blow on the head must have left him a bit foggy.

The colonel searched among the passengers wandering around outside, but there was no sign of the woman. He talked to the trainmen, but they had not seen her. In fact, no one had seen her, at any time before or after the crash. The colonel was told that after he had boarded the train at Carlisle, the door to his compartment had been locked as was customary. No one could have entered the compartment. When he insisted that the woman had been there, the trainmen acted odd and evasive, as if they just didn't want to discuss the subject anymore.

It was months before Colonel Ewart found out more about his fellow passenger. He had described his experience many times, and one day he told it to a railway official he happened to meet. The man's reply was startling.

"So it happened again."

"What happened again?" demanded Colonel Ewart.

The railway official then told him that a few years past there had been a particularly horrible railway accident on the Carlisle to London run. A bride and bridegroom had been traveling on the line. It was the young man's first trip to London, and he was very excited. He was looking out the window and stuck his head out a little too far. His neck was caught by a wire, and the impact completely severed his head. The headless body fell back into the young bride's lap.

No one on the train had any idea of what had happened until the train pulled into London and they found the young woman sitting in the compartment holding the headless body. She was rocking back and forth, singing a lullaby to it. The shock of the ghastly accident had completely unhinged her mind.

The poor woman was committed to an institution but survived only a few months and never regained her sanity. She would sit for hours looking into her lap, rocking back and forth and singing the same lullaby.

From time to time after her death, the passengers on the Carlisle to London train had reported seeing the tragic and awful figure.

THE GHOSTLY WANDERER   One of the punishments that God laid upon Cain for the killing of his brother was that "A fugitive and a vagabond shalt thou be in the earth" (Gen. 4:12). Thus legends of accursed wanderers, such as the Wandering Jew and ghosts forced to wander the earth, have merged into several oft-repeated folkloric tales. A very popular version of this tale is one that was first told in the Boston area early in the nineteenth century. A complete version of this story is said to come in a letter from a man named William Austin, who claimed to have actually seen and spoken with the ghost.

In the letter Austin said that he first encountered the wanderer in 1826 when he was taking a coach out of Boston. The coach was so crowded that he was forced to sit up front with the driver. They had gone a few miles when Austin noticed that the horses were becoming very nervous. The driver then told him that they were about to have a storm. This seemed very strange to Austin since there wasn't a cloud in the sky. But the driver said matter-of-factly that they were about to meet "the storm breeder"—the horses always knew first.

The storm breeder was a man driving an open carriage and who was accompanied by a young girl. The carriage drove by quickly, but it seemed to be pursued by rain clouds. Shortly after the carriage passed, the rain clouds disappeared.

The driver of the coach told Austin that he had seen the man and child many times before. Once the man had stopped and asked the way to Boston; the driver pointed out to him that he was going in the wrong direction, but the man simply refused to listen. After that the coach driver decided that he would no longer even bother to speak to the obstinate fellow. He had no idea who the man was, and from what he heard from other drivers, he learned that the man stopped only to ask the directions to Boston and insist that he had to reach it that very night. However, he never paid any attention to the directions he was given.

Three years later, when Austin had nearly forgotten the strange incident, he met the wanderer again. He was staying at a hotel in Hartford, Connecticut, and one evening while standing on the front porch of the hotel, he heard a man say, "Here comes Peter Rugg and his child. He looks wet and weary and farther from Boston than ever!" From a distance came the same carriage, the same driver and passenger, and the same trailing storm clouds that he had seen on the road to Boston. The carriage was heading straight for the hotel.

The stranger told Austin that he had seen Peter Rugg twenty years earlier. He had been asked the way to Boston; when he was told he was going in the wrong direction, Rugg replied:

"Alas! It is all turn back! Boston shifts with the wind and plays all around the compass. One man tells me it is to the east, another to west, and the guideposts too, all point the wrong way!"

As Rugg neared the hotel, Austin decided to speak to him. He stepped out into the road and waved down the carriage.

"Are you Peter Rugg?" he asked.

"My name is Peter Rugg," said the man. "I have unfortunately lost my way. Will you please direct me to Boston?"

"You live in Boston? On what street?"

"On Middle Street."

"When did you leave Boston?"

"I don't know exactly, it must have been some time ago."

"But how did you and your child get so wet? It has not rained here today."

"There has been a heavy shower up the river. But I shall not reach Boston tonight if I tarry. Which road do I take to Boston?"

Rugg was then told that he was in Connecticut and over one hundred miles from Boston, but Rugg refused to believe this and insisted that he was forty miles or less from Boston. He drove off rapidly.

Austin now had a clue to the puzzle, and he decided that the next time he was in Boston, he would try to find out more about the mysterious traveler.

When Austin did get to Boston, he found an old lady named Croft who had been living on Middle Street for many years. The woman told him that she had actually been visited by Peter Rugg. One evening Rugg had come to her door asking for a Mrs. Rugg. She told him that a Mrs. Rugg had once lived in the house, but that she had died many years ago and was quite old at the time. Rugg insisted that there must have been some sort of mistake and he asked a lot of questions which indicated that he did not know that Boston had grown and changed. His horse became impatient, and Rugg rushed away muttering, "No home tonight."

For further information Mrs. Croft directed Austin to the house of James Felt. Felt was over eighty and had lived in the same home for fifty years. He knew the story of Peter Rugg, for he had heard it from his grandfather.

In about 1730 a man named Peter Rugg had lived on Middle Street. Rugg was a stubborn man with a fierce temper and would take advice from no one. One autumn morning Rugg took his little daughter for a drive to the town of Concord. On the way back he stopped at the house of a friend who warned him that a storm was approaching.

"Let the storm increase," swore Rugg. "I will see home tonight in spite of the storm, or may I never see home!"

With these words, he whipped his horse and disappeared into the night. He did not get home that night or the next or any other night. No trace of him or his daughter was ever found.

See also: THE FLYING DUTCHMAN

THE HIGHLAND SOLDIER   There are endless tales of ghosts returning in order to avenge their murder, but this one related by Francis Thompson in his book *Ghosts, Spirits and Spectres of Scotland* has a rather curious and singular twist.

A young man who worked at a hunting lodge was having his hair cut by the coachman. The coachman remarked that the young man had a lump on the side of his head that was not there the last time he had his hair cut. When he heard this, the young man became extremely pale and upset. He said that he now could tell his story, and he asked the coachman to invite others in to hear it.

"You know that it is part of my duty to cross Cnoc-na-moine very often after it is dark, and many a time I did it, but although there were strange stories about the little hollow near the top, I did not think much about them, and if they did come into my mind, I just whistled to myself to keep my courage. Exactly one year ago today I was going home along the path as usual, but I felt quite cheery, as I had got a good tip from the gentleman who was leaving the lodge. Suddenly, just at the nasty place, I was met by a big strong fellow, well dressed in full Highland garb, but just a little old-fashioned, I thought. I said in Gaelic: 'In the name of the Trinity, if you come from heaven or hell and have anything to say, I shall listen.'

"The ghost replied: 'That is why I am here. I was murdered on this very spot one hundred and twenty-four years ago, and I am allowed to visit it once a year ever since on the anniversary of the murder to tell it to someone ere I can be allowed to rest in the place I have been sent to. I have never met anyone before who spoke to me, and I want to tell you that I was coming home from the south with some money when two brothers of the name A——who lived at B—— set on me, killed me, and took my money and then buried my body. As my people did not know that I was coming, the murderers were never found out and were never suspected to be what they were. They built a good house with the money, and their descendants occupy it to this day, and now I want you to tell the people of the place who murdered me.' "

The young man's reply was "Mr. A—— will hate me and try to do me harm if I tell such a story of his ancestors, and they are good enough neighbors to me just now."

The ghost said, "If you don't tell, you will find that I can do you harm. You will find that if you keep my secret soon a lump will begin to grow on your head and will press on your brain so that you will become mad, and in your madness you will tell the secret. It is better for you to tell it before that happens."

The ghost of the highland soldier then disappeared. The young man said that he was afraid to tell anyone, but now that he had cleared his conscience, he hoped that the lump would also disappear.

Once the story spread, it was thought that the A—— family would deny it, but they did not. It is not recorded whether the young man recovered or not.

⊔IGH SCHOOL AND COLLEGE GHOSTS   Ghost stories

of one sort or another are an integral part of high school and college life in the United States. Often the tales are local variations of popular legends, such as the phantom hitchhiker. But there are some stories that are firmly rooted in a particular area. Here are some examples:

At the University of Indiana there are some very old buildings on campus. One of them, now a girls' dorm, is reputed to be haunted. Generations of Indiana students have passed down the story of how this haunting came about.

This particular building had once been a men's dorm, and there was a medical student who had a room on the third floor. He had been sneaking his girl friend into the room for some time. One evening, when they were up in the room together, she told the medical student that she was pregnant and that they would have to get married.

With that announcement the medical student saw his whole world crumbling. Everything that he had worked for and dreamed about would be suddenly swept away. If he had to get married, he would never be able to finish medical school. Besides, he had tired of the girl anyway.

It was all her fault, he thought. The medical student became enraged, almost insane with fury. He grabbed for one of the scalpels that he kept for dissection and stabbed the girl in the throat. She died without being able to make a sound.

The medical student then waited until it was very late and the corridors of the dorm were deserted. He carried the girl's body down to the building's huge basement and hid it in an unused passageway, hoping that it would never be found. But after the girl was missing for a few days, the police began making inquiries. They found out the medical student was her boy friend, and when they began to question him, he broke down and confessed what he had done. He then led them to the body he had hidden.

The murdered girl's ghost, it is said, still haunts the old building, which has since been turned into a girls' dorm. Those who have seen her say that she has long black hair and wears a yellow nightgown.

A fairly innocuous ghost is said to haunt Payola High School in Kansas. The story of the ghost runs this way. In the school band there was a trumpet player who played second chair. He was a very ambitious young man and anxious to make first chair. He practiced and practiced, but although he was good, he was never quite good enough to make first chair. Still he kept right on practicing.

One night the band was playing out at the football field, and the band director realized that he had forgotten some important sheet music at the school. He called for a volunteer to go back to pick up the music; the ambitious trumpet player shot his hand up first. The sheet music was stored in a room above the stage that could be reached only by a winding flight of metal steps. The footing on the stairs was tricky, and as the trumpet player came down the steps, his arms laden with sheet music, his foot slipped and he fell, striking his head on the metal steps. The blow to the head killed him.

But today, so the story goes, if you drive past the front of the high school on a warm summer night when the school doors are kept open, you can hear the sound of a ghostly trumpet coming from inside. It's the trumpet player still practicing, still trying to make first chair.

A far more ominous legend is attached to a park in New Orleans. The park is haunted by the ghost of a girl called Marie. In life Marie was a teenager who was very much in love with a worthless fellow named Bob. She became pregnant by him and wanted to marry him.

Bob had other ideas, and he had no intention at all of getting tied down with a wife and kid. So one night he took Marie walking in the park, and when they reached a deserted spot, he stabbed her and hoped that the killing would be blamed on some unknown mugger or sex maniac. Bob wasn't very bright, and the police found plenty of evidence linking him to the crime. When the police brought him in for questioning, he broke down and confessed, and he is still in prison today.

Marie's ghost is still in the park. The ghost carries the bloody knife with which she was murdered and is supposed to perform horrible mutilations on any young man caught in the park at night.

It has been rumored that this story was actually encouraged or even begun by the New Orleans police in order to keep teenagers out of the park at night.

See also: THE PHANTOM HITCHHIKER

HOMER'S GHOSTS   To the ancient Greeks ghosts were to be more pitied than feared. This attitude is expressed most clearly in Homer's *Odyssey*. When Odysseus asks how long it will be before he returns home from his wanderings, he is told that he must descend into the underworld and question the ghost or shade of the great prophet Tiresias.

As Odysseus descended into the gloomy twilight world, the phantoms of the dead crowded around him but were so weak and insubstantial that they hardly had enough strength to speak. Odysseus dug a pit and filled it with the blood of sacrificed animals, but he had to keep the ghosts at bay with his sword until the spirit of Tiresias appeared to drink first.

The lot of these shades in the underworld was a miserable one. The great hero Achilles, now a pale shade, informs Odysseus, "I had rather be a poor man's serf than king over all the dead."

But if the underworld was bad, the prospect of roaming the

earth as a spirit was even worse. Not only were such spirits miserable, they were a potential danger to the living. Greek soldiers would sometimes cut the feet off of enemies they had slain in battle. The hope was that the crippled ghost would then be unable to pursue its killer effectively.

The best way to assure that the spirits of the dead would rest easily and not trouble the living was to make sure that the body was properly buried. While in the underworld, Odysseus met the ghost of one of his sailors who had been killed but had not been buried. The ghost warned Odysseus not to tempt the wrath of the gods by allowing his corpse to remain unburied.

The Greeks and many other ancient peoples would go to great lengths to make sure that their dead were properly interred. One of the greatest of all the Greek plays concerns the efforts of Antigone to obtain a proper burial for the remains of her brother. Even today the elaborate lengths to which people will go to recover the bodies of the dead can be traced back, at least in part, to the ancient fear that if a body lies unburied its ghost may return to torment the living.

La LLORNA   Among the Mexicans and Mexican-Americans there is a widespread belief in a ghostly figure called La Llorna— the weeping woman. There are many different versions of the La Llorna story, but the basic theme is this: La Llorna is the spirit or ghost of a woman who had several children but had fallen in love with a man who didn't want any children. In order to please her lover, she drowned her own children, but then, overcome by remorse, she drowned herself. Now her ghost, usually dressed in a flowing black garment, can be seen walking along the side of the river, eternally weeping for her lost children.

In many versions of the La Llorna story, the figure has become a symbol of impending death—like the banshee in Ireland. Anyone who sees La Llorna is destined to die within a year. Or less drastically anyone who sees the figure will have extremely bad luck within the next year.

In other versions of the story, however, La Llorna is more human; people have reported meeting and actually talking to her, and she tells them her terrible story. In some places La Llorna has become the hitchhiker in the popular phantom hitchhiker legend. A man is driving along a deserted road and sees a weeping woman standing by the side of the road. He stops to pick her up; she tells her story and then disappears from the car.

See also: THE PHANTOM HITCHHIKER

THE PHANTOM HITCHHIKER   Unquestionably the most popular and widespread ghostly legend in the United States is the story of the phantom hitchhiker. It is told in all parts of the country with endless local variations. Basically the story is this:

A young man is driving home very late one rainy Saturday night. He finds himself on a deserted road. Suddenly his headlights catch a figure in white standing by the side of the road. As he gets closer he sees that it is a girl of about sixteen or seventeen who is wearing a white party dress. She is trying to hitch a ride. The young man pulls up near the girl in the white dress and asks her where she is going. She gives him an address in the city; he says he is going by the area and will take her right to the door. She thanks him and climbs into the backseat of the two-door car. The man now sees clearly how wet and sad-looking the girl is. She has been thoroughly chilled by the rain and is shivering, so he offers her his jacket. She takes it and thanks him.

He starts the car up and delivers a short lecture on the dangers of hitchhiking, particularly at night. The girl in the back seat does not respond. The driver wants to ask her what she was doing on such a deserted road at that time of night, but he figures that she is tired and has fallen asleep so he doesn't want to disturb her. "Besides," he thinks, "it's really none of my business."

It takes about half an hour to get to the city. During that time the car doesn't stop once, and the girl says nothing. The driver cannot even see her in the rearview mirror, and so he assumes she is stretched out on the back seat.

He finally reaches the address which he has been given and stops the car. The house looks rather deserted, so he turns around to ask the girl if this is the place. When he looks in the back seat, he discovers that it is empty.

He has driven for half an hour without stopping once—there is no possible way anyone could have gotten out of his two-door car without his knowing about it, and yet the girl is gone. Puzzled and now more than a little frightened, the man gets out of the car and goes up to the house. It looks empty, but when he knocks on the door, he sees a light go on and hears the sound of slippered footsteps scuffing down the hall. The door is opened by a frazzled-looking middle-aged woman who has obviously been roused from a deep sleep. There is something about her that seems familiar, but the young man can't quite put his finger on what it is.

He apologizes for waking her, but says that he has just had such a strange experience that he feels compelled to talk about it. As he tells his story, the man realizes just how crazy it sounds. But the woman does not slam the door in his face or laugh at him as he fully expects that she will. Instead she listens silently with a sympathetic look on her face. When the story is over, the woman says quietly:

"I was expecting you, because you're not the first young man to come by and tell that story. The girl you picked up is my daughter! She's dead; she was killed in an automobile accident on the road where you found her ten years ago. She was coming home from a party on a rainy Saturday night just like this one when the car she was riding in skidded out of control. Ever since then on rainy Saturday nights people have found her hitchhiking. We think that she's trying to get home."

The man is quite startled by what he is told. He goes back to his car thinking that this is all some sort of dream or hallucination. He tries to convince himself that he has never picked up a hitchhiker at all. When he gets back to his car he feels cold, so he reaches for his jacket. It's gone. He has given it to the girl in the white dress.

Now the young man knows that something has happened. He goes back to the house and checks the name on the door. The next day he goes to the cemetery and finds the family plot. He locates the grave of the girl and finds she has indeed died ten years ago. And there, on top of the tombstone, neatly folded, is his missing jacket!

This is the basic story. Sometimes it is told in a shortened version which ends simply when the woman says that's my daughter; she's dead. In other versions the man recognizes the photo of the girl on the wall.

As with most folklore the story is generally localized, so that no matter where it is told, it always seems to have happened just a few miles away. These hitchhiking ghosts sometimes become locally famous. One Chicago version of the phantom hitchhiker is known as Resurrection Mary because she is supposed to have been buried in Resurrection Cemetery.

There have been more exotic variations of the legend, some with religious overtones. From time to time there have been reports of drivers who pick up a bearded stranger hitchhiking. This stranger makes some prophetic statements about the end of the world and then disappears. At other times it has been a hitchhiking nun who makes the prophecies and disappears.

Among the Chicanos there is the ghostly figure of La Llorna, the weeping woman. And so among the Chicanos the vanishing hitchhiker sometimes is La Llorna.

No one seems to know where this particular legend began, but it has been making its way around the country for at least a century. There are also similar tales from other countries, but whether they are directly related to the phantom hitchhiker story is impossible to say.

See also: LA LLORNA, RIDE WITH THE DEAD

THE PLEA FOR HELP   The ghost who tries, usually in vain, to summon help for a person about to die is a common theme in legend, lore, and supernatural fiction. One version of this tale appeared in a December 16, 1890, edition of a Russian newspaper, the *Citizen* of St. Petersburg. It concerns a young man who was visited by a priest. The priest, it seems, has been told by an old woman he does not know to go out and administer the sacraments to a sick man in the apartment. But the young man is the only occupant of that apartment, and he is not sick. The priest then recognizes the old woman who told him to make the visit from a painting on the wall of the apartment.

"That is the portrait of my dead mother," says the young man. He takes the sacraments, and that evening he is dead.

The story was reported as one that is "going about town" and is "worthy of attention." It must be noted, however, that Russian newspapers of that era, like many other newspapers of the time, were extremely fond of printing hoaxes, stories that were totally without foundation but presented as regular news items. The newspaper hoax might almost be considered a separate literary genre. The readers of the time were usually aware of the nature of the material that they were reading, but later researchers have sometimes been taken in.

However, a tale very similar to this one was also collected by the British Society for Psychical Research in the 1920s, and it appears in one of their journals.

In the United States the tale often involves a doctor who is visited by an elderly lady and told that he must rush to the bedside of a gravely ill patient. When the doctor arrives, he finds the prospective patient alive and well. But then he sees the portrait of the lady who visited him hanging on the wall. The "patient" announces that that is a portrait of his long-dead mother. Within a few hours he falls prey to a mysterious and rapidly fatal disease.

Folklorist Jan Harold Brunvand, who has studied this tradition, points out that the story many similar to the extremely popular phantom hitchhiker legend. Often in that story the person who has picked up the hitchhiker sees a photograph and identifies it as the girl he picked up who has disappeared so mysteriously from his car. The response is always something like this:

"That is a picture of my daughter. She was killed ten years ago at the very spot that you picked up the hitchhiker."

See also: THE PHANTOM HITCHHIKER

RIDE WITH THE DEAD

An Armenian tale from Turkey tells of a young man who was traveling on horseback through a part of the country with which he was not familiar. He had been badly delayed on his trip and now felt compelled to ride straight through the night.

Just as it began to get dark, he passed a cemetery and saw a young lady sitting at the roadside crying softly. He stopped his horse and asked her what was wrong. She told him that she was due in a distant town by morning, but that she was far too tired and weak to make the entire journey at night.

Since the young man happened to be going past that very town, he told the girl to climb onto his horse and he would take her along. He had her sit in front of him so that he would be able to keep a good grip on her lest she fall off.

As they rode into the night, the girl didn't say a word, and the young man noticed that she was becoming harder and harder to hold. It almost seemed as if she were getting heavier. At first he thought it was his imagination and that the feeling that she was getting heavier was brought on by fatigue. But soon there was no mistaking it, the girl was really getting heavier. He tried to stop his horse, but the horse seemed to be driven by some powerful fear and refused to stop.

Finally at dawn the rider reached the town that had been the girl's destination. The horse suddenly stopped of its own accord. When he dismounted and tried to help the girl down, she tumbled off the horse and sprawled on the ground. She was dead. He had ridden through the night with a corpse!

A few early risers had gathered around to watch the scene, and the young man was suddenly frightened by the thought that they would think that he was somehow responsible for the girl's death. He tried to explain what had happened to them, though the explanation didn't really make much sense even to him. But the onlookers merely nodded their heads in agreement and said that they understood.

They went on to explain that this sort of thing had happened before. The dead girl on the ground had once lived in the village but had been killed in a distant town some ten years past. Her family decided to bury her where she had died, but each year, on the anniversay of her death, she appeared to make an attempt to return to her native village. The villagers assured the young man that the girl's relatives would be by in a short time to claim the corpse and rebury it.

See also: THE PHANTOM HITCHHIKER

RADIANT BOYS   Throughout Europe there are legends of Radiant Boys, the apparitions of a young boy usually surrounded by a glowing light or flame. Some believe that the Radiant Boys are creatures of the spirit world who have just taken on the form of human boys—but were themselves never human. However, majority opinion holds that the Radiant Boys are the ghosts of children murdered by their parents.

Everyone agrees that the appearance of one of these glowing figures is a portent of evil for all those who see it.

The most celebrated of the many tales concerning Radiant Boys is the one about the apparition's appearance to the early-nineteenth-century English statesman Viscount Castlereagh.

While still a young man, Castlereagh was out hunting in Ireland. A sudden and violent storm broke and caused him to lose his way. He was fortunate to be able to locate a large house, and though he had never been to the house before, he knocked on the door and asked for shelter from the storm

The house was already filled with guests, many of whom, like Castlereagh himself, had been forced to take shelter from the storm. The host said that he was sure his butler would be able to find a place to accommodate yet another guest. So after a good dinner Castlereagh was shown to his room. It was a strange sort of room, for though it was quite large, it contained no furniture of any kind and had obviously not been in use for many years. The only thing for the guest to sleep on was a mattress hastily thrown near the fireplace, which was blazing with an unusually large fire.

Castlereagh was far too tired to worry about the oddness of his accommodations. He lay down on the mattress by the fire and was soon sound asleep. A couple of hours later he was awakened by a sudden increase in the light. At first Castlereagh thought that the room was on fire. Yet when he looked into the fireplace, he found the fire had actually died out.

The light was coming from the form of a beautiful young boy who seemed to be gazing intently at him. After a moment the form began to fade and finally disappeared entirely.

For a moment Castlereagh was frightened, but as he thought about what had happened, he became convinced that somehow he had been made the object of a practical joke. He was not a man known for his sense of humor, and so he rapidly became extremely angry.

The following morning Castlereagh announced to his host his intention of leaving the house at once. When his surprised host asked him what had happened, Castlereagh grudgingly told of his experience the previous night, adding that he was sure he was the victim of a hoax. His host at first seemed inclined to agree with the hoax theory but insisted that he had nothing to do with it. The other guests were questioned, and all swore they knew nothing.

Finally the host called his butler. He asked the servant where Castlereagh had slept. Haltingly the butler admitted that he had put the extra guest in "the boy's room" because there was no other place available in the crowded house. The butler added that he had lit a blazing fire to keep "him" out.

The owner of the house was furious and reminded the butler of his strict instructions that under no circumstances was anyone ever to spend a night in "the boy's room."

He then took Castlereagh aside to explain what had happened. The glowing figure, he said, was the spirit of one of his own ancestors. Many years ago the boy, who was only nine or ten at the time, had been murdered by his own mother during a fit of madness. The murder had taken place in the very room in which Castlereagh had spent the night. Since the murder the boy's blazing spirit had been seen in the room from time to time.

Unfortunately there was more to the story, and this part Castlereagh's host related slowly and gravely. The appearance of the glowing phantom was thought to be an evil portent for anyone who saw it. It meant two things; first it meant that the person would have a period of great prosperity, but then at the height of his power he would die violently.

This news did not greatly trouble Castlereagh. At that time he was only the second son of the Marquis of Londonderry and not destined to be heir. His older brother was in excellent health. In the normal course of events he had no reason to expect great prosperity. He had chosen a military career, and so the warning of a sudden and violent death did not surprise or worry him.

But within a few years Castlereagh's prospects took a dramatic turn. His eldest brother was drowned in a boating accident and he became heir apparent. He then left the army and went into politics, where he displayed talents that had not previously been suspected. Very rapidly he became one of the most powerful men in England.

Though his political accomplishments were enormous, Castlereagh was never a popular man. He was a cold and often hostile person who made few friends. He was also a complex and deeply troubled man, and by 1822 his contradictory nature and the great strains of his work began to take their toll. He became violently suspicious of everyone around him. His mental state became so alarming that he was confined to his country home. His family feared for his safety, so all razors and other sharp objects were removed from his rooms. But on August 12, 1822, Viscount Castlereagh found a penknife with which he was able to cut his own throat.

There are a number of versions of the Castlereagh story extant. One told by the author Edward Bulwer-Lytton (later Baron Lytton of Knebworth) places the appearance of the apparition much later in the viscount's life.

According to Bulwer-Lytton, Castlereagh had stayed at Knebworth, the seat of the Lytton family, during his grandfather's time. One morning Castlereagh came down to breakfast looking haggard and pale. He told his host that he had seen a strangely dressed boy with long yellow hair sitting in front of the fire in his room. The boy drew his fingers across his throat three times, then vanished. A short time later Castlereagh cut his own throat.

Bulwer-Lytton called the phantom the Yellow Boy and would challenge guests to spend a night in "the haunted room." Lytton would occasionally sneak up to the room and frighten his guests. He had an odd sense of humor.

Bulwer-Lytton had another Radiant Boy story. This one concerned his own family. One of Bulwer-Lytton's eighteenth century ancestors, Thomas Lytton, was known in his own day as the Bad Lord Lytton. He was reported to have seen one of the flaming apparitions shortly before the end of his own dissipated life.

The figure of a boy dressed in white appeared beside his bed one evening and announced that he had very little more time to live. "How long?" demanded Lord Lytton. "Weeks, months, perhaps a year?"

"You will die within three days," replied the figure.

Lytton was very much alarmed and depressed by the grim prediction. He told his servants and friends about it and tried to maintain a brave front by saying that he felt as well as he ever had in his life.

But as he went to bed at eleven in the evening of the third day, Lord Lytton was almost beginning to feel as cheerful as he had tried to sound. "If I live over tonight, I shall have jockeyed the ghost, for this is the third day," he told his servant.

The servant left the room briefly; when he returned Lytton was having a choking fit. Lytton had been subject to such fits before and the servant might have been able to help him. But with the ghost's prediction weighing on his mind, the terrified servant dashed from the room, and the Bad Lord Lytton died before the clock struck midnight.

The most persistent of the Radiant Boy legends in England are attached to a place called Corby Castle, owned by the Howard family. The house isn't really a castle but a pleasant country manor house. However, the site on which it stands had been used as a fortification since Roman times. Part of the ruins of a Roman tower had been incorporated into the structure of the house. The room haunted by the Radiant Boy is in the older part of the house adjoining the Roman tower.

No one seems to know how the Radiant Boy stories became attached to Corby Castle, but the Howard family certainly did not take them seriously until September 1803. At that time the family held a large house party, and the haunted room was given to the rector of Greystoke and his wife. The next morning the couple fled, refusing to give any explanation for their sudden departure.

A few days later Howard visited the rector, who had recovered a bit from his experience and was able to talk about it. He said that in the middle of the night he had been awakened by a bright flame. Like others who have confronted the Radiant Boy, the rector too first thought that the room was on fire. Then he saw a boy with long golden hair and all clothed in white standing near the bed.

While the rector of Greystoke was terrified by his experience, he was also acutely embarrassed, for such things were not supposed to happen to clergymen. He made Howard promise never to speak of the incident. However, the rector himself began repeating the story in a few months.

In this case no evil seems to have befallen the person who saw the Radiant Boy. The rector of Greystoke was still repeating his tale of the encounter with the Radiant Boy of Corby Castle twenty years later.

See also: LA LLORNA

THE SLEEPING KNIGHTS

THE SLEEPING KNIGHTS   The legend of the "sleeping hero" is a common one throughout the world. The best-known version of this legend concerns King Arthur, who was supposed to have been gravely wounded in his last battle and borne off to the Isle of Avalon where he "sleeps," until some future time when he is needed and will awaken to again lead his people. The location of the Isle of Avalon was never specified in the legends, so there are all sorts of locations throughout the British Isles where Arthur is supposed to "sleep." The ghost or form of the sleeping king is reported regularly at certain places associated by tradition with Arthur, Glastonbury Abbey, for example, or Tintagel Castle in Cornwall. Some traditions hold that he is allowed to awaken one day a year.

The power of the sleeping hero legend is not to be underestimated, for it has not always been regarded as merely a charming tale. More than once an impostor claiming to be the reawakened form of some fallen king or hero has come in out of the wilderness and convinced a large number of people of the truth of his claim.

Frederick II, the Holy Roman Emperor, had a remarkable if brief career. During his lifetime there were many prophecies proclaiming that he was the new messiah—a story that Frederick may have actually encouraged and possibly even believed. His enemies were as fanatical as his friends, for they proclaimed him to be the

Arthur being taken to the Isle of Avalon

Antichrist. When he died suddenly in 1250, there was a sense of shock and disbelief, for during his lifetime he had seemed more than human.

The legend spread that Frederick was not really dead but merely "sleeping" and more than thirty years after his death, two different imposters, each claiming to be the reawakened Frederick, appeared in widely separated parts of Germany. One of them gathered a huge following, including several powerful princes who probably didn't believe the story but were using it for their own political advantage. Eventually both pretenders were executed, but not before they had caused the established authorities a great deal of anxiety. Rulers often went to great lengths to prove that their predecessors were really dead and not just sleeping.

Arthur is only the most celebrated of the sleeping heroes; in Britain there are many others. Most of these tales represent a mixture of ghostlore, magic, and historical myth, and it is generally held that bad luck will come to anyone who encounters the sleepers.

Typical of the legends of the genre are the stories attached to a small spur of the Eildon Hills in Scotland. The spot is known as Lucken Hare. It has associations with King Arthur as well as with the legendary magician and seer Thomas the Rhymer.

A popular story dating from the eighteenth century tells of an amorous horse trader named Dick Canonbie. One night, when Dick was on the run from a jealous husband, he tried hiding out in Lucken Hare. Though the area was usually completely deserted, Dick met an imposing white-bearded old man wearing a flowing cloak. Dick asked the old man what he wanted, and the old man replied that he wished to buy some black horses and was willing to pay a good price for them. Always on the lookout for a favorable deal, Dick sold the man all the black horses he had and was paid in gold coins with strange symbols and pictures on them. Strange or not, the gold was good, and Dick was well pleased with his bargain. The stranger then offered to buy more black horses the next month for the same price. Dick readily agreed.

The horse trader made several sales to the strange old man at Lucken Hare, always receiving the same kind of gold coins in payment. Finally Dick began to get curious about his customer and asked him where he lived, since there seemed to be no habitations about. The old man tried to put him off. Dick persisted in his request, and the old man finally agreed to show him his home. But he said that Dick would see things that would test his courage and if his courage failed the results might be disastrous for him.

Dick followed the strange old man up the slope of Lucken Hare and to the entrance of a deep cave. The vast interior of the cave was lighted by flickering torches on the walls.

There was more to come, for carved into the walls of the cave were stalls, and in each stall stood a coal black horse. At the foot of each stall lay a knight in black armor. Both horse and knight seemed to be alive but were unmoving.

At the center of the cave was a massive oaken table carved with mystic signs and symbols. On the table lay a sword and a hunting horn. The old man said, "Since you have been rash enough to intrude upon the realm of mystery and secret knowledge long forsaken and forgotten by the world of men, a choice is forced upon you. Either draw the sword or blow the horn. One or the other you must do. Chose correctly and you will reign here as king; chose badly and you forfeit your life. Trifle not with me for I am Thomas the Rhymer."

When he heard the name of the great magician and seer, Dick knew that he was in serious trouble. He thought, what if the knights should awake and see him with a sword. It was better to awaken them first with the horn.

He blew the horn, and the knights began to stir, but the glances they gave him were not friendly. He grabbed the sword in order to defend himself, but against such a horde any fight would be hopeless. The magician had disappeared, but Dick could still hear his voice echoing through the cave: "Woe to the coward, that ever was born; who did not draw the sword, before he blew the horn."

The knights set upon him and then carried his nearly lifeless body out of the cave and dumped it on the hillside. He was found the next morning by shepherds who tried to help him, but it was too late. Dick lived only long enough to gasp out the story that has been related here.

See also: GHOSTS OF FAIRYLAND, THE GHOSTLY MONKS OF GLAS-TONBURY

ANNOTATED

BIBLIOGRAPHY

Any attempt to list all the books on ghosts is as hopeless as an attempt to list all the ghosts. What follows is a listing of books that I have found unusually useful in compiling this encyclopedia and books that I found interesting, significant, revealing, or just plain enjoyable, even if I did not make extensive use of them.

No serious student of ghosts, spiritualism, and psychical research should overlook Frank Podmore's classic study, *Mediums of the Nineteenth Century*. It was republished in two volumes by University Books in 1962. As an investigation of the spiritualist or psychic scene, this book has never been surpassed and probably never will be.

In 1962 University Books also republished a revised edition of *Phantasms of the Living*, edited by Eleanor Sidgwick, a collection of the best of the investigations of the founders of psychical research. And while on that subject, Alan Gauld's *Founders of Psychical Research* (New York: Schocken Books, 1968) provides a great deal of insight into the lives of these extraordinary individuals.

In specialized areas there are books like the revised edition of G. N. M. Tyrrell's *Apparitions* (London: Gerald Duckworth, 1953) and D. Scott Rogo's *The Poltergeist Experience* (New York: Penguin, 1979), which also contains an excellent bibliography of other poltergeist books, and

305

there are lots of them. Perhaps the most complete book on animal ghosts is Raymond Bayless's appropriately titled *Animal Ghosts* (New Hyde Park, N.Y.: University Books, 1970).

The skeptical magician Milbourne Christopher tells of his experiences with poltergeists, among other things, in his book *ESP, Seers and Psychics: What the Occult Is* (New York.: Thomas Y. Crowell & Co., 1970). Christopher's biography of Houdini, *Houdini: The Untold Story* (New York: Thomas Y. Crowell & Co., 1969) gives one version of the Houdini–Margery–Arthur Ford situation.

E. J. Dingwall, K. M. Goldney, and Trevor H. Hall's demolishing of Borley Rectory and Harry Price, *Haunting of Borley Rectory* (London: Gerald Duckworth, 1955) is another must for serious students, as is Dingwall's and Hall's *Four Modern Ghosts* (London: Gerald Duckworth, 1958) and Hall's *New Light on Old Ghosts* (London: Gerald Duckworth, 1965) and *The Spiritualists*, the story of Florence Cook and William Crookes (New York: Helix Press, 1963). Dingwall, Hall, and Goldney are all pillars of the British psychical research establishment, but they have made themselves unpopular by exposing some of the follies and frauds of their colleagues.

There have been a fair number of popular books on early spiritualism in America and England. Three that I enjoyed were Slater Brown's *The Heyday of Spiritualism* (New York: Hawthorn Books, 1969), Ronald Pearsall's *The Table-Rappers* (New York: St. Martin's Press, 1972), and Robert Somerlott's *"Here, Mr. Splitfoot"* (New York: Viking Press, 1972).

The best-seller type of ghost books such as *The Amityville Horror* by Jay Anson (Englewood Cliffs, N.J.: Prentice-Hall, 1977) and *The Ghost of Flight 401* by John G. Fuller (New York: Putnam, 1976) can be read for enjoyment or simply because everybody else is reading them, but they should not be treated as serious psychical research.

There are hundreds of books of "true" ghost stories, mostly, it seems, from England. These should also be read strictly for entertainment. One that I enjoyed is *Haunted Houses* by Joseph Braddock (London: B. T. Batsford, 1956). Any of the numerous books by Elliot O'Donnell or Peter Underwood are also good. There are, of course, many regional ghost books as well, often put out by regional publishers and difficult to obtain outside of the area. Two examples of this genre are *Ghosts and Witches of the Cotswolds* by J. A. Brooks (Norwich: Jerrold Colour Publications, 1981) and *Ghosts: Washington's Most Famous Ghost Stories* by John Alexander (Washington, D.C.: Washington Books, 1975). No devotee of ghosts should miss *Lord Halifax's Ghost Book* (London: Geoffrey Bles, Ltd., 1936).

If you are to have only one book of fictional ghost stories in your library, it should be *The Supernatural Omnibus*, edited and with an introduction by Montague Summers (New York: Doubleday, 1932). If you have room for a second, make it *Classic Ghost Stories* (New York: Dover Publications, 1975).

Finally, for folklore of ghosts try *Things That Go Bump in the Night* by Louis C. Jones (Syracuse, N.Y.: Syracuse University Press, 1983) or the scholarly look at modern folklore *The Vanishing Hitchhiker: American Urban Legends and Their Meanings* by Jan H. Brunvand (New York: W. W. Norton, 1981).